The Texas Pan American Series

History of the Inca Empire

An account of the Indians'
customs and their origin
together with a treatise on
Inca legends, history, and
social institutions
by *Father Bernabe Cobo*

Translated and edited by
Roland Hamilton from the holo-
graph manuscript in the Biblioteca
Capitular y Colombina de Sevilla

Foreword by John Howland Rowe

UNIVERSITY OF TEXAS PRESS
AUSTIN AND LONDON

1979

*The Texas Pan American Series is published
with the assistance of a revolving publication fund
established by the Pan American Sulphur Company.*

Library of Congress Cataloging in Publication Data

Cobo, Bernabé, 1582–1657.
　　History of the Inca Empire.

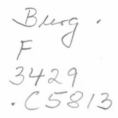　(Texas Pan American series) SN M
　　Selections translated from Historia del Nuevo Mundo.
　　Bibliography: p.
　　1. Incas.　2. Indians of South America—Peru.
I. Hamilton, Roland, 1936–　II. Title.
F3429.C5813　　985　　　79-12672
ISBN 0-292-73008-X

Contents

BOOK II

Foreword

Roland Hamilton has provided us with the first English translation of any substantial part of one of the classic Spanish sources on Inca history and institutions, the *Historia del Nuevo Mundo* (History of the New World) by the Jesuit scholar Bernabé Cobo. Cobo was an Andalusian by birth, but he spent most of his adult life in the New World. His interest in the Incas was probably aroused by his experiences as a student of theology in Cuzco from 1609 to 1613, but his book about them was not finished until 1653, when Cobo was seventy-three years old.

In using Cobo's work, it should be remembered that we are dealing with a work of seventeenth-century scholarship. Relatively little of the part about the Incas is based on first-hand observation or interviewing living informants. For the most part, Cobo relied on earlier written sources, many of them in manuscript, which he simply paraphrased and combined. His paraphrasing usually involved some condensation and sometimes interpretation of the original, and he had to make difficult choices when he found contradictions in the sources available to him. His object was to weave the materials he had into a coherent narrative.

Not many seventeenth-century writers acknowledged their sources for particular information. Those most likely to do so were theologians and jurists who felt the need to support their statements by citing authority. In this tradition, Cobo gave specific references when he was debating a problem with theological implications, such as the peopling of the New World or the identification of the New World with the Ophir mentioned in the Old Testament. When he came to the subject of the Incas, he gave a generalized account of his sources, identifying only a few of the principal ones specifically. We can identify some but not all of the sources he did not mention. A printed one which falls in this category is the *Symbolo catholico indiano* of Luis Jerónimo de Oré (Lima, 1598) from which Cobo took some incidents in his account of the deeds of Mayta Capac; he also had at least one manuscript source on Inca history, probably a lost work by Cristóbal de Molina written before 1575. Much of his information on Inca laws was derived from sixteenth-century testimony by García de Melo; another of his sources on Inca institutions was a report by Francisco Falcón, probably the one Falcón presented to the Second Provincial Council of Lima in 1567. None of these sources was acknowledged, though Cobo did name another work by Cristóbal de Molina which he used in his chapter on Inca origin legends (Book II, Chapter 3, of the translation) and elsewhere in chapters on Inca mythology and religion not yet translated.

The complete work of which these two books are a part was clearly inspired by the *Historia natural y moral de las Indias* (Natural and Moral History of the Indies), written by the earlier Jesuit scholar José de Acosta and published in Seville in 1590. Cobo refers to Acosta occasionally, although not as often as his intellectual debt to his predecessor would lead a modern reader to expect. Cobo's handling of the problem of the peopling of the New World, for example, is based directly on Acosta's. The chief difference is that Cobo devoted special attention to the argument, which he did not accept, that the Ophir of the Bible was Peru or some other part of America. Cobo's preoccupation with the Ophir theory, which Acosta had refused to take seriously, may have been motivated by something he had read (see the translator's note 6 to Book II).

In Cobo's time, the most detailed published account of Inca history was the *Commentarios reales . . . de los Yncas* (Royal Commentaries of the Incas) of Garcilaso de la Vega, which had appeared in Lisbon in 1609. Cobo referred to this work in discussing his sources, and he evidently used it. Since Garcilaso's mother was an Inca princess, and he claimed that he had gotten his version of Inca history from members of her family, his account had the appearance of considerable authority. Garcilaso's version of Inca history is in fact largely fictitious; most of it seems to be a pious fraud perpetrated by Garcilaso himself, rather than a narrative concocted by his mother's relatives. Cobo might have been able to detect the fraud if he had asked his Inca friends in Cuzco for their family traditions, but there is no indication that he did more than record the traditional list of Inca rulers during his stay in Cuzco. The chief point that appears to have concerned him in Cuzco was the number of Inca rulers, the length of the dynasty. Garcilaso's account was not very deviant in this respect; he added only one ruler to the traditional list, and Cobo did not accept the addition.

The chief matter on which Cobo accepted Garcilaso's version against other evidence was the timing of the Chanca attack on Cuzco and the crucial victory which saved the Inca state. Garcilaso quoted the accounts of the Inca victory over the Chancas given by Jerónimo Román y Zamora and José de Acosta, both of whom attributed the victory to Pachacuti, but Garcilaso said that both authors were confused on this point, and that the victory was won by Viracocha, one reign earlier. Cobo evidently allowed himself to be convinced by Garcilaso and adjusted his narrative accordingly.

The decision is understandable in the light of Garcilaso's apparent authority, but from our perspective it was a mistake. The sources not available to Cobo which have come to light in more recent times indicate clearly that Román y Zamora and Acosta were right in this case, and Garcilaso was wrong. The section of Cobo's narrative affected by the influence of Garcilaso is that between the reigns of Inca Roca and Topa Inca. Cobo's material on later Inca history is not based on Garcilaso and preserves valuable testimony from better sources.

The section of Cobo's work dealing with Inca institutions is chiefly based on one or more reports by Juan Polo de Ondegardo, though Cobo also used other sources which he did not cite, as was noted earlier. Polo de Ondegardo was an investigator active in the mid-sixteenth century who is generally trusted by modern scholars. He certainly had good opportunities to inform himself. Two major reports of Polo's were known to William H. Prescott, the pioneer American historian of the conquest of Peru, and both have subsequently been published. Polo wrote in a somewhat convoluted and legalistic style, with much repetition, and his original reports are consequently not easy reading. Where Cobo summarized Polo, Cobo's presentation is clearer, so that the meaning, as Cobo understood it, is more accessible.

What makes Cobo's work important for modern readers is that it provides a synthesis of Inca history and culture which is based in large part on sixteenth-century manuscripts, many of which have been lost since he wrote. The two books translated here, plus the two which follow them in the original work, constitute the most comprehensive treatise on the Incas written before the present century.

John Howland Rowe

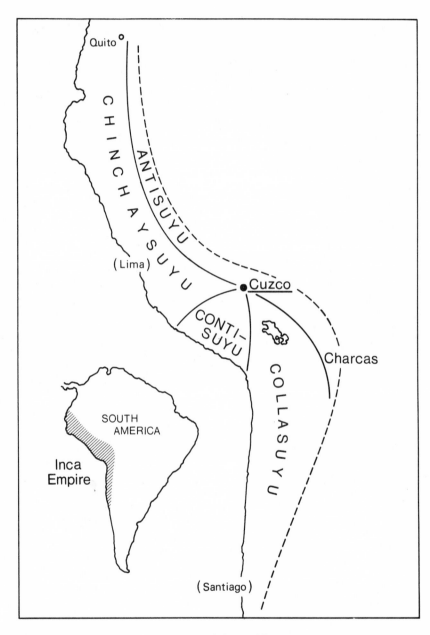

MAP 1. *Tahuantinsuyu: Four Quarters of the World.*

Introduction: Father Cobo and His

Historia Bernabe Cobo (1580–1657) became one of the
New World's outstanding historians. Born in
southern Spain,[1] he spent a year on Hispaniola[2] before continuing on
to Peru in 1599.[3] He was to remain in Peru for the rest of his life, except for a trip to New Spain between 1629 and 1642.[4] Cobo was edu-
cated as a Jesuit and did extensive missionary work with the Peruvian Indians at intervals from 1609 through 1629.[5] During his sojourn
in New Spain and thereafter in Peru, he spent much of his time in
the capital cities of Mexico and Lima doing research in archives and
libraries for his monumental *Historia del Nuevo Mundo*, which he
finally completed in 1653.[6]

In the prologue to the *Historia*, Father Cobo explains that his
work contains forty-three books divided into three parts; the first
part deals with pre-Columbian America, the second with the discovery and conquest of the West Indies and South America, and the
third with New Spain. Unfortunately, most of the *Historia* has been
lost; what remains is only the first part, composed of fourteen
books, plus three books from the second part concerning the foundation of Lima. The loss of such a large portion of Cobo's *Historia* is
not as regrettable as it may seem because, for contemporary scholars, the account of pre-Columbian Peru is his most important piece
of scholarship. He collected a vast amount of material in Peru. This
includes the judicious use of the best written sources on the Incas,
which Cobo tells us he confirmed through interviews with the descendants of the royal Inca lineage in Cuzco around 1610.[7] Cobo
also took careful note of the customs of the plebeian Indians with
whom he did his missionary work. This mass was then organized
into the most comprehensive and lucid study of its kind. As the
eminent Peruvianist John H. Rowe so aptly put it, Cobo's account
"is so clear in its phrasing and scientific in its approach that it is
pleasant as well as profitable to work with."[8]

The manuscripts of the *Historia* found their way to Seville,
where they remained unnoticed until around 1790, when Juan Bautista Muñoz had copies made for his collection in Madrid. Muñoz's
research assistants used two separate manuscripts; one was a large
volume containing the ten books from the first part which deal with
natural history; the other had the three books on the foundation of
Lima.[9] Today the holograph manuscripts for these two volumes are

housed in the Biblioteca Universitaria de Sevilla, identified respectively as MSS. 331–2 and MSS. 332–33.

There is a third manuscript including Books 11–14 of the first part; this volume, dealing mainly with pre-Columbian Peru, is located in the Biblioteca Capitular Colombina de Sevilla, and, for the sake of brevity, I will refer to it as the Colombina-Cobo MS. It does not bear the author's signature, and it has never been adequately described. The first sign of it came in 1892–1893, when the contents were published by Marcos Jiménez de la Espada, but he made no reference to the manuscript.[10] This was done by Philip A. Means: "The original manuscript, holograph, is in the Muñoz collection in the Royal Academy of History in Madrid."[11] Although Means is a very trustworthy scholar, in this case he made the mistake of using González de la Rosa (see note 1) instead of inspecting the primary sources in Spain.[12] I have personally studied the manuscripts for Cobo's works in the Muñoz collection in Madrid. These are only the copies made around 1790, and they are in the Biblioteca del Palacio Real. Moreover, this collection does not even include a copy of the Colombina-Cobo MS.

The only scholar to identify the Colombina-Cobo MS. was R. Vargas Ugarte; under the heading "Biblioteca Colombina—Sevilla," he states as follows: "416.—MSS. 83–3–36. 1 vol. en 4.º encuad. en pergamino, 363 pág. n. Al dorso: Historia del Nuevo Mundo. 2 p.p. 1 Historia del Nuevo Mundo, 1a. Parte. Libro Undécimo. Cap. 1 Que la América estaba poco poblada y por qué causas. Comprende hasta el Libro Decimocuarto, inclusive. Escrito todo de una misma mano. Origl. Se trata, como el lector habrá advertido, de la obra del P. Bernabé Cobo . . ."[13] The only error here is the call number. When I visited the Biblioteca Colombina in 1974, the call number was 83–4–24. It should also be noted that this text is done in a clear and careful style of handwriting which makes it easy to work with.

Later scholars who have used Vargas Ugarte have either been noncommittal or have not accepted his identification of the Colombina-Cobo MS. as the original. Porras Barrenechea does not say whether the Colombina-Cobo MS. is original or not,[14] and Francisco Mateos indicates that the originals are missing.[15] In order to remove all doubts about the matter, I have made a comparison of the three surviving letters signed by Cobo and the Colombina-Cobo MS. All of the letters were written in New Spain. The first is dated 7 de Março de 1630 in La Puebla; the second, 21 de Junio de 1633 in Mexico; both of these letters, reports of Cobo's trip through New Spain to members of the Jesuit Society in Peru, are now in the

Biblioteca Nacional de Lima.[16] The third letter, dated in 1639, was written in an effort to get the *Historia* published in Seville; it is in the Biblioteca Universitaria de Sevilla.[17] I have studied the entire text of the Colombina-Cobo MS. as well as the known handwriting and signatures of Cobo as found in the aforementioned letters. I have paid particular attention to the proportional size, spacing, and slant of the letters as well as the use of upper- and lower-case letters and the lack of abbreviations. There is no question that the Colombina-Cobo MS. is the original holograph.[18]

Now that the manuscripts have been identified, it must be pointed out that none of the originals were used for the publication of Cobo's works. The botanist D. Antonio Josef Cavanilles did the first publication of parts of the *Historia*. He used the Muñoz copies for an article that came out in 1804.[19] The scientific accuracy of Cobo's descriptions of New World flora was illustrated with extensive quotations. As a botanist, Cobo was far ahead of his time, but even by the latest scientific standards of the early nineteenth century, his practical approach, with special emphasis on medicinal plants, was more valuable for ethnobotany than for natural science.

Next, M. González de la Rosa published the *Historia de la Fundación de Lima* in 1882, using a copy found in the Biblioteca Colombina.[20] It is unfortunate that he did not find the original, also in Seville. This work remains an important source of information on early colonial Lima because many of the documents that were used have now disappeared and Cobo is an original source for events in Lima during the first half of the seventeenth century.

Finally, between the years 1890 and 1893, Marcos Jiménez de la Espada published all fourteen books of the first part of the *Historia*.[21] Unfortunately Jiménez de la Espada died before finishing the introduction, and he never told which manuscripts he used for this edition. However, since he was working in Madrid, he probably used the Muñoz copies for Books 1–10, and, although it has been assumed that he used the Colombina-Cobo MS. for Books 11–14, I have found evidence that he had a copy that now seems to have disappeared with the notes for the introduction. The fact that a copy was made is borne out by a number of emendations and omissions. For example, the Colombina-Cobo MS., f. 66, v., reads "vilcas," but the printed editions read "Vilgas" [Vilcas] (BAE, 92: 53); the Colombina-Cobo MS., f. 117, v., reads "Collatupa," the printed editions have "Coya-Tupa," and note 17 says "Probablemente Colla-Tupa o Tupac" (p. 90). The Colombino-Cobo MS., f. 134, r., reads "unbuhio"; the printed editions have "bujío" [buhío] (p. 102). Furthermore, the Colombina-Cobo MS., f. 49, r., reads "y de los animales peregrinos, y estraños que vemos en algunas islas, como no quedo casta en otras partes?" This whole passage was omitted (p. 40). Other examples of omissions are found in the following places: Colombina-Cobo MS., f. 50, v. (p. 41); f. 76, r. (p. 59); f. 177, r. (p. 134). The list could be extended, but this is sufficient; no doubt these emendations and omissions were based on the shortcomings of a copy made for Jiménez de la Espada.

In fine, the manuscripts of the *Historia*, all located in Seville, are in excellent condition. Nevertheless, all published editions are based on imperfect copies. Therefore, new editions, based on the holograph MSS., are urgently needed, especially for the account of pre-Columbian Peru contained in the Colombina-Cobo MS.

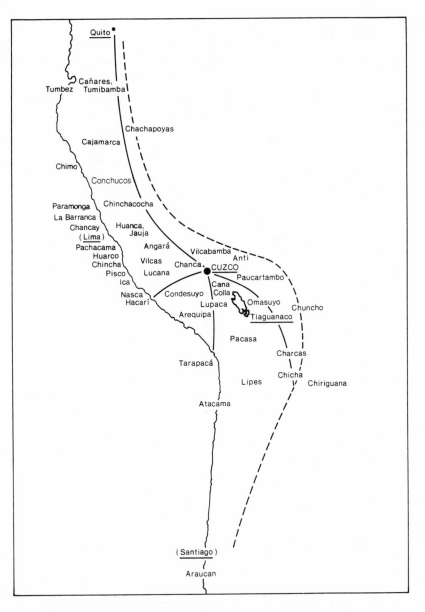

MAP 2. *The Inca empire: tribes and provinces.*

A Scientific Outlook of the Seventeenth Century

Father Cobo's standards of excellence were based on the crowning achievements of early seventeenth-century Spain. To him the Spanish Baroque cathedral embodied the highest ideals in art, architecture, and music, symbolizing the only true faith, Christianity. On this basis Cobo was very favorably impressed with the Inca's public architecture, roads, bridges, irrigation system, farming methods, weaving, and metallurgy, but he found their music and dance to be monotonous and uninspiring. In comparison to Spanish houses, the plebeian Indians' one-room huts, or *buhios*, seemed primitive and dirty to him, as did their habit of going for months without either bathing or changing their clothes. Moreover, as a priest who had labored long and hard in missionary work with the Indians, he was singularly exasperated by the Indians' lack of receptiveness to the subtleties of the Christian doctrine. Nevertheless, Cobo was intrigued by the religious beliefs of the Indians.

These seventeenth-century European values did not alter Cobo's sincere desire to reveal the scientific and historical facts in his writings. He was a genuine scholar, dedicated to ferreting out the truth. In this respect, Father Cobo was at variance with the prevalent attitude of his own times.

There was still a strong insistence on the authority of the Bible, the Christian fathers, and Aristotle and Pliny. Cobo was influenced by these authorities, and, like that of the other European scholars of his day, his historical framework was strictly Biblical. The bench marks were roughly the following: Creation, 4000 B.C.; Flood, 2300 B.C.; Solomon, 1000 B.C., etc. Nevertheless, Father Cobo drew most of his conclusions from reports by painstaking investigators such as Juan Polo de Ondegardo and from his own personal observations. On this basis Cobo found empirical evidence in ancient ruins indicating that continuous human habitation in Peru antedated the Universal Flood by centuries. How could this be reconciled with the Christian dogma which taught that Noah and those on his ark were the only survivors of the flood and repopulated the world? Cobo's solution to this theological dilemma provides a good example of his tendency to rely more on experience than authority. He theorized that the Indians were not really affected by the Flood and were not descendants of Noah. Cobo based his conclusion on the fact that neither in their physical features nor in their technology or culture did the Indians resemble the Hebrews. Although Father Cobo was definitely opposed to introducing miracles to solve such historical problems, he made an exception in this case. He suggested that after the Flood God must have replaced the flora, fauna, and indigenous population unaltered in their original habitat in the New World.

In order to fully appreciate the validity of Cobo's works, the reader should interpret certain outmoded terms. For example, when Cobo speaks of "barbarians," it should be borne in mind that he means what we would call "primitive people." Cobo's insistence on the Indians' "false religion" and their "devils" or "false gods" would be rendered today as "myths" or "animistic ideology." Once substitutions like these are made, the reader will see that Cobo's thinking is really quite scientific.

As I have suggested, the material covered in the present translation is the most important part of Cobo's *Historia del Nuevo Mundo* for the modern reader. The title *History of the Inca Empire* was selected because it is the focal point of the part of Cobo's work presented here. The subtitle was added to clarify the exact contents of the work. It is divided into two books (Books 11 and 12 of the *Historia del Nuevo Mundo*, which constitute the first half of the Colombina-Cobo MS.). In the first part of Book I (Colombina-Cobo Book 11), Father Cobo treats the general aspect, character, and dress of the Indians. In the second part, he analyzes several theories concerning the origin of the Indians. He concludes that they came from Asia by taking a northern route. Then Cobo systematically refutes all other theories, especially the belief that the New World or Peru was the Biblical land of Ophir. Book II (Colombina-Cobo Book 12) contains a superb treatise on Inca legends, history, and social institutions. It also includes careful descriptions of some important ruins from pre-Inca civilizations as well as Inca roads, bridges, canals, and buildings. Thus Father Cobo's reliance on empirical evidence and detailed descriptions of the Indians, their environment, and ancient ruins and monuments makes him a precursor of modern anthropologists.

A Note on the Translation

This is the first rendering of Father Cobo's works into English, or any other language for that matter. It is also the first edition of any of Cobo's works based entirely on the holograph manuscript, in this case the Colombina-Cobo Manuscript. So far as possible the English version expresses the exact meaning of Cobo's original. Therefore, I have preferred a free to a literal rendering where the latter would result in an obscure or unintelligible passage, and I have broken up the long, periodic sentences which characterize Cobo's style.

In interpreting the meaning of archaic or obscure words or passages, I have used reference works which reflect seventeenth-century Spanish. The most important dictionaries are the *Tesoro de la lengua castellana o española* (1611) by Sebastian de Covarrubias and the *Diccionario de Autoridades* (1726–1729) by the Real Academia Española. For the numerous expressions from indigenous languages, I have used the early Spanish-Quechua vocabularies, especially the anonymous *Vocabulario y phrasis en la lengua general del Peru* (1586), the *Vocabulario de la lengua general de todo el Peru* (1608) by the Jesuit Diego Gonzalez Holguin, and the *Vocabulario de la lengua Aymara* (1612) by the Jesuit Ludovico Bertonio. In my Madrid dissertation I have shown that Cobo was familiar with all three of these vocabularies. Of all the modern guides to the usage of the chronicles, the most valuable is the *Amerikanistisches Wörterbuch* (1944) by Georg Friederici. In addition to the works listed here, I have consulted numerous other reference books that were useful for limited aspects of the project as well as many translations of other chronicles.

With regard to the mechanics of rendering seventeenth-century Spanish into modern English, proper nouns and Indian words have caused some special problems. The need for both fidelity to the MS. and clearness for the nonspecialist has led to the following solutions. Proper nouns have either been transcribed exactly as they appear in the MS. or translated into their common English equivalents. For example, where the MS. reads Nueua Espana, the translation is New Spain; Cristoual Colon is Christopher Columbus. In other cases I have put the modern version of a name in brackets: Guamanga [Ayacucho]. Where a familiar name like Mancocapac is run together in the MS. I have transcribed it Manco Capac. In keeping with the orthographic standards of his times, Cobo generally did not use the written accent mark in the MS., so I have not added it to names like Bernabe. In general I have transcribed all loan words from Indian languages exactly as they appear in the MS. Words such as *ayllo* may seem strange at first, but they are just as strange to those who read the original text in Spanish. In fact, Father Cobo was aware of this, and he generally uses some equivalent word or phrase such as "lineage" along with the Indian word.

There are a number of spelling inconsistencies in the MS. With regard to place names the more familiar form was preferred. Cobo used the spelling Caxamarca most of the time; Cajamarca appeared only once in the MS. Nevertheless, this latter spelling was preferred for the translation. Similarly, Jauja was also spelled Xauxa and in one instance Xauja. Trujillo was usually spelled Truxillo in the MS. The name of the northwestern quarter of the Inca Empire was given as either Chinchaysuyo or Chinchaysuyu; the latter spelling was preferred in the translation. I have followed Cobo's spelling of Condesuyo for the province and Contisuyu for that quarter; Cobo also uses the spelling Cuntisuyu. All three are actually variants of the same name. There was also inconsistency in the spelling of the name of the third Inca. First it was spelled Lloqueyupanqui, then Lluquiyupanqui thereafter. Lloque Yupanqui was preferred in the translation.

Most of these inconsistencies can be explained. They stem from the fact that the Spanish alphabet used in the seventeenth century was inadequate for making a precise transcription of Quechua. The Spanish vowels *i* and *e* as well as *u* and *o* were used interchangeably to approximate two Quechua vowels which are half way between each pair. Thus *cumbi* or *cumbe, camayu* or *camayo* represented the same two Quechua words. The Quechua sound *w* was usually represented as either *gu* or *hu*. Thus Quechua *wak'a* was spelled *guaca* by Cobo and most other writers of the seventeenth century; however the same word was also spelled *huaca*. This same principle applies elsewhere. For instance, Cobo used the spellings Guayna Capac and Guamanga. These same names were spelled Huayna Capac and Huamanga by some other writers.[22]

The notes to this translation are meant to clarify the meaning of Cobo's MS. No effort is made to correct Cobo's errors in judgment. In the first place, Cobo's writings are generally very accurate. Moreover, the intent here is not to take issue with Cobo whenever it could be done; this is an undertaking that will be left for future studies. On the other hand, some of Cobo's ideas require an explanation for the modern reader. For example, I have indicated that the belief in giants was so prevalent in Cobo's day and so many signs of them were found that the most perceptive historians accepted the legends.

This translation was originally initiated on the suggestion of the eminent anthropologist John H. Rowe. His advice and the example of a translation he did of one fragment from Cobo's works have served as a model for my own rendering. I must also mention the valuable advice of two colleagues, Professors William Moellering and José Cerrudo.

R.H.

BOOK I

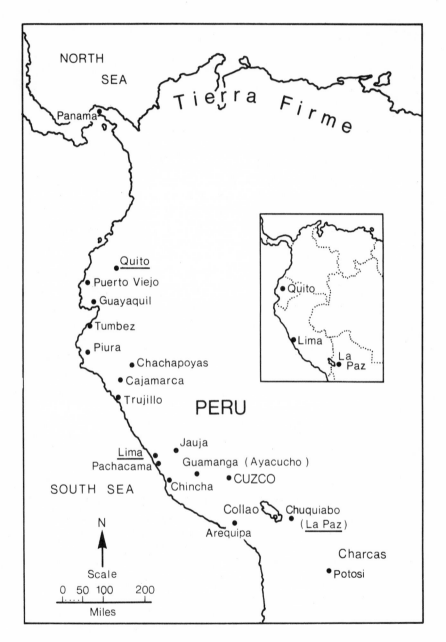

MAP 3. *Peru and Tierra Firme in the early colonial period. The map at the right shows modern national boundaries. Modified from the map in* The Men of Cajamarca, *by James Lockhart (Austin: University of Texas Press, 1972).*

Chapter 1: Concerning the sparse population of America and its causes

I will begin the treatise concerning the nature and characteristics of the Indians who inhabit America by explaining why the first Spaniards who came here found such a small number of them. Certainly, if all this fourth part of the universe,[1] which is so expansive, were as densely populated as any region of Europe, no monarch of past centuries would have been as powerful as our King of Spain. In fact, no one is shown on historical records to have possessed such a large portion of the world. But since the number of people that inhabited it was so small, and since the number it has at the present time is even smaller in proportion to its size, this empire turns out to be less impressive than is indicated by its immense boundaries, which extend from pole to pole. Though it is true that some provinces were found to be more densely populated, such as the province of Mexico in North America, and in South America the provinces of Santa Fe de Bogota in the New Kingdom of Granada, those of Cuzco and Quito in Peru, Chile, and some others, nevertheless, the sparsely populated and nearly unpopulated ones were more numerous. This circumstance cannot be attributed to a recent settlement of these lands; rather, based on the evidence which I have observed and considered, it may be concluded that America was populated before the Flood. As will be demonstrated, there are some traces and ruins of towns of so strange a kind that they permit no less an estimate of antiquity. And there is clear evidence that resettlement started many centuries ago.

In order to remove whatever doubt might arise as to how a land so extensive, rich, and fertile as this could be so sparsely populated, even though it has become famous throughout the world for so many great and marvelous things, I will explain here the causes of its sparse population; my conclusions are based on observations made during the more than fifty years that I have lived here.

The first and most general cause is the lack of water; the problem affects extensive parts of the New World. In some places it never rains, in others there is not enough rain for cultivation; and in both instances either there are no rivers or not enough water for irrigation. For example, on the coast of Peru it does not rain and there are only a few rivers in comparison to the large amount

of fertile land which could be planted if there were plenty of water.
The plains of the coast extend from north to south for more than
six hundred leagues and are from ten to fifty leagues wide. Because
of the lack of water, not a twentieth of this large stretch of land
is productive. Here there are many unpopulated areas extending for
twenty, thirty, and up to fifty leagues² which lack even enough
water for foot travelers to drink, as can be seen in the provinces
of Piura and Atacama; so the Indians did not settle in these plains
except on the river banks, and the rest was devoid of man or beast.
In the inland areas of this same Kingdom of Peru, we also find
large stretches of land which, though not totally useless like the
land of the plains, are almost as uninhabitable. Here it rains sometimes during the year, but not enough for crops. A lot of it is not
inhabited either for lack of rivers to irrigate or because it is very
broken and the mountains are too rugged for irrigation ditches. In
spite of all this, it produces grasses and firewood with the few rains
that it receives; thus it is not completely unutilized.

The second cause, which is almost as general as the first, is the
excess of water which other lands have; this also makes them uninhabitable. These waters are distributed among lakes, rivers, estuaries, marshes, and swamps. The lakes occupy large areas because,
in addition to those that are famous for their unusual largeness,
such as the Lakes of Chucuito [Titicaca], Paria [Poopo], Lipes [Coi-
pasa], Maracaibo, and others which are found in New Spain, there
are innumerable other smaller and lesser-known ones which are
from eight to fifteen or twenty leagues around; if it were not under
water, the ground covered by these lakes would be sufficient to
support large cities and provinces. Large rivers which spread across
this land cover just as much ground. Some of these rivers run over
six hundred and even a thousand leagues from the beginning of the
flood plain to where they empty into the sea; for this entire distance
they are one, four, ten, twenty, forty, and up to fifty leagues wide.
Apart from the large amount of ground which the riverbeds occupy,
the rivers cover much more with their floods, spreading their water
over the riverbanks for six, twelve, twenty, and more leagues on
both sides, making the land uninhabitable because it is marshy the
year round. The water of the lakes and rivers is added to the sea
estuaries so that these also take up a stretch of land; for this reason, along the ocean a great deal of land is left uninhabited. Since
this land is very low and flat, the sea flows into it at high tide,
forming large estuaries so covered with mangroves and underbrush
that it is impossible to walk through them.

Many other ponds and estuaries result from the rains on the flat lands; these bodies of water last most of the year without drying up. Besides these, there are many swamps, caused either by springs or by the extreme humidity of the soil, from which water is always pouring forth without draining in any direction; and in areas with much rain there are extensive flood lands and quagmires which will not even hold up under foot traffic, let alone permit habitation.

As a result of this abundance of water, there is another equally troublesome hindrance to human habitation: the many forests and *arcabucos* which grow in the hot and rainy lands of *yunca* climate. These forests were never inhabited by man; no trace of settlements can be seen in them because these forests are very high and dense. There are great trees, many thickets, and much underbrush; moreover, the soil, which is never reached by the sun, is very boggy. The Indians who lived in these woodlands and forests had their dwellings on the high banks of the rivers. They sustained themselves more by fishing than by agriculture because of the difficulty which they experienced in having to clear the *arcabucos* to make their cultivated fields. Whatever is cleared one year sprouts again the next year with such vigor that the luxuriant growth overcomes the industry and strength of man. This is especially true of people who, for lack of our tools, had to put in an incredible amount of work and zeal to clear a space no larger than the palm of the hand. To the inconvenience which these woody lands cause must be added the abundance of wild beasts and poisonous vermin which ordinarily inhabit them; they are no small bother and even consume the local residents. In fact, we know of provinces which are kept nearly uninhabited because of the multitude of savage tigers [jaguars].

Although other places neither lack water nor have excessive amounts of it, as we have just stated, but have enough to cultivate and populate the land, nevertheless large stretches of land are left unused. This is true on the one hand because of the rigors of the climate, and on the other hand because of the physical make-up of the soil. As a result of the excessive cold which produces killing frosts, none of the lands of the first zone of the sierra[3] can be used to grow fruits and vegetables. This zone, with such a severe climate, is composed of the punas, the paramos, and the snow-capped cordilleras of Peru; and we can even include here a good measure of the land of the second zone of the sierras, which also has uninhabitable paramos. Nevertheless, in this second zone, a large amount of native livestock and Castilian sheep and cattle is raised. Because of the physical make-up of the soil there are lands

which, though they have a good climate, nevertheless are not suitable for cultivation, owing to one of three causes: first, because
they are saltpeter beds, such as the ones we see in many parts of
Peru; second, because the ground is very sandy or rocky, both in
the countryside and in the mountains; and third, because some of
these mountains have numerous crags and rough, brambly ground
covering many leagues. Other mountains have good soil, but they
are so rugged and lofty that they cannot be worked. All of these
causes make the majority of the Indies impossible to cultivate and
uninhabitable, as I have noticed numerous times while walking
through many of the provinces.

The fertile lands were not uniformly populated; some were
densely populated, others sparsely. This uneven distribution of the
population was comprehensible; the great and powerful kingdoms
were much more densely populated than the smaller provinces
ruled by caciques and than the tribal groups and *behetrias*.[4] Some
of the more densely populated areas are the kingdoms of New Spain,
Peru, the New Kingdom of Granada, and others.

The reason why the powerful kingdoms were more densely populated is that the vassals of the monarchs and great princes lived
longer because they did not make war among themselves and were
better able to defend themselves against outsiders. Since the tribal
groups and *behetrias* were continuously at war, they would destroy
and consume each other. These Indians would go around hunting
their neighbors in order to sustain themselves. In fact, nations of
cannibals were found that annihilated entire provinces, leaving
them uninhabited. And, without going farther afield, the Chiriguana
Indians of Peru will suffice as an example: they have eaten up many
Indian nations and now they possess the lands of their victims. The
Chiriguanas wreaked so much havoc along the borders of this Kingdom of Peru during the times of the Inca kings that although it
was among the most populous lands of the Indies and the best and
most fertile in Peru, its borders were uninhabited. For this very
reason, the Spaniards forced the Chiriguana Indians out to the
roughest part of the woods and founded rich farms, as we see in
the entire Diocese of Charcas, especially in the provinces of Tarija,
Pazpaya, Tomina, Mizque, and Cochabamba. While it is true that
some of the fertile lands were densely populated when the Spaniards
arrived, the contrary is true of other fertile lands. This is easiest
to prove in Peru, where the whole kingdom was distributed among
its conquistadores and settlers. In the densely populated provinces,
it was possible for them to have large, rich encomiendas[5] of Indians,

but in other provinces, although the climate there was good and the land fertile, repartimientos[6] of Indians were not designated for the Spaniards. This is because these provinces were uninhabited. In many of them, which have been populated since the Spaniards arrived, no vestige of an ancient population is found. If they had been populated previously, it would be impossible for this fact to be unknown now because some vestige or ruins of the previous population would be left, as we see in other places; and, more importantly, because if there had been many Indians, they would have been mentioned in the first repartimientos, just as the few Indians that used to inhabit them are mentioned.

Besides these arguments, there is another very strong one in the reports and histories concerning the discoveries and conquests of diverse provinces of the Indies. In some of them we read how it happened that our Spaniards found no people in large areas of land, and that for this reason many of them died of hunger; this happened because the provisions which they were carrying were used up, and in such large, uninhabited areas they did not find any kind of sustenance. And even if all the previously stated arguments were not to hold, the knowledge that we have of many expeditions which have been made in recent years into the lands of heathens from this Kingdom of Peru is sufficient proof of this truth. The entire eastern side of this kingdom for more than seven hundred leagues borders on several of these nations; all of these heathens live in *behetrias*, under caciques with very small domains, located beyond the uninhabited areas which lie between the boundaries of this Kingdom of Peru and its first settlements and farms. Within the domains of the heathens it is amazing to see the small number of people found wherever one may travel. For example, the priests of the Society of Jesus, who went on two expeditions made by order of the Archbishop of this city of Los Reyes, Gonzalo de Ocampo, found, throughout the large expanse of land which they crossed, only a few Indians and such small *cacicazgos* that the biggest one had no more than fifteen hundred subjects; and all of them were so engaged in wars that the priests were unable to make any headway in converting them.

Chapter 2: Of the names which were given to the natives of the Indies and of their color

The Indians had no general name for all the peoples of America; they had no equivalent to our names African for everyone from Africa, Asian for everyone from Asia, and European for everyone from Europe. This was not because they did not have information concerning all this fourth part of the globe (although it is true that they were not informed about it). It is because they were not accustomed to giving such general names for all the inhabitants of an entire region. Even though the Peruvians had all of the boundaries of this kingdom very clearly delineated, they used no single name for all of its inhabitants. They had a proper name for the natives of each province, no matter how small it might be; this name applied to all of the inhabitants of a province and to them only. For this reason we find so many different names in Peru, each one for a different nation, such as Charcas, Amparaes, Chichas, Carangas, Lipes, Quillacas, Pacages, Lupacas, Collas, Canas, Collaguas, Chumbivilcas, Cotabambas, Chocorbos, and innumerable others. There is only one name from the Quechua language which we can say has now taken on a universal meaning among the Indians of Peru; it refers to all of the Indians who are native to America; this word is *runa*. Although in their language it signifies "man," the Indians of Peru have restricted it and applied it to the Indians, distinguishing them from the Spaniards and people from other nations of Europe. Moreover, they use the name *viracocha* for all white men. And in accordance with this, when they talk with us and mention some man who is coming or is looking for us, they distinguish between Spaniards and Indians with these names, and they want us to speak in the same way when we make reference to someone whom they do not know; therefore, they ask us if he is *viracocha* or *runa*. With the word *runa*, they mean only the Indians, despite the fact that it used to signify "man" in general. But *runa*, in this sense, is only used by the Indians of this kingdom and by us when we speak with them.

There are three names that the Spaniards have given to all the natives of this New World: Indians, Natives, and Americos; all of them are modern and artificial, invented since this land was discovered. The name Americos is not very widely used; the other two are more common. The name Indians was given to them because this land was called the Indies by the ones who discovered it, and the name Natives was given to distinguish them from the Europeans who live here. But, although these two names have the same meaning, there is a slight difference between them in our usage. The word Indians is used when we Spaniards speak to each other; but since its meaning is now derogatory, we do not use it when we speak with Indians (if we refer to them specifically), although we do use it if the ones we are speaking about are not present. I will give an example: I am talking with some Indians; if I make reference to other Indians from some other place, I could use this name and say: "Look, brothers, the Indians of New Spain, of Chile, etc." But if I make reference to them, personally, I would use the term Natives, which is accepted as more respectful, and I would say: "You Natives have this obligation, etc."

One of the most surprising things that we find in the Indies is that although it is such a big land with such a wide variety of climes[7] and weather, inhabited by an infinite number of people of different languages, customs, and rites, nevertheless, with regard to their appearance, physical make-up, and natural properties, especially with regard to their color, the inhabitants of the Indies look as similar to each other as Europeans born in the same province and within the same European clime.

The Indians are rather dark in color; this is commonly described by our writers with words such as the following: dark brown, olive, tawny, yellowish-brown, the color of cooked quince, light chestnut-colored, and, the one that describes it best of all, mulatto-colored. It must be pointed out that, although the color of a Spaniard is always of the same hue of white, in the Indies it varies by being more or less reddish, according to the characteristics of the land where he lives. In the sierra of Peru the Spaniard conserves the same colors which he had in Spain, and he has a white, reddish face, with rosy cheeks; but if he dwells for very long in *yunca* lands, which are very hot and humid, he loses his good color and takes on such a pale hue that he seems to be sick. If he comes again to the sierra, in a short time he regains his colors. In the same way, the sierra Indians can be distinguished from the *yunca* Indians, but not by the hue of whiteness, because they are all the same in this respect, rather in that the sierra Indians have a more reddish color, while the *yunca* Indians are as pale as a dead man, similar to the color of cooked quince. But if those of the *yunca* land go to live permanently in the sierra, they take on the same color as the sierrans; and if the sierrans move to *yunca* land, they take on the same color as the *yunca* Indians.

In regard to the color of the Indians, I have often heard wise men discuss the matter and argue about whether it is inherent in their race or if it comes from the atmospheric conditions of the land. In the latter case, this land would not produce only white men, as in Europe, or only blacks, as in Guinea; rather it would produce men of an intermediate color like that of the Indians. This is as general a problem as the one concerning the inhabitants of different regions of the world; some people are very white and others coal black, and between these two extremes there are different hues. What I hold to be certain is that the clime where a person is born does not cause this variety of colors; rather, it is inherent in men and we get our color by nature, in spite of the fact that we all come from the same source, from Adam and Eve. Actually, God ordained this diversity of colors in order to beautify the universe and to demonstrate his infinite wisdom and omnipotence. I will briefly tell the reasons which move me to feel about this matter as I do. The first is (returning to our Indians) that if the clime and the mellowness of the land were the cause of their color, in America there would have to be men of as many different colors as are found on the whole globe, some whiter than Germans or Flemings, others blacker than the Ethiopians of Guinea, still others moderately white, like the Spaniards, and others of as many different colors as are found in different regions of the world. In fact, just within the torrid zone of the Indies, between the tropics, we find as many different climates as are known in the world; there are lands colder than Flanders or Germany, as extremely hot as Guinea, as temperate as Italy or Spain, and there are places not only with all the different kinds of climates on earth, but also with all those that the human mind could imagine; and outside of the tropics there are regions in both hemispheres, northern and southern, of the same latitude, climate, and characteristics as those of Europe. In spite of all this, the natives throughout America are the same color and the same hue of whiteness, both those that live within the torrid zone and those that live outside of the tropics in the temperate zones up to the fiftieth and sixtieth parallels of latitude toward either pole. Therefore, although some Indians from distant provinces may be somewhat different from each other, this difference in color is al-

ways within the same hue of white. This is borne out by the fact
that there are no people in the Indies who are as white as the Spaniards or as dark brown as some East Indians from Malabar whom
I have seen.

The color of the Americos cannot be attributed to their nudity
because they do not all go naked; nor are the ones who cover their
nakedness with clothes of wool and cotton whiter than the others.
We can see in Peru that the caciques, who were always well dressed
and enjoyed all the luxuries of the land, are no different in color
from the common folk and the *mitayos*. And another factor which
adds not just a little to this opinion is that the Indians are born
with the same color as their parents. Actually, if this color were
so accidental and extrinsic as to be contracted from the inclemency
of the heavens, rain, sun, and wind, it could not be inseparably
transmitted to them in their mother's womb.

The strongest argument is, in my opinion, that the Spaniards
who live here do not slowly lose their color and take on that of
the Indians, which inescapably would have to be the consequence
if, in fact, the characteristics of the land determined the color of
the natives. If the clime really caused the Indians' color, it would
produce the same effect on the Spaniards who are born here. Thus,
in the course of time, everyone, Spaniards and Indians alike, would
come to be the same color. However, the experience of one hundred
and sixty years which have passed since the Indies were discovered
and first populated proves the contrary because the Spaniards born
here are as white as those who come from Spain. In spite of the fact
that there are a great many Spaniards born in this land who are
the sons, grandsons, and great-grandsons of criollos (a name we commonly give to the Spaniards born in the Indies), there is no difference between them and those who come from Spain. The sons of
Spaniards here turn out to be as handsome, fair, and blond as in
Spain. Moreover, I have often heard many people assert, and their
opinion does not displease me, that there are more beautiful children reared in this city of Lima and in Mexico City than in many
Spanish cities.

It is equally important to note that just as the Spaniards born
here are white, the sons of blacks from Guinea turn out to be similar
to their parents in their color and in their tightly curled hair; and
the sons of Flemings and those of other northern nations are blond.
In short, we notice that the sons of an Indian mother and a Spanish
father get half their color from each parent, and that the farther

they become removed from either of their parents, as generations pass, the less they retain of that parent's color. All of the preceding is sufficient proof that the clime and weather of various regions do not cause the diverse colors which we see in men of different nationalities, nor do the atmospheric conditions of this land cause the color of its natives.

Chapter 3: Of the physical make-up, body proportions, and facial features of the Indians

Concerning the stature of the Indians, the only thing that needs to be said is that just as the various regions of the world differ in that some produce taller and heavier men than others—although the differences are not excessively disproportionate to the average stature—so too, the men who are born in the various regions of America show this diversity. Some regions, like Tucuman, Paraguay, the Strait of Magellan and, in North America, the lands near the pole of that hemisphere, generally produce tall men. Others produce short ones, and still others produce individuals of average stature. The difference between individuals in any of these regions is not so great as to cause surprise, for in all of them there are well-proportioned men who reach the perfect stature of two varas.[8] And, if it is true that many do not reach this height, many others surpass it, for they are not all cut from the same pattern, a fact which is as valid for this land as for other lands of the world. It is true, however, that in the tropical zone there are many more of those who do not reach the perfect stature than of those who surpass it, just as in other provinces there is a larger number surpassing this stature than falling short of it.

We find greater differences among individuals in the fact that some lands, by virtue of their fertility, produce stronger, more robust men and consequently men with more physical stamina than other lands, which are sterile, for the very things which affect plants and animals also affect the human body. Just as the Kingdom of Chile surpasses the rest of the provinces of the Indies in fertility and in the production of nourishing foods and stronger animals, especially horses, so too its natives show a superiority over the rest of the Indians in being more robust and possessing greater strength and courage. If it is evident that a person takes on special characteristics from the region and climate in which he is born, as philosophy teaches and as we see by our own experience, it becomes much more evident in the physical make-up and tendencies of the human body.

Without exception, the Indians of all of the provinces of the New World share the following characteristics. They all have black eyes; there are no Indians with either green or blue eyes. Their upper and lower eyelids are so closely connected near the nose that they barely show the entire whites of their eyes. This distinguishes them from the Spaniards, because the corners of our eyes are well pronounced. For this reason, to find out if one is a mestizo or if he is partly Indian, when the rest of the signs are inconclusive (since there are some very light complexioned mestizos and *cuarterones*),[9] all we have to do is look at their eyes and this will clear up all doubt, for the more Indian blood one has, the more occluded the corners of his eyes will be.

A second common characteristic of all Indians is their hair. It has five properties. It is black, thick, and straight, and it is certainly noteworthy that one cannot find an Indian with curly, soft, or blond hair. This is not only true of the men and older women but also of the children, among whom not a single one will be found with blond or curly hair. They all have it thick and almost as coarse as bristle. Thus, on those who cut it as we do (for there are many who have it sheared), it stands up on end, almost straight, and does not lie down on their heads. The other two properties of the Indians' hair are that it seldom grays and, if it does, only among the very aged, and that it seldom falls out, resulting in baldness.

They are also alike in that they have very little hair on their bodies, as one can easily see by observing those who go about naked. And on those who dress like the Peruvians, we can tell by their exposed arms and legs, which are as smooth as a baby's skin. Their beards start to grow later than the Spaniards'. They are sparse, not well distributed, and as coarse as the hair on their head. They all generally pull out the hairs of the beard with copper tweezers as soon as they appear, allowing no hair to grow on their faces except for the eyebrows and eyelashes. This custom, together with that of allowing their hair to grow long, was so universal among the Indians that there was no nation which did not practice it. Thus, they were all very surprised to see the bearded faces of the first Spaniards who came here. Imitating the Spaniards, some Indians in this kingdom are already letting their beards grow—with no small loss in looks, because their whiskers look more like a handful of horsehair than a man's beard.

All of this provides copious material for the philosopher to investigate the secrets of nature, which are great indeed, as we have seen in the make-up and qualities of the Indians; for even though the Spaniards live here among them, breathing the same air, drinking the same water, and eating almost the same foods, we still see great differences between them. The Spaniards' beards begin to grow before they turn twenty, and they become gray before they reach forty. Many become bald when still young. Some have blond, curly hair, and all Spaniards have thin, soft hair. Finally, insofar as these physical variations are concerned, the Spaniards born in America turn out the same as those born in Spain. The fact that all of this is the opposite among the Indians causes one to marvel.

Based on what has been stated in this chapter, one can infer that the accounts that some people have written about the various types of Indians who are said to be found in this New World, and whose make-up and appearance is different from that of common men, are mere fables. Such is the case with the Indians described by the friar of the Seraphic Order of Saint Francis, Father Pedro Simon, in the first part of the *Noticias historiales de las conquistas de Tierra Firme*, gathered from writings and accounts of people expert on New World matters. In it he states that men have been found in different parts who, like those who live in California, have such long ears that they drag on the ground; that others who live nearby sleep under water; and that the men of another neighboring nation, lacking the ordinary tract to rid their bodies of waste, sustain themselves by smelling flowers, fruits, and herbs; they cook these only for this purpose. He also says that the same kind of people are found in one of the provinces of Peru, where Captain Pedro Sarmiento de Gamboa, on the trip he took to Spain from Peru by way of the Strait of Magellan in 1580, found giants measuring more than three varas tall. Finally, he states that in the expedition made by Governor Juan Alvarez Maldonado from the city of Cuzco to the provinces of the Andes, the party found two pygmies who did not measure a cubit and a gigantic monster measuring more than five varas tall.

It seems to me that all of these stories told by the author mentioned above are false, as are so many other fake accounts invented by men who are fond of novelty in order to impress people. The truth is that all of the Indian people have the same form and body structure that we do and that all the physical differences to be found among them are very incidental and are those which I have described in this chapter. In effect, the California Indians and all their neighbors are in every way like those of New Spain I saw in Mexico City. And besides, the Franciscan father, Juan de Torquemada, who was in Mexico when the provinces of California were explored by order of the Viceroy, wrote extensively about their exploration in his *Monarquia indiana*, and he does not mention anything about those prodigious long-eared Indians, nor about the ones who sleep under water (so contrary to man's nature), nor about the others who sustain themselves with flowers. Likewise while I was in Mexico, the Viceroy, the Marques of Cerralbo, authorized a journey to California, from where many pearls were brought; I learned from those who went all they were able to see and understand about the nature of the land and its inhabitants, and they did not find any such Indian nations. Nor do I know about any province in Peru where there are Indians who can sustain themselves by smelling flowers, despite the fact that I have traveled on foot throughout almost the entire kingdom and during the fifty-six years that have passed since I came to the Indies I have been in touch with many persons who have traveled throughout all its provinces.

Concerning the giants that Father Simon says Pedro Sarmiento found in the Strait of Magellan, I can only state that I was in touch with Hernando Alonso, the pilot who sailed the flag ship of Pedro Sarmiento through the Strait into the North Sea; with General Hernando Lamero, who was at that time the pilot of the admiral's ship; and with many other persons who have been in those provinces of the Strait of Magellan and have seen their inhabitants; and they confirm that although the Indians are corpulent, they are not so big that they can be called giants, for their height does not exceed that of the tallest men in Europe. Two of the Indians from around the Strait whom I saw in this city of Lima and who were sent to the Viceroy, the Marques of Guadalcazar, by his nephew Luis de Cordoba, governor of Chile, were no taller than what I have said, for they did not even reach two and one-half varas in height.

Finally, concerning the pygmies and the monstrous giant Father Simon says Governor Juan Alvarez Maldonado found in the provinces of the Andes, I cannot imagine how this story was so widely spread that it came to the attention of Father Simon, though he was so far away, and not to mine, even though I was in touch with and interviewed in the city of Cuzco not only Governor Maldonado, but also many persons who went on that and other journeys which were later made to the same area. These people told me all about it, and I never heard anyone say he had seen or heard of such monstrous men in those provinces.

Chapter 4: Of the natural make-up of the Indians

In the preceding two chapters we dealt with the exterior characteristics of the Indians as seen through our eyes; it follows that we should say something about their interior characteristics and humoral composition. All of them are phlegmatic by nature, and since natural phlegm makes the substance of one's limbs soft and moist, their flesh is very soft and delicate. As a consequence, they tire easily and are incapable of working as hard as Europeans; in Spain, a single man does more work in his fields than four Indians will do here. They are slow in all they do, and if someone hurries them while they are working, they will refuse to do anything; but if they are left to work at their own pace, they are successful at any task they undertake. They are extremely patient in learning our trades. That is the reason why they make such excellent craftsmen. They are especially proficient in those crafts that require patience to learn. As a consequence, there are already many Indian master craftsmen, especially in the more intricate trades. They are not fond, however, of those trades that require physical labor. They are very adept in vocal and instrumental music, in painting and in sculpture, and as embroiderers, silversmiths, and similar tradesmen. But above all, the Indians of Peru show their exceptional patience in enduring the slowness of the llamas, their beasts of burden. These animals walk so slowly that the Spaniards are incapable of tolerating them without becoming angry. The Indians, however, follow them at their pace, without ever becoming impatient, no matter how many times the llamas stop or lie down, as they often do, with their loads still on.

Besides being phlegmatic, the Indians are extremely sanguine, and as a consequence, they are excessively warm. This can be confirmed by touching their hands, which even during the coldest seasons will be noticeably warm. Further proof of this can be found in that they wear scanty clothing which gives them very little protection and merely serves to cover their bodies. When they travel, they sleep out in the open wherever nightfall catches them, even in the cold paramos. And if eight inches of snow happen to fall on them, they will sleep as restfully as if they were on soft, comfortable beds. Their excessive warmth can also be appreciated by the quantity and quality of foods they put in their stomachs, which are stronger than that of an ostrich. Notwithstanding the fact that their foods are very ordinary and coarse, they are able to digest them very quickly, even though they ordinarily eat them unseasoned and almost raw. And although they are frugal when they eat at their own expense, when they eat at the expense of others, they are like wolves. The Uros from Peru are good examples of this. They are such big gluttons that if an Indian happens to steal a pig weighing from four to six arrobas,[10] two of them will eat the whole thing raw in one night. Just as surprising is the fact that they need no knife or any other such instrument to kill the pig and cut it up into pieces. They rely on their thumbnails to do the job, using them as if they were sharp knives. Stomachs which are gorged with so much meat have to be hotter than a forge to be able to digest it.

I have found equally important evidence of the warmth of these people in the fact that those who are born in the paramos and very cold punas of the first and second zones of the sierra survive and develop better than those born in the warm and hot lands. It is therefore in the cold lands of this kingdom that we see the healthiest and most prolific Indians. The opposite is true of the Spaniards' children born in such lands. The majority of them do not survive. That they are killed off by the extreme cold is proven by the fact that those who survive owe it to the great care taken in keeping them warm. The facts stated above cannot be countered by saying that the Indians are in their natural environment and that because they are raised naked and without the same care as the Spaniards, the inclement weather makes them tougher. To the first allegation, I will respond that since the children of the Spaniards are conceived and are born in the same land and atmospheric conditions as the Indians, the land and clime is already as natural for them as it is for the Indians. To the second allegation, I will respond that the children of the caciques and rich Indians are raised with equal or better care than the children of many poor Spaniards and that, despite this fact, the difference in survival remains the same. This difference can be seen best in the mestizos, *cuarterones*, and all those who have some mixture of Indian blood, for even though they are often raised with the same care as the pure Spaniards, their rate of survival is proportionately higher than that of the Spaniards according to the amount of Indian blood they possess. Therefore, there is now a common saying taken from everyday experience to the effect that the children who have some Indian blood have a better chance of survival in cold lands than those who do not have this mixture.

I can think of no other explanation more in keeping with the facts than the one I have given; that is, that the warm physical make-up of the Indians protects them from the rigors of cold weather. Thus, the more of this physical make-up a child inherits along with his parents' blood, the warmer he will be; it therefore follows that those who come closest to the nature of the Indians run a lower risk of being killed by cold weather than those who do not, as happens with children of pure Spanish stock.

Some people say that the phlegmatic and sanguine make-up of the Indians originates in important traits which are not found in the Spaniards of the Indies. The first one is that all the Indians have such excellent and strong teeth that they last an entire lifetime. This is true, for rarely do they have toothaches or cavities, and few old Indians are toothless. The other trait is that there is scarcely an Indian who suffers from problems of the urinary tract, or from gallstones. The effects can be clearly seen. Whether they result from the Indians' natural make-up or from the food and beverages they consume, I am not prepared to say; let each one make up his own mind. What I can say is that the Spaniards would like to possess these traits since countless numbers of them in this land are, even in their youth, subject to the pain and suffering of urinary problems, gallstones, rheumatism, cavities, and toothlessness.

Chapter 5: Of the extreme ignorance and barbarity of the Indians

In lands as broad and spread out as the regions of America are, it is evident that the people who inhabit them will differ from each other in intelligence, speech, and customs; these differences between individuals will be greater or lesser depending on the remoteness of their place of birth and on the unusualness of its soil and atmospheric conditions. Thus, it is difficult to measure them by the same standard and find unity where it does not exist in such a multitude of nations and peoples. In spite of all this, we still find some customs, rites, and vices which all of them, or at least the majority, have in common, even in such a diverse multitude of languages, inclinations, and usages held by so scattered a people. Here I only intend to discuss the most general customs without going into details about what is peculiar to each nation (of the Peruvian nation and others, a good deal will be said later). Moreover, now many of these Americos have received the light of the Holy Scriptures, and with it and by their association with our Spaniards, they have become much more human and orderly; nevertheless, still others (who constitute the majority) are left in the darkness of their heathen ways and barbarous ignorance. It should be noticed, however, that what is said here of their rudeness and barbarous customs is what we find in the heathen Indians, and the lesser barbarousness of those who have become Christians should be attributed to the culture, virtue, and efficiency of our sacred religion, which is powerful for making human beings who live by reason and virtue out of savages nearly as uncouth and inept as unfinished logs.

Although some of these nations surpass others in intelligence and ability, nevertheless all of them generally coincide in lacking that spirit, that human, courteous, and noble manner at which the courtly people of Europe excel; for this reason the name *barbarian* is a most apt designation for them. Furthermore, if (as defined by noteworthy authors) barbarians are those who, without following the dictates of proper reason, live outside of the usage and customs commonly accepted by other men, it can clearly be seen how well this definition fits these people, for they embrace and consider proper many things, owing to the fact that they live in the darkest ignorance and corruption, which are repudiated by the light of reason

and both natural and human law. In order to clear the way through
such a thick and uncultivated jungle, so covered with the weeds
of ignorance and savage customs of these barbarians, which are not
worthy of men who possess some measure of reason, in this chapter
I will discuss only the extraordinary ignorance, vulgarity, and intellectual vagueness which these Indians exhibit in their manner of
living. In the four chapters that follow, I will discuss the perversity
of their customs, which is the result of their limited and cloudy
powers of reason and which has been ingrained by the usage of so
many years; it will also be seen that these customs corrupt and
degrade the illustrious faculty of human volition. The human happiness that men can by nature attain in this life consists, as Aristotle
says, partly in the operation of volition tempered with virtue, and
partly in the search for truth. The more that one may practice and
excel in the use of these noble powers that give him the excellence
which he possesses by virtue of being a man, the more he will
achieve the accidental perfection which his nature calls for and of
which he is capable; and the less he achieves in this activity, in
that measure will he fall short of making his life worthy of a man
who makes proper use of his free will.

Therefore, we must measure the Indians by this standard to find
out to what extent they achieve this perfection which is characteristic of man, beginning with the richest jewel we possess, the
excellent faculty of reason. There is no one who is not surprised
and frightened to see that these people's power of reason is so dull;
this is not so much because they are short on reasoning power,
as some have alleged, as it is because of their very limited mental
activity. On the one hand this is because they have no written
literature, sciences, or fine arts, which generally cultivate, perfect,
and make the mind quicker in its operations and reasoning powers.
Generally they had no natural sciences, nor did they usually show
craftsmanship in making the things that they needed to use for their
existence, except for a few of the more advanced nations, which in
some works of the mechanical trades showed fine craftsmanship,
as we will see. On the other hand, since the ingrained, savage vices
to which they are commonly given have nearly become innate,
these vices have dulled their ingenuity and obscured the light of
their powers of reason. If this unusual coarseness is the result of
their vices, in my opinion, the most prejudicial of them all is intoxication; it is the most universal and common, and the Indians fall
prey to it so frequently and so unrestrainedly that, by calculating
how much time they spend unconscious either drunk with wine or

asleep, it follows that they do not even enjoy the use of their powers of reason for as much as one-third of their lives. This single evil, which is the source of innumerable others, would be sufficient to account for the inability and dullness of these people. Speaking in general about the harmful effects of drinking on men, whether they be wise men or fools, Pliny calls it the death of the memory. And Saint Basil says that it extinguishes prudence. Since this evil does so little to improve memory and prudence and so much to promote ignorance, forgetfulness, and savageness, as can be seen in these miserable Indians, what light could it cast on them, if not one as faint as an oil lamp on the verge of going out in the middle of a pitch-dark night?

The Indian children's lack of instruction and manners stems from the above. They are brought up without any kind of education in the principles of virtue, orderliness, or praiseworthy habits. Their parents let them grow up like so many little beasts; left to their own devices, they are never reprimanded for wrongdoing or corrected or warned to be good. In fact, their parents do not even know what it means to be good, much less set a good example for them as they should. In no way whatsoever do they take notice of the presence of their children and subdue their extreme sensuality; thus the despicable habits of the parents are so permanently impressed on the children that they turn out very much like them, and parents and children alike are almost incapable of receiving any kind of good discipline. They do not know what proper respect and courtesy are; they lack the advice and prudence to choose what is good for them and shun that which could be prejudicial. They display such limited use of logic and such senselessness that it seems as if they go around stupefied, without thinking about anything. Often, in order to investigate this matter myself, when I see them standing still or sitting down, I ask them in their own language what they are thinking about. To this they ordinarily answer that they are not thinking about anything. I used to know an intelligent, bilingual Indian who was a tailor. Once while he was sewing, the Indian was asked by a friend of mine what he was thinking about. The Indian answered by asking how he could think about anything while working. In truth, this, I think, is what causes the Indians to do so well at any mechanical trade which they decide to learn. Their attention is not distracted to some other thing; rather all their faculties are employed exclusively in the task at hand.

Finally, they have the light of their reasoning powers so clouded and darkened and they use so little deliberation or logic that they display little more ability than dumb animals, whom they imitate in that they concern themselves only with outward appearances and with the present. They lack any type of providence; in fact, their thoughts are so close to this earth that they do not raise them two inches above it. Their bestial coarseness is such that it resulted in one of the most notable things that ever happened in the world, which is that some of the first Spaniards who came to the Indies doubted whether they were really men of the same nature as us. Some held that they were not, and therefore they should be considered incapable of freedom, or of control over the things that they possessed, or of receiving our Holy Faith and the sacrament of the Church. In order to put a stop to this error from the beginning and close the door on innumerable evils which would have been ushered in with it, the sovereign pontiff determined with apostolic authority, as an article of faith, that all the Indians, as rational men of the same species as the rest, were capable of receiving the divine sacraments. And since this is one of the rare cases in history on this subject, I decided to insert here the Bull of His Holiness as it is reported by Father Fray Agustin de Avila Padilla, of the Order of the Preachers, in the account which he wrote about the foundation by his sacred religious order in the province of Santiago de Mexico. It is of the following tenor:

> Pope Paul the Third extends to all the faithful Christians who may see this decree his salutation and apostolic blessing. When he sent the preachers of his faith to exercise this function, we know he told them the truth itself, which can neither deceive nor be deceived: 'Go and teach all peoples—to everyone he said regardless—because everyone is capable of receiving our faith.' Upon seeing this, the common enemy of mankind, who always opposes good works, was envious, and so that these good works would perish, he invented a method, unheard of before, to stop God's word from being preached to the people and stop them from being saved. Some of his ministers, who wanted to satisfy their greed, presume to affirm repeatedly that the Indians of the West and those of the South and the rest of the people of whom we have been informed in our times have to be treated like dumb animals and brought into our servitude. This is justified on the assumption that they are unfit for the Catholic faith, and on the pretext that they are incapable of receiving it, they are brought into servitude, and they are so afflicted and harassed that even the servitude to which animals are subjected is no greater than that of these people. Although we are unworthy, still we are God's representatives on earth and we try with all

our strength to find his lost sheep in order to convert them to Him; after all, this is our profession. We know that these Indians are true men; and they are not only capable of Christ's faith, they take to it very promptly, as we can certify. Since it is our wish to provide a proper remedy for these things, by apostolic authority in the tenor of this decree we determine and declare that said Indians and all the other peoples of whom Christians may be informed, although they may not have faith in Christ, are not deprived, nor should they be, of their freedom or of ownership of their possessions; and they should not be brought into servitude. We further declare that said Indians, and everyone else, should be called to the faith of Christ by preachers of the divine Word who set an example of good living. And anything that may be done contrary to this determination, let it not be binding or of any value in itself, notwithstanding all things to the contrary, not those aforestated or any other of any type. Given in Rome, the year 1537, the 9th of June, the third year of our Pontifical term.

It certainly is something very worthy of consideration that the ignorance and coarseness of the majority of these Indians would have given rise to such a dispute. Thus we can appreciate how much the preachers of the Gospel have done and do in these regions where they have to implant it in people who would seem to be so inept.

Chapter 6: Of the usages that the Indians have regarding their individual houses, clothing, and

sustenance Not all of the nations of this New World
live in established towns; in fact, there are some
which are so savage that they do not even have houses or a permanent
campsite. Among those who do construct houses for their living
quarters, whether in villages or settlements on their lands and *chacaras* in the manner of farm dwellings (which are used by the majority of the Indians), we normally find the following difference: the
houses of the lords and caciques are somewhat more luxurious than
the ones occupied by the average citizen. This difference is not so
much in the workmanship and design as in the size and quality of
the materials. With regard to the form and style of the floor plan, all
the houses are the same and those of the lords do not have more
rooms than those of the vassals. Except for the houses of caciques,
the rest are so humble and so poorly designed and constructed that
they should really be called huts or cabins rather than houses; and
therefore, since we do not consider them worthy of this name, normally we call them *buhios* (the name of the straw houses used by
the Indians of Hispaniola). They are all simple, one-story constructions with a single room, which is at the same time entrance hall,
living room, bedroom, pantry, wine cellar, kitchen, and even stable;
in fact, not only does it serve the purpose of the different rooms
which are devoted to household work in our houses, but it is even
used as a pigsty where the domestic animals which they raise sleep
right along with the people. And since they do not have different
rooms, it is necessary for everyone, parents and children alike, to
live and sleep together with the whole family, whether they are in
good health or ill; even if they want to withdraw from one another,
the smallness of the hut gives them no room. This is the reason why
these *buhios* are never any cleaner or more orderly than their inhabitants require. In the cold lands the huts are as black from smoke
and soot as a fireplace, and the floors are covered with rubbish
because they never bother to clean house. This is clearly proven by
what I have seen *baquiano*[11] Spaniards do. When they are looking
for some Indians and they find them drinking in their houses and
when the Indians are summoned, they often turn a deaf ear to the

Spaniards in order to continue their drinking bout. At this point, the Spaniards take a stick and pound and shake the roof of the *buhio*; this causes so much soot and dust to fall on the Indians and on their drinks that they cannot stand it and they come forth at once—they do not just saunter out. The valuable ornaments of their homes are none other than pots, earthenware jars, pitchers, and cups; all of them are instruments of Bacchus. The floor serves both as table and bed; they use no mattress or comfortable bedding other than an ordinary blanket, half underneath and half on top. (This is the custom in the cold lands; in the very hot lands, they sleep in hammocks or in similar beds.)

Their garments are no more costly and difficult to make than their habitation. Actually, half of these barbarians go around as naked as the day they were born, and those who do wear clothes hardly cover half of their bodies with them. In fact, the ones who are the best and most warmly dressed leave their arms and legs uncovered. They use simple clothes and they never put on more than one piece at a time. Their clothes are so poorly designed that they do not cut them to measure for each individual; nor do they need scissors to shape and adjust them. Their full dress is limited to only two pieces: a wide tunic without any collar or sleeves, and, in place of a cape, a four-cornered blanket which is somewhat longer than it is wide. They generally make these clothes of cotton, except for the sierrans of Peru, who make·their clothes from the wool of llamas, as will be explained. Once the everyday garment is put on, it lasts them until it is worn out; they never change clothes except possibly when they celebrate certain festivals; at this time they may put on their festive garments. These differ from the everyday ones only in that they are more colorful and of somewhat better quality. They do not undress at night; and since they go to bed with their clothes on, they save themselves the trouble of getting dressed in the morning. They do not keep their garments any cleaner than they keep their houses, since they never, or at least rarely, wash them; and since they have no other tablecloths or napkins when they eat, nor other towels or handkerchiefs to wipe themselves with, anyone can imagine the mountain of filth with which they are covered.

They sustain themselves with anything produced on the land or in the water which can be eaten without ill effects; in fact, this is their only criterion, and they are not the least bit finicky. Although it is true that not all the Indian nations eat everything, nevertheless, if they are all included, no living thing whether plant or animal is excluded from their diet, from the most noble one, man himself, to the most revolting vermin and filth in the world. Human flesh is eaten by the *caribes* or cannibals, who bear this name for that very reason; others sustain themselves by hunting and fishing; the majority kill and eat whatever vermin and filth they run into, without passing up snakes, toads, or any kind of worms. They are so barbarous, voracious, and dirty in this that, even though the Mexicans and the Peruvians are the most intelligent and orderly nations to be found in the Indies, the first considered human flesh to be a delicacy and the second ones ate a thousand different kinds of repulsive vermin, including their own body lice. So much for their main dishes.

The bread is not the same everywhere either; the most common is maize; next comes cassava bread, which is eaten in many provinces; in others bread is made from various roots, such as *yucas* [manioc], *papas* [potatoes], *ocas*, and other species of vegetables. In short, there is hardly a nation that does not have a very ordinary food which takes the place of bread.

In preparing their dishes, they are not the least bit clean; the most scrupulous Indians are satisfied to eat their food nearly raw, poorly roasted, or half-cooked. They do not bother to season it with anything but water and salt and a few little herbs, and they hardly go to the trouble to wash it first because they pay no more attention to the cleanliness of their food or other things they use than to that of their persons. Ordinarily they let themselves get so dirty that it is nauseating, and since they hardly ever change their clothes or wash them, they have a foul smell; but it is not offensive to them, nor is any other odor, because they do not appreciate fragrance, and they show no delight in sweet odors or disgust at bad ones. This is because the Indians are all so filthy.

Ordinarily they eat little, but they do this more as a result of misfortune and want than from abstinence, because, when they have the chance, they gobble the food down like wolves, and this usually is when they eat at the expense of Spaniards.

However, granted that they were always as frugal in their eating as they seem to be when they eat their own food, and though they may even abstain in this, they go to the opposite extreme by getting intoxicated, because they drink to excess and all the fruits of their work go down this drain. Water is their worst enemy; they never drink it pure unless they are unable to obtain their beverages, and there is no worse torment for them than being compelled to drink water (a punishment which the Spaniards sometimes give them, and they resent it more than a whipping). With the word *chicha* we make reference to all of their drinks, which are commonly made of maize and other seeds and fruits; in New Spain the pulque is made of maguey; in Tucuman the *chicha* is made from algarrobas, in Chile from strawberries, in Tierra Firme from pineapples. In this kingdom, in addition to making *chicha* from maize, they also make it from *quinua* seeds and *oca* roots, from the berries of the *molle* tree, as well as from other things. Also in other places they make wine from a certain liquid which flows from the heart of palm trees after they have been cut down; in still others, from the *guarapo* made of sugar-cane juice. In short, there is no nation of Indians that does not have their wines and beverages on which to get intoxicated, although formerly they had no knowledge of true wine made from grapes. All of these *chichas* are intoxicating; some are more stupefacient than others, and some are as strong as or even stronger than wine. The Indians are so addicted to these *chichas* that drinking is the height of their glory, and they do not consider it a disgrace to get drunk. They usually spend their days and nights drinking and dancing to the tune of their harsh-sounding drums and songs, which sound sad to our ears, although to the Indians they are joyful. They never celebrate an event, whether joyful or sad, in any way other than by dancing and drinking to excess; thus, for them the funeral and burial of their parents and relatives is just as festive an occasion as the birth and weddings of their children, for in both cases the principal activity is to drink until they cannot stand up. They are so overpowered by this vice that it is impossible to make an exaggerated account of the situation; it will suffice to say that their supreme joy is to drink until they pass out; in fact, to this end they prefer the strongest *chichas*, and in making them they customarily put in strong things so that the *chicha* will knock them out more rapidly.

Chapter 7: Of the most general customs common to all of the Indians

In people who were so subjected by the devil that he made them render to him the honors and adoration owed only to the Creator, it is not difficult to see the kind of transgressions, cruelties, and assortment of vices which they would have learned from such a perverse teacher. They are all idolaters, given to infinite superstitions and auguries, except for isolated cases of nations made up of men who were so gross and savage, indeed so beastly, that they neither recognized earthly or heavenly deity, nor practiced any kind of religious ritual. And even though many of the people of this New World have already received holy baptism, there are still many more who to this day are in the darkness of their infidelity. What else could sprout from such contagious pestilence as is idolatry, which the Holy Scriptures call the beginning and end of all evil, if not the corruption of customs and the stream of vices and misery in which these unfortunate people were submerged. Since they lack the light of truth and the knowledge of their Creator, they also lack the study and exercise of virtue, love, and honesty, the appreciation and love of justice, clemency, piety, continence, and other apparels and ornaments of the soul.

Beginning, therefore, with the side of man which because of its weakness is the first to be attacked by the devil, especially in people over whom he reigns and who are given to the vice of intoxication, one cannot describe (nor is it worthwhile to dwell on it; rather, we should pass rapidly over such a foul-smelling quagmire) the sewer of turpitude and indecency in which these idolaters wallowed and in which they delighted like filthy animals. Because they never knew the splendor and beauty of chastity, they never appreciated it; indeed, the virginity of their women was very offensive to them. They said that those who were virgins had never been loved by anyone. As a matter of fact, very few remained virgins until the day of their marriage. This was so, first of all because since childhood they were brought up with complete freedom. Their parents did not shelter them or look after their modesty and chastity. Nor did they prohibit them from going out by themselves whenever and wherever they wanted. Even when they went to distant towns, upon returning, they were not obligated to account to anyone for their actions. The parents themselves would take them to drunken gatherings and to work in the fields, where, as a rule, there were many men, both relatives and strangers. Second, they consented to being deflowered because they wanted to be free of the shame which the chaste had to endure simply for being virgins. Hence, no excess in this respect was considered a crime or, for that matter, considered reprehensible.

In accord with this depraved custom, when an Indian chooses a woman to be his wife, he does not try to find out whether she has led a virtuous or a licentious life because, among them, this is not a matter which adds to or detracts from her worth. The foremost consideration is how much wealth she possesses. Second to this he considers whether she is a hard-working woman who will delight him and serve him well. But since this second question is difficult to determine unless it is done through direct experience, to gain it, he usually takes her as a concubine first, keeping her on a trial basis for a few months and, at times, for years. If she pleases him, he marries her; if she does not, he gets rid of her and selects another one.

The women serve their husbands like slaves. They do most of the work, because, besides bringing up the children, they cook, make *chicha* and all the clothing they, their husbands, and their children wear, and they even do more work in the fields than the men. The husbands are incapable of doing anything without the company and help of their wives. Even when traveling, the men go empty-handed, while their wives are loaded down like donkeys. For this reason, the possession of many wives was a sign of greatness and wealth among them. Only the commoners made do with one wife, but the nobles and caciques had as many as they wanted, even though there was one principal wife whom the others recognized as such. The men do not watch over them, nor take the trouble to shelter them, and least of all do they pay attention to their faithfulness. Even if the wife runs away, they will accept her when she returns, even when the absence has been long. Moreover, they will seek her assiduously, asking their friends to help find her, and when she returns they will welcome her with a show of happiness and will celebrate her return by getting drunk.

To better illustrate what usually happens in situations of this nature, let me relate the following example. The wife of an Indian ran away but returned after a long absence. She asked a priest whom I know to reconcile her with her husband. The husband was about to do so, but on finding that she was pregnant, he asked the priest how he could be expected to take her back in that condition. The priest convinced the husband with this argument: "Come on, brother; if your dog left the house, would you refuse to take her back because she returned pregnant?" To which the Indian answered: "You are right, Father"; and so he took his wife back without bringing up again what she had done.

Both in their marriages and in their licentious sexual conduct they paid little attention to blood relationships, except between mothers and sons, although even they, at times, committed transgressions. This was the case because these people are wantonly inclined to the vice of lechery, which was spurred by the indecency of a way of life which imposed no limits on their relations.

A universal custom of all of these barbarous nations has been to show more concern for the place they were to be put after death than for the dwelling in which they lived. The type of graves and burial customs varies greatly, because in each province there were different rites. However, they all share the practice of burying their dead in a lavish fashion, wearing the best dresses, all the jewels and finery with which they usually adorned themselves when they were alive, with the weapons that they used in war, and in many places with the tools of the trade they had practiced during their lifetime; thus, if a person was a fisherman, he was buried with his nets and other fishing gear; the same was done for other trades. They would place food and drink on top of the corpse and, in the case of caciques and lords, they would bury them with some of their servants as well as some of their favorite wives. Some of these were strangled first and then thrown in dead, but others were made drunk and then buried alive, an end to which many went willingly. The funeral took place with the accompaniment of relatives and friends, who escorted the remains to the cemetery in the midst of mournful chants, dances, and heavy drinking. The duration of the ceremonies was greater or lesser according to the rank of the deceased. In their chants they recalled and repeated the heroic and most memorable deeds they knew about him. They told of the places where he had lived, the good deeds that he had done for them, and anything that might be cause for compassion and weeping.

All Indians are inconstant, docile, and completely unreliable. They are easily led far astray by passions and licentious affection, and are incapable of curbing or moderating their appetites. Their fear of adversity and disasters cows them and subjects their will to such an extent that they become weak and pusillanimous and then they give up; and to avoid a lesser evil, they will often opt for a greater one and at times for the greatest evil of all, which is death. Thus, in desperation, many will hang themselves or jump off a cliff for the slightest reason. They are so untrusting in their commerce and social intercourse that they are suspicious of one another; the children are even suspicious of their parents. A small amount of prosperity will make them vain and haughty, and they will show contempt for everyone. They lie openly and do not feel confounded or ashamed if they are caught in a lie. Moreover, on being caught, they confess openly that they lied.

They will not show any loyalty or keep their word unless there is something to be gained from doing so. Once the profit has been made, they will break their word without any regard for being ac-cused of treachery. They are extremely puerile in their behavior: the men frolic about and engage in children's play with the boys, much as the children of Spain frolic about and play tricks on one another. They are by nature extremely attracted to a life of idleness and indo-lence. Hence, if they have enough to eat and drink on a given week, they will not work of their own free will during the entire week, un-til they have drunk everything they have. They will do this unless they are threatened and forced to do otherwise, for they cannot con-template doing it differently, out of either love or duty. This is so because they are not moved or spurred on by any sense of honor or respect. When they are children, they are happy and loving and show promise of ability, virtue, and good manners, but on reaching the age of fifteen, when they begin to drink, they turn out like the rest. They quickly forget what they have learned because they seldom make a practice of studying or repeating what they are taught, except when they are forced to go over it.

To sum up, they are a people with such mundane, vile, and cowardly spirits that they value only the visible reality which is perceived through the senses. This is the only thing they prize and the only thing they seek; they do not know or appreciate any other form of good or happiness except that of pampering and gratifying their stomachs and their licentious appetites.

Chapter 8: In which the same topic is continued

Still to be discussed are the customs and vices of the Indians which are contrary to the virtue of justice; that will be the subject of this chapter. The caciques and lords of the people were those individuals whose right to govern was based solely on forceful subjugation; and since the acquisition of power was tyrannical and cruel, so was their government. They did not look after the welfare of their subjects, but tried to satisfy their own ambition and greediness. They thus forced their subjects into such an abject servitude that it was no different from slavery. The poor subjects lived under such oppression and were so frightened by the tremendous punishments which they saw with their own eyes perpetrated upon those who incurred them through some disobedience or disrespect for their caciques that they did not respect them, but rather worshiped them. They did this with such extraordinary submission and fear that when they were in the presence of their caciques, they would not dare raise their eyes from the ground or look them in the face. Nor were they the masters of their homes and properties, not even of their own children, for everything was at the disposal of the tyrants. The subjects were not allowed to utter any complaints against them, regardless of the injury or affront suffered, not even when their wives and daughters were taken away from them. No laws or privileges were observed other than the will and whim of the caciques. They would do or undo anything as they wished and would absolve or condemn as they pleased without being even-handed in punishing or rewarding. Thus, at times they meted out atrocious punishments for small crimes; at other times, they ignored serious crimes, unless they were committed against them personally, in which case they were implacable and inhuman. In their punishments they commonly included the innocent, punishing the individual along with his closest relatives even if they had no part in the crimes. Nowhere were these caciques more inconsistent than in the establishment of laws and statutes, which they changed repeatedly, and in the lack of uniformity in the execution and application of the law to all people without exception. Since they obeyed only out of fear, the subjects worked for the public good and that of their masters only because they could not escape their wrath and cruelty. But, if an opportunity to commit a crime presented itself where there were no witnesses and no chance of getting caught (even if it involved treachery), driven by their evil inclination, they would perpetrate the crime.

The injustices committed by tribes and nations upon others were of the same gravity. Each was always scheming to destroy his neighbor; they were in a perpetual state of war with each other, justifiably or not, sometimes on account of the boundaries of their districts, and other times on account of their pastures, rivers, and fishing rights. On other occasions, they tangled with each other to avenge an offense committed upon a member of one group by an individual of another group. They would kill and rob each other without pity or compassion. The thing which best reveals their barbarous fierceness is the fact that they really loved these quarrels and wars and that they looked for opportunities to engage in them because they always expected to make a prey of their enemies, whose flesh they consumed.

Their transactions and contracts were few because they were satisfied with little. Each one would sow and harvest what he needed to sustain his home or he would hunt and fish; the latter was a practice common to many tribes. Rarely was there commerce between nations, for their rudeness and cruelty caused them to distrust one another. Even though they knew about and prized gold, silver, and other metals and made varied use of them, they did not make coins out of any of them, nor did they use coins anywhere in America until they were introduced by the Spaniards. Instead of buying and selling they bartered. Payment for rent was made in goods. (Outside of these two types, no other kinds of contracts were known to them.) It is true that some things were more common for this use and served as money to buy everything necessary to live on. These were ordinarily the foods they used instead of bread, except in New Spain, where cacao beans were used as money. In this Kingdom of Peru, maize was used for this purpose, and even to this day, the Indians use it to buy other foods. This custom has been introduced in the towns of the Spaniards where the Indian women (who are the ones that commonly sell the vegetables, fruits, and things of this nature in the plazas and marketplaces) exchange their products for bread, and thus these minor provisions are usually bought with bread. There was no standard of valuation imposed by public authority in these *rescates* (the name given in these lands to this type of exchange or purchase). The matter was left to the satisfaction of the people trading, as it is seen today in almost all the Indian towns of this kingdom. On holidays, the women come to make *rescates* in the plazas. Each brings the goods she has: some bring out fruit, others bring maize, others cooked meat, others fish, raw meat cut up in pieces, salt, coca, agi pepper, and likewise the other things they trade. And they make their *rescates*, exchanging a plate of fruit for a pot of stew; some buy salt with agi pepper; some buy meat with maize, and so on. In this way, they all get what they need in exchange for their surplus goods. And in fact, it is not a bad pastime for the Spaniards who are present to observe how these transactions and exchanges are made, which is unique, as I have seen sometimes among these people. It is done in the following way: The Indian women put all their goods, or part of them if they are fruits or things of this nature, in small piles arranged in a row; each little pile is worth about one-half to one real; if it is meat, it is cut up in pieces of equal value, and likewise with the rest of their goods. The Indian woman who comes to buy with her maize instead of money sits very slowly next to the one selling and makes a small pile of maize with which she plans to pay for what she is buying. This is done without exchanging a single word. The one who is selling looks at the maize, and if she thinks it is too little, she does not say a word or make any sign. She continues looking at it, and while she continues in this pose, it is understood that she is not satisfied with the price. The one buying has her eyes on the seller, and during the time she sees her uncommitted, she adds a few more grains to her pile of maize, but not many. If the seller remains inflexible, she adds again and again to the pile, but always in very small amounts, until the one selling is happy with the price and declares her approval—not with words, which from the beginning to the end are never spoken, even if the transaction lasts half an hour, but rather by deeds. The seller reaches with her hand and brings the maize toward her. They never stop to think about whether or not these exchanges are in keeping with the principle of just and equitable commerce. Nor do they ever show scruples at having gotten more than they justly deserved; they are not obligated to return an excessive gain and are even less obligated to return anything usurped from their neighbor, even if they definitely took advantage of him or robbed him. They are inexorably driven to this by their natural inclination, because once they have taken possession of another's property, it never occurs to them to unburden their conscience.

They show very little or no respect for and obedience to their parents. This disrespect is so excessive that they seem to base it only on the principle of power and physical strength. Only when they are inferior to their parents in this respect do they serve and obey them with some humility. They never show very good manners or love for them. (They never had any manners anyway.) Once they grow up and become as strong as their parents, their submission ends, for Peter is as good as his master (as they say here). Moreover, as soon as the poor parents begin to grow weak with age, their ungrateful children forget the natural debt which they have to serve and respect them with even greater care, love, and compassion. As they grow stronger than their parents, they start taking the parents' place. The children will become masters of the poor old people and make them obey and serve them. Not only do they use them as vile slaves, but they also treat them as cruelly and inhumanly as if they were dogs or some other inferior animal. This clearly shows their barbarity and brutal ignorance, for besides taking advantage of them in this manner, they mete out heavy punishments for very light offenses, such as not catering to their whims or the like. When they are drunk they vent their wrath on their parents. This beastly custom was so much a part of their nature that they have not shed it altogether even after being taught about Christianity. Every day we see barbarous examples here of children who raise their hand against their parents and mistreat them, which demonstrates the barbarity and disorder in which they lived before the introduction of Christianity. These acts of parental disrespect committed by the children were so frequent that they have ceased to horrify us as much as they did in the beginning. Not long before the moment of this writing, an Indian came to his priest and in my presence complained about one of his brothers who had mistreated his mother. When I asked him what horror had been done to her, he told me that the brother had knocked her teeth out. This type of crime would be abominable among civilized people and would not be allowed to go without severe punishment. And yet it did not startle those of us who were present much because we are already used to seeing such excesses.

How could people who show no respect and courtesy for their parents show respect for one another? They never showed reverence and politeness other than submission, humbleness, and fear when they spoke with their caciques. Thus, to this day, we see that when two Indians pass each other on a road, they proceed without greeting each other or saying a single word. And if they stop together at the same place to spend the night, each begins to eat what he is carrying without inviting the other or being civil in any way, even if one is eating and the other is staring at him. The young show no respect for the elderly, nor the common folk for the nobles if they are not their caciques, for only to these will they show reverence, and they will pay no attention to the rest. They did not know the meaning of mercy and charity for the poor, the needy, or the sick; they lacked compassion for people in grief, and they would fail to come to their aid even if they were able to do it. Their inhumanity was so great that even if they saw someone dying they were reluctant to lend a helping hand.

Once while I was talking with some friends about the hardness and inhumanity of the Indians they told me the following story which occurred in that very town:

A child happened to fall down in view of the town's priest, a religious father whom I knew, who, because he was at a distance from the child, was not able to pick him up. Since the child had been hurt from the fall and could not get up, he just lay there on the ground crying. At this point an Indian woman passed near the child, and even though she saw the boy lying on the ground covered with dust and crying, she went by completely unruffled without making any effort to pick him up and help him, as if she were a dumb animal. When she reached the priest and was reprimanded for being cruel and not having felt enough compassion for that little angel to lift him off the ground, the Indian woman answered with these words: "Did I give birth to him?"—an answer which, of course, shows the barbarous inhumanity of these people.

They do not provide special treatment for the sick, nor do they make their beds more comfortable or give them better food. When the healthy members of the household sit down to eat, they give the sick person the same food that they are eating; they put it at his bedside and leave it there so he can eat it if he wants to or leave it if he does not. No matter how little his appetite or how weak he may be, there is no attempt to use loving words in encouraging him to eat. Nor do they ever feed him themselves. Thus, many of those who die among these people perish more because of this unusual neglect than from the sickness itself.

The poor live in extreme indigence because of the lack of charity from those who are in a position to provide it. All of them are merciless and avaricious, showing no trace of liberality in sharing their wealth with those in need. But the ones who experience the greatest need and misery are the elderly. This is so, on the one hand, because of their lack of foresight; they live by meeting the bare necessities (as they say) and only for today, without providing for the future, and once they lose the strength necessary to work, they also lose their sustenance. On the other hand, the elderly experience the greatest need and misery because among these barbarians there is nothing more hateful and vile than old people. So small is the respect they show for venerable old age! Thus, the young men will mock and mistreat them as if they were unworthy of living in the world; such is their lack of mercy and compassion. In this they show their ignorance and lack of reason, for even if they were to use only their common sense and realize that they would all be needy on reaching old age, they would understand the advantages resulting from giving aid to the poor old people who are not able to sustain themselves by working. They pay absolutely no heed to the conventions of friendship. Their friendship lasts only as long as it is beneficial to them, and when the benefits end, so does the friendship. They also forget the conventions of gratefulness for benefits received and are so thoughtless that if someones does them a favor, they will not even honor it with its remembrance.

Chapter 9: Of the many languages used by the various nations of Indians, and how these all seem to have a common origin

Whoever may have given careful considera-
tion to what has been said up to this point concerning the intelligence, living conditions, and customs of the Indian nations of this
New World certainly must have noticed the extraordinary uniformity and similarity which does in fact exist among them. Often I have
pondered this matter and I have tried to determine why the Indians
are so similar not only in color, appearance, size, and physical make-
up, but, what is more, in their personalities, interests, and customs,
in spite of the fact that some of the Indians are more distant from
each other than America is from some parts of Europe, Africa, or
Asia. I can find no other explanation which is more satisfactory than
the theory that all these people have a common origin; without
doubt it was some nation or family of men who came to populate
this land, and as their numbers increased and multiplied, they began
spreading out all over this land until they had filled it with the
multitude of peoples which we find here now. It certainly took them
many centuries to complete this process.

The only counterargument which I could make against this
opinion is the incredible number of languages which these people
use; in fact, although no one to date (that I know of) has taken the
trouble to count them, considering the many languages about which
I have been informed in the lands discovered so far and estimating
on that basis the innumerable ones which there must be among the
barbarians who live in the interior of this immense expanse of land
which is included within the coastal areas we possess, I think it is
probable that there are more than two thousand of these languages.
Actually, there is hardly a valley to be found of any size whose inhabitants do not have a different language from their neighbors. But
why do I say valley? There is a town in this Archbishopric of Lima
that has seven *ayllos* or tribal groups; each one of these *ayllos* has a
different language. More about this will be seen in the general description of the provinces which I am putting farther ahead.[12] But
this argument, which in some people's judgment should prove the
contrary, is so much in my favor, that even if the other ones which

move me to feel this way were lacking, this one alone would be sufficient to convince me to hold this opinion. In fact, if, on the basis of the multitude of languages which these Indians speak, we were to infer that many nations had populated the Indies, it would be necessary to assign each language to a single nation. Anyone can see that this is impossible. From what parts of the world could two thousand nations have come? And even if we were to accept this incredible possibility, how could these people have conserved only their particular languages and at the same time have become so strikingly similar in everything else?

Still it could be held that although we might concede that this land was populated by different peoples, it would not be necessary to postulate as many different nations as there are languages at the present time. Rather there could have been a much smaller number of nations, each one possessing separate languages; and from these few, by a process of mixing and transforming the words of the several nations, with time the number of languages would have multiplied and expanded until it reached the enormous number in existence today. Even though this line of reasoning may be sufficient to explain the introduction of this multitude of languages, it is not necessary even for that, nor does it fit in with the other facts. First of all, this line of reasoning conflicts with the uniformity in physical features and customs of these people. I am more convinced that they descended from a single origin on the basis of this uniformity than from multiple origins on the basis of their many languages. In the second place, I do not find it necessary to postulate the existence of a great many nations in order to account for the many languages which they speak today. Just as a few languages could multiply to become so numerous by a mixing process, in the same way, from only one nation and language, the ones we see now could have been propagated. The families and towns which proceeded from that first nation would have slowly spread throughout the various regions of America, and at the same time their individual languages would have taken shape.

Moreover, I think that there are sufficient reasons to persuade us that this process of introducing among these people such a large number of languages is reasonable and in accordance with the nature and way of life of these Indians. The first reason is the lack of writing; this not only impairs the development of all the sciences and good arts, but without it the usage of the people cannot be conserved pure and invariable for very long. This is caused by man's natural tendency to be inconstant and changeable. We are always looking for something new in all the things which we use in our daily lives; when we are tired of our old suit, the new one which we invent pleases us and alleviates our boredom. In this respect, our sense of hearing is no different than that of sight or the other senses. Old words and an archaic style are annoying, and modern usage composed of new and unusual words causes delight. This is why we have experienced such notable changes and variety in our own Spanish language in only a few centuries, as can be seen by comparing modern texts with ancient ones. If such a change occurs among us, a people with writing who have continuous and frequent relations and communications with all the towns of our nation and republic, why should we be astonished that these barbarian nations, lacking in everything that could keep them united in their original language, have come to have so many different languages? They have had no books in which to conserve their language as they received it from their elders which could serve as models that they could follow and therefore maintain unity among themselves in accordance with that principle of philosophy which holds that if many things are regulated and molded to a third, which is like a model for them, they will become like it. Who does not know that if many men read the same book, they will assimilate the style and type of speech which the book has?

In fact, besides not having writing, which is in my opinion the most efficient mode of conserving a language, these Indians did not have any commerce with one another either, which, for the matter at hand, is nearly as effective a means of language maintenance as writing. Each one of these nations was content to live with the things which were available within its own boundaries, without caring for or seeking anything produced by its neighbors. Moreover, they had no need of anything else for their way of life, because it differed only slightly from that of animals; as long as the pastures had sufficient feed for their livestock, they would not move on to others. Thus their lack of refinement and luxury in their food and in their clothing (most of them went naked) explains why the individual nations were not dependent on one another.

Their natural rusticity and savageness, contrary to the humane and benevolent relations which characterize people of reason and restraint, contributed all the more to the Indians' aloofness. Moreover, as their numbers increased, at first they divided up and established themselves in the unpopulated lands which were suitable for settlement. Since communities or families had remained isolated within their own borders and admitted no communication with those who were not members of their tribal group, it is certain that in a reasonably short period of time their language would have changed considerably from that of their forefathers. Owing to the fact that, at the same time that their language was changing, the Indians were constantly spreading out to new places, within a few centuries their speech was probably so modified that even the people of neighboring towns would hardly be able to understand one another. Since the cause of these language changes has continued to be present among the Indians from the time that they started to settle in this land down to the present time, there is no reason why we should be surprised that their many languages could all have evolved from a single one. In order to confirm the truth of this line of reasoning, I am only going to rely on firsthand experience. The fact is that, even though the nations which are very far apart spoke languages so different that at first they seemed to be unrelated, nevertheless, the languages of neighboring nations were very similar, just as the people themselves were closely related. In order to avoid boring details, I will only give for my examples the Quechua and the Aymara languages, which are the ones most generally used in Peru. Since these two languages are from two neighboring nations, they are so similar in vocabulary and grammatical constructions that anyone with even a limited knowledge of them, as I have myself, would find it impossible to deny that these languages had a common origin, in the same way that Spanish and Italian evolved from Latin.

Chapter 10: *In which all the Indian nations are divided into three categories*

As has been stated before, all of the Indians who are native to America are barbarians, for, like barbarians, they share a lack of orderliness, humaneness, and respect for law, which distinguishes them from men who observe these practices and regulate their lives and customs by the laws of reason and justice. Although this is so, nevertheless, due to the fact that among barbarians there are great differences, some barbarians being superior to others in many things (not all barbarians are cut from the same pattern), we will make a general division which will include all of them and will serve to make more distinct and clear what will be said in the course of this writing.

These people can be divided into three groups or classes, using the kind of government and political structure they have as the principal criterion for this classification. In the first group of barbarians I am placing those who live in *behetrias* and have no towns, kings, or lords; these are the most crude and savage of all. Some wander about in the open lands and deserts in bands like animals, recognizing no one as their leader; others live in small communities made up only of members of the same lineage or family. These will obey, in the things they wish, the head of the family, who is usually the oldest relative, or the one among them who is superior to the rest in knowledge and ability. The second group is more like a republic, because it includes all the barbarians who live in communities made up of different families and because they recognize a chief or cacique, whom they obey but who does not have any lords with vassals under him. The third group includes the Indians who are more orderly and have better political organization. These live together in large communities and republics which are controlled by powerful kings who have as their subjects other caciques and lords with vassals.

Besides the stated differences, the three groups of Indians usually stand apart in that many of those in the first group do not have homes or permanent campsites; rather they move from day to day and from one place to another in search of food, much as animals do when they shift from pasture to pasture. Consequently, they sustain themselves by gathering wild fruits and by hunting and fish-

ing, for they do not cultivate or sow the land. Those in the second
and third groups sow and gather their seeds and vegetables. They
both live in houses and in towns. Of the two, the former live in
settlements made up of a small number of houses and ordinarily
divided along family lines. The latter live in large orderly towns
with many small villages in the immediate area, each one belonging
to its particular *ayllo* or lineage.

They differ, moreover, in that many of the nations belonging
to the first two groups go around naked, unlike those of the third,
which never do. In addition, the farther they progress from the first
group, the more religious practices and superstitions they have. Inasmuch as the Indians in the first group surpass the other two in
their degree of barbarity, they are also the least idolatrous of the
three, because practically none of them practice any kind of worship. Those belonging to the second group recognize and worship
some false gods, but this is done with few ceremonies and offerings.
The Indians belonging to the third group were the ones who worshiped the most gods, observed the greatest order in their cult and
celebrations, and had the most priests, temples, and sacrifices. Outside of what has been said, very little dissimilarity between these
three groups of barbarians can be seen, because if we look at their
rudeness, inhumanity, and fierceness, all three had plenty of these.
Even within the most noble and orderly group, there were nations
of *caribes*, eaters of human flesh, who offered human sacrifices to
the devil. The third group was superior to the other two in that its
members were meeker and more domestic, because they were more
accustomed to obeying their kings, and in that they were also more
assiduous and skillful in some of the crafts they practiced. In addition, their great kings, through their practice in government, had
acquired much experience and adroitness in good administration
and preservation of their kingdoms, as is exemplified by the governments of the Mexican and Peruvian kings.

The first group of barbarians is the largest and the most widely
distributed. In it are included the Chichimecs of New Spain, the
Indians from Florida, those of California, and innumerable other
peoples that live in that northern part of America. In this southern
part, the Indians belonging to this group are all those who inhabit
the provinces of the Strait of Magellan, most of those in Tucuman,
Paraguay, and Brazil, and almost all of those from the coasts of the
North Sea, together with all those found inland from there, along
the banks of the great Marañon River up to the borders of this Kingdom of Peru. Throughout the length of this kingdom, there are in-

numerable peoples who inhabit the provinces of the Andes and the *yunca* lands of the East from the district of Charcas, continuing north all the way up to the lands which border on the provinces of Quito and the Kingdom of New Granada.

The second group includes the brave Indians of Chile, those from Popayan, and some nations from Tucuman and Paraguay. Many of the people who became extinct after the arrival of the Spaniards also belonged to this group, as did the natives of the island of Hispaniola and other *cacicazgos* from the surrounding islands, the inhabitants of Tierra Firme, and many other nations of the coasts from the north of Peru.

In the third group we include the populous republics that observed the highest degree of humaneness and reason, and which were governed by powerful kings. They were few in comparison with the innumerable *behetrias* and settlements and small dominions that existed. They were the Kingdom of Bogota within the Kingdom of New Granada, the Mexican Empire, and the Inca Empire of Peru, together with lesser kingdoms found in New Spain, among which one can include the Kingdom of Tlaxcala, which was a free republic in the manner of the city-state of Venice.

Regarding the origin of these three classes of barbarians and the time at which they began to differentiate from each other on the things mentioned above, one can determine (taking their earliest recollection and tradition, which hardly date back five hundred years) that all the people of this New World were very barbaric and savage in ancient times. Among the tribes which we still find today in this first stage of development are the Chichimecs, Chunchos, Mojos, Chiriguanas, and many others who are still infidels. It has also been determined that, in the course of the last few centuries, a few of the men who possessed greater ability and valor than the rest came up from the ranks and encroached by skill and by the force of arms upon the freedom of their people and that of their neighbors. And despite the fact that in the beginning these fierce and untamed people were not accustomed to bearing such a burden and upon feeling the yoke of subjugation tried to cast it off, in the end, because of the rigorous punishments meted out by the tyrants on those who resisted them, the people became domesticated and surrendered to this cruel and tyrannical power. And once these dominions and *cacicazgos* were founded, the descendants of those who established them continued to inherit them and with the passing of time continued to make them more secure and to enlarge them. This was the way in which the first class of barbarians gave origin to the second, and from this one came the third. Some of the caciques grew so powerful and had so many vassals that they were able to subjugate their immediate neighbors and to have as subjects other lesser caciques and lords with vassals.

I have written at length and have told as much as possible about the nature and customs that the Indians have in common, moved only by the wish to record the truth about how they were in their state of paganism. I did not do it so that we would disdain them and consider them inferior because of their ignorance and misfortune, but rather so that we would show compassion for their needs and in the spirit of Christian charity make an extra effort to help win them for Christ and show them the road to salvation. This effort will be all the greater on behalf of those who were and still are in the darkness of their infidelity and under the tyrannical dominion of the devil. I have also written this account so that those who should see the abundant fruit borne by spreading the divine word among these people who were so far astray of the path of righteousness will know its admirable virtue and effectiveness. It was also written so that the great work done in only a few years by the preachers of the gospel to further the education and refinement of the Indians will be recognized and to encourage those who will come later to imitate them and carry on with this glorious enterprise.

Chapter 11: On the origin of these peoples of America

I would consider it to be frightfully audacious if, without more proof than that which is based on the subtleness of his own ingenuity and reasoning power, someone should venture to determine as true what he may have imagined about the origins of the Indians. Actually this matter is so refined and difficult that to this day no one, of all that have written on the subject, has gone any farther than to propose his own opinion to us, without asking that we confirm it by anything other than probability. Being fearful of committing the same error, I will content myself with merely expressing plainly what I feel about this complicated matter; and I will relate the conjectures and explanations which induce me to adopt this view, leaving the determination of the truth to whoever may find other more solid explanations and bases upon which to support it. In my opinion, it would be very difficult to prove conclusively, since the guiding light which usually shows the way to reason in such disputes is lacking, but we will have to infer what we judge to be reasonable by discretion and good judgment, rather than by outside authorities and evident arguments. Not even in ancient writings, whether they be holy or profane, do we find any trace of this point; much less among the Indians themselves do we find any memory or tradition concerning where they came from. It is true that the Indians of this Kingdom of Peru tell fictitious tales concerning their origin, but these stories are not pertinent to the matter at hand; so I will mention them later.

Let us take for granted, before anything else, the universal truth that the Holy Scriptures teach us, that is to say, that all the men in the world come from a single first man, and that all perished in the Universal Deluge; no one escaped alive except the patriarch Noah and his sons and their wives; and they repopulated the earth. Therefore it follows that the first men to populate the Indies came from some regions of the Old World, from where the restoration of the universe began. The second assumption is that we do not have to recur to miracles where they can be dispensed with; at this time we are not investigating what God could have done in order to populate the whole world, but rather what is most in accordance with the natural course of human events. With these fundamental ideas set down, which are considered infallible by all who write about this matter, it is left for us to inquire what route the first settlers who came here could have taken. Being so obscure and doubtful, this business has given those who have written about it occasion to each go their separate way. Some say that the settlers of this fourth part of the world came by land, spreading little by little from region to region; for this reason they suppose that America is connected with Asia somewhere. Others hold that they came by sea, possibly impelled by a storm, or on a planned voyage; and writers are not lacking who point out the nations and provinces from which they came. Some state that all these Indians spread out from one nation, and these people came from Phoenicia and Carthage. Since they were very skillful in the art of navigation, these people came by their own design in a flotilla to this land, of which they had had some information. Others say that these Indians descended from those Ten Tribes of the Hebrews, who (as they say in the Book of Esdras)[13] were transported to a very remote region beyond the Euphrates River, where people had never lived before, and that from there, through Tartary, they came to North America, from whence they spread throughout the other part of the Indies. Still others say that they were descended from the inhabitants of that legendary island called Atlantis by Plato. Others are of the opinion that the natives of this New World are descendants of Spaniards, because they say that from them the Canary Islands were populated; and from these islands they came here. Others feel that the Romans populated this land at the time when their empire was largest and most powerful. To others it seems that the Indians descended from the Tartars and the Chinese. Finally, others say that they did not come from one single nation, but from all of those mentioned above; nor did they come by one single route, but by many different routes, some by land and some by sea; some came by chance, others planned their passage.

In conclusion, due to the uncertainty and obscurity surrounding the period when America was populated, everyone has taken the liberty of adopting the conjectures that his thoughts have brought forth; and since none of them have any other basis than that which those who build their reasoning around these conjectures attempt to give, the support and stability of the opinions based on such conjectures are so feeble that in order for them to weaken and topple, it is not necessary to refute them by other more powerful opinions. But, though it is a very easy thing to cut to pieces what I consider to be false concerning the beginning and origin of the Indians, nevertheless, I consider it to be a very arduous and difficult business to hit upon the truth of this matter. And certainly if the

process and order of this history did not oblige me to say what I
think about this matter, and if the description previously made
about the condition and quality of the land and its inhabitants did
not give promise of throwing some light on the truth of this matter,
I would very gladly abstain from going into it and expressing my
opinion. In the last analysis, I am aware that no matter how hard
I may work to defend and substantiate it, in the end my opinion
will have to stand in contrast with the other opinions that I try
to refute.

In starting to disentangle this difficulty, the first thing I will
say is that, considering what I have proven in Chapter 9 of this
book, namely, that all these people descend from one lineage, the
opinion that they were from many nations of the Old World is
cut to pieces. It is no obstacle to put aside the first objection which
presents itself, that it would be impossible for so many far-reaching
lands to have been populated by one single lineage of men. In fact,
from just one lineage the whole world has been filled with the innumerable peoples that inhabit it today; and certainly, without any
difficulty, the first ones to put their feet on this land, no matter
how few in number they may have been, along with their descendants, could have, in the course of time, slowly spread out and occupied all this land. In the little more than one hundred and fifty
years that have passed since our Spaniards discovered this land,
in spite of finding it full of fierce and warlike people who offered
and still offer stubborn resistance, our Spaniards have penetrated
it all, have occupied the majority of it, and have founded so many
cities and provinces. So why should it astound us that with it unpopulated and desolate, without anyone to offer them resistance
or interrupt their passage, the first settlers populated it in a few
centuries? There probably were enough settlers to have sufficient
time not only for this land to be filled by its first owners, but for
some areas to become overpopulated and end up without sufficient
room within their borders. This probably led them to wage war
on their neighbors, destroy them—as a result of the rigors of war
and their barbarous cruelty—and occupy and populate their provinces. We have an example of this that is not very ancient in the
Chiriguana Indians; being valiant and warlike, at the time or a few
years before the Spaniards entered this Kingdom of Peru, they left
their country, Paraguay, in bands and traveled more than four hundred leagues across the intervening provinces, destroying the natives of these provinces. They arrived at the area that now adjoins
the province of Charcas, took this area from its inhabitants, and

usurped it for themselves. It is now well populated by Indians of the Chiriguana nation. Another example is the Indians of Brazil, who got as far as the province of Chachapoyas during the time of President Pedro de la Gasca; from their homeland to the end of their journey, these Indians traveled more than a thousand leagues. Now I ask, if in so few years about ten or twelve thousand Chiriguana Indians have overrun and occupied such large provinces, fighting and destroying their inhabitants and filling them with their own colonies (and they would have expanded even more and dominated more lands if the Spaniards had not stopped them, curbing their arrogance), how swiftly the first inhabitants must have multiplied and spread, especially because of the brutal intemperance of these barbarous people, who, owing to their heathen ways, multiplied almost as fast as the most prolific livestock. Therefore, I am finished with this first point, and I consider the basis for resolving this matter to be the fact that one single nation of men came over to populate these Indies, and from it are descended all of the innumerable nations that possess this land today. It was very easy for them to be propagated by that one nation because of the many centuries that have elapsed. Although there may not be definite proof of the time when men came here, still the antiquity of ruined buildings that we find, and what has been stated above concerning the division of these people into three classes of barbarians and their innumerable languages—all of this supports the view that the settlement of this New World had started only a few centuries after the Universal Flood was over.

The second assumption I will make is that the men who settled in this land were, at the time they came, ignorant, primitive and savage, illiterate, unskilled, and lacking any sign of law and order. I am convinced of this in view of and considering the nature and properties of the land and the character of its inhabitants, so different in everything from the people of Europe and their neighbors; it is certainly true that if the first settlers had come from some civilized nation with writing, after a long time without contact with other people, their descendants could have degenerated from the existence and luster of their progenitors, and they might have ended up in the unrefined barbarity where we find them; but the unusual strangeness and divergence of their qualities and customs which have been explained do not give cause to think this. If this had happened, some traces would remain as an indication of the greater value and excellence of their ancestors, and what we find the farther into the past we inquire and investigate is more coarseness and savagery. But since I will continue to expand on this subject, I do not want to go into it any further here. By virtue of this second assumption, the opinion of those who would have it that these Indians descended from the nation of the Jews or from any of the other European nations is refuted; and, therefore, it must be concluded that their progenitors did not come on a long planned voyage by sea, as has been stated; nor was there ever any information in Europe about these Indies, as we will show.

Chapter 12: In which the same is continued

In accordance with the assumptions which we have set down in the last chapter, we will move ahead in our investigation by inquiring from what part of the Old World the first settlers came to this New one and how they could have made such a long trip. For this inquiry, though it is true that we have no easy way, nor even any sign or trace that we can follow with assurance, I think that the way in which I am directing my line of reasoning is the truest and most reliable, as will be shown by the conjectures which prompt me to proceed in this manner. In the first place, let us make an imaginary trip around this fourth part of the world which we call America, circling it along its coasts and borders, and on the way let us observe and notice, as from a watchtower, what land lies nearest to it; and once this has been found, let us look over the inhabitants and see if there are any points of similarity in temperament and characteristics between them and these Indians. As a consequence of this, we will soon be faced with the doubt which the cosmographers and geographers have not been able to clear up, namely, whether the northern part of this land is connected with any of the northernmost regions of Asia.

And truly there is very much reason to doubt this connection because of the reports brought by those who have navigated along the northern coasts through both the North and South Seas with the sole intention of exploring the boundaries and limits of this land. Even though by sailing along the shore they have gotten as close to the Pole as they could, going more than sixty degrees above the equinoctial line, the excessive cold in that place during the months of June and July has not permitted them to go past that point; nor have they discovered the end of the land, nor has it been determined whether or not the land continues until it joins with Asia; thus remains the doubt. And if there is a sea strait between Asia and America, as the cosmographers put on their lists (they call it Anian), it probably is not very wide, because the northernmost parts of this land come so close to Asia. Therefore, it is certain that the northern area comes closer to the Old World than any other.

Up to this point we have been speaking of the common opinion based on the views of geographers; but, in my opinion, there is no more doubt, considering what I said in Chapter 14 of Book 1, Part One,[14] and the fact is that I consider it most probable that this land is joined with the northernmost part of Asia. According to this opinion, the first settlers came to this land from the latter region of Asia, made up of China, Tartary, and the Archipelago of Saint Lazarus, which includes the Philippine Islands. This point of view is greatly strengthened by the second line of reasoning that we were investigating, which is the similarity between these Indians and the people that inhabit the coast of Asia. This similarity cannot be denied; rather, it is very great. Not only are the men of China and the adjacent islands beardless like these Indians and similar to them in color, but they are also similar in temperament, disposition, and customs. The people of America, like those of China and the Philippines, are pusillanimous, inconstant, and docile; and the very delicate Tartars from China must also have the same qualities because they are from the same area. The one who gave me the first report that America is connected with Asia, in addition to what has been said, assured me that the Tartars, near the Chinese border, use the same type of books that the Mexicans had, in which they told their history with characters.

And what contributes much in support of what we are saying is to see the great similarity which these Indians of America have with all the nations of people that have been discovered on trips both by sea and along the coast from this land toward the west and north. Those who have sailed from Peru to the Solomon Islands have encountered throughout the entire trip many islands densely populated with Indians up to the Solomon Islands, and from there on to the Philippines and the coast of Asia. And in the same way, explorers have gone to discover the end of this land along the coast, through the South Sea as well as the North Sea, and all the people that they found in all the places where they came ashore to explore the land are very similar in every way to our Indians of America.

The manner in which those first settlers made their way here could be difficult to explain; however, it certainly does not seem difficult to me when you take into consideration the fact that the same men who left did not necessarily carry out such a large trip to the far reaches of this land; rather, the same thing that happened in the settlement of other parts of the world must have happened: as the men were propagating themselves and multiplying, they spread out and divided up by families and bands, occupying the nearly virgin provinces that they found uninhabited. Therefore, the first men who left Asia probably occupied the first land of this America, which from there was the closest. To the extent that they multiplied, they must have been spreading and occupying new lands without making long stops on the way, avoiding the difficulties of stopping in the densely populated provinces. They probably tried to spread out across only those that they found uninhabited and suitable for them to be able to maintain themselves. And as those filled up with more people than could comfortably be supported there, the families, like swarms of bees, would produce and extend themselves across the adjoining provinces, without undertaking long journeys that would separate some groups from others. This is true because the whole route that we have discovered in this direction is continuous. Thus, following one another in the continuation of this trip in this way, the first settlers having started it, their descendants carried it forward. After a few generations the last ones would finish the trip.

Upon occupying all the provinces of this large mainland (which would take at least several hundred years), when the multitude of inhabitants had no more room, some would cross over to the nearest islands of the great archipelago of America.[15] Since these islands are close to the mainland and linked together from the coast of South America to North America, the settlers would not have found any difficulty that would impede their passage to all of them, until they completed the long course of the journey—initiated by their ancestors—in the most distant and easterly islands of that archipelago. And truly, if the wide gulf of the Ocean Sea, which lies between the eastern coast of America and the western coast of Africa, did not divide these two parts of the world, these Indians might have gone so far as to get in touch with the Africans, if they found, as they have so far, continuous land passage or if they did not lose sight of land on the way.

That this was the type of journey and route taken by the settlers of these Indies and those who populated the other regions of the world, and not long, planned voyages, is in my opinion strongly supported by the fact that in our days many unpopulated and virgin islands have been found, for no other reason than they are very distant from the mainland—previously there had been no knowledge of them—for example, the Cape Verde Islands, Madeira Island, San Juan Island, the Terceira Islands, or the Azores, which the Portuguese have discovered and populated. I do not doubt that if ancient man had discovered them, he would have settled there as the Portuguese have done. And in this South Sea, when they were found by the Spaniards, all the islands that are nearby and in view from the mainland were well populated with Indians; however, the islands that are very distant were uninhabited, for example, the Islands of Juan Fernandez off the coast of Chile which are sixty leagues away, and the Galapagos Islands, across from the province of Guayaquil, about one hundred leagues out to sea.[16]

Chapter 13: How the animals and birds that we find here must have come to this land

We find these Indies well populated not only with men but also with many and varied animals, some of which are native and others are of the same species that occur in the Old World, especially Spain: for this reason inquisitive people are not satisfied that we point out the way by which the first men who populated these Indies came, but also want us to make way for the birds and animals, on the assumption that this matter is either dependent on or related to the other one. And although, in my judgment, these two matters are not related, nevertheless I will try to satisfy those who are not sure how land and air animals, and even men, could have come here if this land were not connected to the first three parts of the world—Europe, Asia, and Africa. Others are not lacking who, admitting and confessing that this land is not connected to the other, make no less effort to find the route of the wild beasts and birds than that of the first settlers. Whether the animals and birds all came by the same route or whether they took different ones, this matter is a dispute which is not really exclusive to the animals of this land; rather it is a general question common to all wild animals and birds that are found in remote places and islands far from the mainland.

Putting aside the various opinions that I find concerning this matter, I will briefly give what I consider to be the most probable, on the basis of arguments which are both reasonable and in accord with the context and sense of the Holy Scriptures. First of all, in the beginning of the world, God created the animals, not just in one place, but in many places, each type in the place and climate which was best suited to its conservation and increase. I am persuaded that it must have happened in this way (going to the root of the matter), because there seems to be no doubt that the production of the plants happened in this manner: on the same day that the Creator decorated the earth with them, all places and regions appeared adorned in this new and cheerful way; first of all, when God ordered that grass and trees sprout forth, there is no evidence that He limited this concept to one single region, province, or territory; on the contrary, from the words in which Moses tells it, the implication is made that God's word was conveyed generally all around the world. Moreover, experience leaves no room for us to believe anything else; the fact is that in different parts of the universe we find noticeably different kinds of plants which have properties so different and contrary that they could not grow and thrive except in different and contrary climates, each kind in the climate that conforms to its nature.

On the basis of this principle and assumption, which I do not think is contradictory, let us go up one more step, by inquiring whether the same thing happened in the miraculous creation of the creatures that came to life on the fifth day; and in truth, I find no arguments or sign of it having occurred in any other way. The fact is that in describing it to us the sacred text makes no change in style or form of words from those in which it tells us of the creation of the plants. From which I infer, for this reason and owing to what was stated before, which is also true for these kinds of creatures which have the diverse qualities of fish and fowl, that they do not have less need of different weather and land conditions for their preservation than the plants. And experience shows that there are diverse kinds of these creatures in different regions, climates, and seas, especially in large, wide lakes which are not linked to the sea anywhere; this is because God provided all the parts and zones of the waters and earth proportionately with fowl and fish on the fifth day, just as he had covered the earth with plants on the third day.

Now let us get to the point, which I presume has been inferred as an evident consequence of the two premises that we have made, since the same reasoning as for the others holds here; the words are uniform with which the Holy Scriptures describe the production of the animals that came from the earth on the sixth day and the words about the plants, fish, and fowl which had been created on the third and fifth days. Actually the variety of qualities with which different kinds of land animals were provided is no less marvelous and comprehensive than the variety which was given to plants and the animals of water and air. For this reason, as well as for them to propagate themselves and endure in the world, God created them in places and climates required by the condition of each species so that in the places which were their natural setting and their native region, they could better establish and conserve themselves; we must confess that Providence itself looked after them. To this, add self-evident experience that shows us in different parts of the earth the same diversity of animals as of plants, fish, and fowl.

Besides what has been said, this opinion is backed up by the

authority of scholars who defend it, such as Father Benito Pereira
(Book I of *Commentariorvm et dispvtationvm in Genesim*) and other exegetes of Genesis. This opinion is further substantiated by what
is stated in the second chapter of Genesis itself, that, after the creation of all the animals was finished, God brought them to Adam
in the Garden of Eden so that he could give each species the name
that it was to have. This happened on the same day that the land
animals and Adam himself had been created. And as the exegetes
of the Scriptures explain how the animals were brought to Adam,
the majority agree that this was done miraculously through the
work of Angels, presupposing that the animals were already spread
out through the entire circumference of the universe. If it happened
in this way, as I consider to be most probable, naturally, if they
had been created together in one place and not throughout the
world, by themselves they could not have spread out all over the
world in only a few hours; nor would it have been necessary for
a miracle to have occurred so that they could be placed in the presence of Adam.

Therefore, I conclude that not only the plants but also the
animals, those of the land as well as those of water and air, were
created by God in diverse parts of the world; each kind was placed
in the region and climate most suitable for its conservation. Thus
He did not give to each region all the species of living things which,
owing to its climate and weather, could live there; rather to each
species He gave the region that best suited it and agreed with its
nature and characteristics, distributing His abundance so systematically that no corner of the entire globe, no matter how remote it
may be, was left without its share of them. And if He did not send
to each region all of those that because of its quality and fertility
it could produce and sustain, He did not fail to do so for being
miserly or less generous, but because, with His supreme counsel,
He wanted to leave this entrusted to man's responsibility. Principally so that some lands would need to make up for what they
lacked with others, He obliged men to communicate with one another as in a fraternal alliance, at least because of the need which
would necessarily ensue for them to trade and exchange the goods
that abounded in some lands and were lacking in others.

We would have been finished with this problem if the ruin
and havoc that the Universal Flood played with the world did not
oblige us to move ahead to discuss saving the animals from it. Ac-
knowledging jointly what we know from the Holy Scriptures, that
is, that all animals of the land and air perished except for the ones

that were saved in Noah's ark, from whence all those that now live on land or in the air originated, consequently, we find ourselves obliged to open the way for them from the place in which the ark ran aground and Noah stepped down from his post, to these regions of America so distant from there, and the crux of this problem lies in this dispersal. But before taking upon ourselves the task of unraveling it, I consider it necessary to find out how Noah gathered together the animals themselves in order to save them in his vessel from the waters of the Flood. To avoid giving several opinions, let it suffice us to explain what the majority of the holy scholars and exegetes of the Divine Scriptures say, and this is that the animals were collected and enclosed in the ark by a miracle of the Angels.

Accepting this opinion as true and certain, I find no better, simpler, and more reasonable way out of the problem at hand than to say and declare that the same divine providence that planned by way of a miracle to save all the species of higher animals, since for its purposes it lacks nothing that is necessary, providence also took the trouble, after the Flood was over, to order the Angels to return the animals to the same places and regions from whence they had brought them. In drawing this conclusion I do not believe that I ought to be accused of resorting to miracles just to avoid and get out of the tight spot in which those who have tried other ways to solve the problem find themselves. I do not feel that a new miracle has been involved here or that this was more than a continuation of the first one, which almost everyone accepts. And if this solution does not meet with approval, I do not know of any other that can be proposed without including in it either special and miraculous intervention by the Lord or enormous drawbacks and absurdities. And in spite of this, scholars of note are not lacking who, so as to avoid admitting the Lord's intervention, although it is nothing more than the continuation of that first miracle, get mixed up and entangled in such an intricate labyrinth, so full of new obscurities and problems, that no matter how many sleepless nights they spend, nor how much they tire themselves trying to hit upon a way out, in the end they are forced to admit effects that go far beyond the style and course that nature usually takes and that cannot be explained logically without special divine assistance.

Chapter 14: In which the same topic is continued

As proof of my opinion in such a case, I will give only one example, and I will note some of the drawbacks and absurdities that those who take any other alternative will necessarily have to accept. The example is the miracle that God performed for Adam by having the Angels bring all the animals to him so that he could give them names. Regarding this miracle, I would like to know if after those animals were put in Paradise, the Angels left them there to return on their own to their native regions, or if they were returned to them by the Angels. The first possibility does not seem reasonable; actually not a few of the holy fathers and scholars of the Church deny that there had even been animals in Paradise (although the majority take a contrary view); thus, because it is more reasonable, I feel that, in order for that miraculous work to be completed, God ordered the Angels to take the animals back to the same places from which they came, because they were brought up in them. Therefore, we can draw the conclusion that, since this miracle occurred in this way, it is not difficult to believe that this other one happened in the same way; in both cases the same reasonable explanations apply.

Those who do not accept this opinion necessarily will have to say that all the animals disembarked together in the same place and that from there each breed and type struck out by itself, and since they multiplied successively, they gradually spread out to the far corners of the earth, in the same way that it was populated by man. In refuting this argument, I say, that to defend it and carry it out, first its authors must admit an unsupportable absurdity, which, normally speaking, we can call impossible; it is that the place and zone which the animals first occupied upon landing was appropriate and agreeable to the various properties and characteristics of all the animals, although this is contrary to what experience teaches us. To this day no land has been found with a climate commensurate with and suitable to all different kinds of animals. This is because some are born only in hot regions, and they die if they move to a cold or temperate one; others are born in the very cold paramos, others in temperate lands, and in this way each species is born in a suitable ambience. And having given them being and life, to give them places and homes in accordance with what the nature of each kind required, God did not create them in one single part of the earth, as has been proven, but in different ones, each type in the place it needed by nature to survive. That divine power that made them this way would have been useless and in vain if, on being produced in one single place, they could naturally survive and multiply in it and go out from there spreading all over the world, as those who are of this opinion will have to confess—although they may not want to—unless they resort to the extraordinary care that God could have taken to preserve them out of their natural habitat. And what else would this be but to add new miracles in order to avoid that first one that I accept? Here we are proceeding on the following assumption: that the course of natural phenomena is in all ages one and the same, invariable. This is because nature (and this is a principle of philosophy) is always directed toward the self-same objective, and in accordance with this principle we must confess that we cannot now naturally raise and preserve all the species of animals in the same climate; this is the way it has been for all time, and the animals were never naturally together in one place or territory.

The second drawback that those who take this view must recognize is contrary to the nature of the animals themselves. Who could be persuaded that the animals would take such a long journey on their own volition, traveling over so many extensive regions with such great differences in climate, many contrary to their nature, innumerable plentiful rivers, and in not a few places swamps, tidelands, and thick, impenetrable forests and jungles? And if, by their own volition, they traveled through so many lands that they arrived here, where they stopped and took up residence, why, not having changed their nature, did they tire so many centuries ago and stop their roving? Now each kind is content to stay in the province or territory where it was born and raised without going beyond its borders to enter into other areas and roam about in them. We could confirm this argument with innumerable instances and examples: Pliny[17] is exceedingly amazed by this, and in his amazement he confesses his inability to grasp the secret of this mystery. I do not want to mention the vicuñas, a species of animal native to this Kingdom of Peru, which never descend from the high sierras and very frigid paramos where they live; I will keep silent about the animals of the tropical *yunca* lands, such as monkeys and others that we never see come out of the hot montaña to go up to the cold climate of the sierra. I will leave out the animals that are native to New Spain, such as the coyotes, wolves, buffalo, and others that, even though land is connected to this kingdom, have not come here; neither have animals from this land, such as the vicuñas, guanacos, and others which are lacking there, gone from here to New Spain. We also find this to be the case in regard to many types of birds: let the example of the crows suffice; although North America is full of them, they never come here to South America, nor are they ever seen in Peru; and even though they come as far as Nicaragua, they never go beyond its borders, nor do the Peruvian ostriches and condors go to New Spain.

Well, what if we were to speak about the animals, both those of the land and those of the air, uncommon and unique, that are found here in the Indies and were never seen before in other regions of the world, nor are they mentioned by the European historians of antiquity, because they had never seen or heard of them? If, as they were multiplying, they kept spreading out little by little until they arrived here, why did not others of the same sort stay in the lands they came from and remain along the way by which they came? And how could those which are found here have come? Why did some of the other kinds that were not present in this land not make the same journey? This seems strange, especially since there are in the broad regions of America suitable climates for as many species of wild beasts, livestock, and birds as are to be found in any part of the world; this has been borne out by experience after our Spaniards brought some of each kind of livestock and tame animals from Spain. Who distributed and picked out the types of wild animals, beasts, and birds that had to cross over to these Indies and prohibited the rest from coming here? I do not know what solution can be given for the many drawbacks that his way of thinking [that the animals from the ark spread out by themselves] presents unless the proponents reply that by an interior impulse some animals were moved to make this journey and others were not, but then the proponents would end up by getting caught in the snare that they seek to avoid by not conceding that the animals were brought by a miracle to this New World.

The third drawback is no less problematic than those mentioned. With regard to the animals that we find in remote islands far from the mainland, it must either be said that they swam across the sea or that they were carried in ships by people. The first argument is not on the right track because, since, as we have seen, they are not accustomed to going from one region to another, even though they can without danger or even getting their feet wet, they would be less inclined to plunge into the waves of the sea, where they would run the risk of drowning. Moreover, all the doubts expressed above can be repeated here, namely: Why did some dare to undertake this journey and not others? And with regard to the rare and strange animals that we see on some islands, why did none of their kind remain in other places? And finally, why are those of today not inclined to swim across the sea, if they are of the same nature and disposition as their original progenitors who crossed it? Perhaps those of the contrary view would like to answer with the second argument. But, who could help but notice how ridiculous it would be, and even absurd, for men to occupy themselves in loading and taking with them wild animals that would not only be of no use to them, but which would be very detrimental, and at the same time fail to take beneficial livestock and tame animals, though this is what the Spaniards who came to this New World have done?

In fact, one of the strongest indications I find in favor of my view is to see that the animals that we find in these Indies and New World of the same type as those of the Old World are wild, and many of them are fierce and harmful; and the domestic and tame ones that the Indians had are unique and native to this land, never before known in Europe or in any other part of the Old World. Putting aside numerous other arguments in my favor which occurred to me, in order to avoid going into lengthy details, I will conclude this matter with what I noted at the beginning of it, namely that this controversy and dispute has nothing to do with the one we have already dealt with concerning the route of the first men who settled in this land; this is because the animals were brought to it in the way that has been proven here.

Chapter 15: In which is given the opinion of those who place within these Occidental Indies the region called Ophir in the Divine Scriptures, to which the ships of Solomon navigated

In the last part of this book we will find out if the people of Europe or those of the surrounding regions of Asia or Africa had any communications or commerce with the people of this New World, or if evidence can even be found in their writings that the Europeans had information about this fourth part of the universe called America which our Spaniards have discovered and populated in our times. Some modern writers have discussed this matter, speculating about the region called Ophir, so highly praised for its wealth in the Sacred Scriptures, which the ships of Solomon navigated to and returned from loaded with gold and other riches; they concluded that Ophir was this Kingdom of Peru or another of the rich and famous provinces of America. In this chapter and in the remaining chapters of this book, we will make a careful inquiry into the probability of this opinion, and from the conclusion of this inquiry it will be possible to resolve this matter in general.

The first person who conceived of this and expressed this opinion was François Vatable; on publishing this idea in his writings, he attracted the attention of others and moved them to imitate him and accept his view and defend it, making every effort to have it generally accepted as valid. In the scholia that Vatable wrote about chapters nine and twenty-two of the third Book of Kings, he states that the region of Ophir is the island of Hispaniola, the site of the first colony founded by the Spaniards in these Indies. However, he makes Ophir extend in both directions, south and north, to include all of America, in his comments about the third chapter of the second book of the Paralipomenon. Many learned men have followed Vatable, attempting to promote and support this opinion; some of them are Guillaume Postel, Goropius in "Hispanica," and Arias Montano in his biblical commentaries and in the section he entitled "Phaleg." The first one contends that Ophir is Peru, and the other two that it is all of America. These authors are followed by Genebrard; Marco Marini in his *Arca Noe*, under the heading "Ophira et Paruaijm"; Bozio Eugubino; David Pomi; Father Manuel de Sá, about chapter nine of the third Book of Kings, although he tends to put it in the Oriental Indies of the Lusitanian dominions; Father Antonio Possevino in *Bibliotheca Selecta*, Book 3, chapter 5; and Fray Rodrigo de Yepes in the "Historia del niño inocente crucificado." All of these authors and some others are quoted by Father Juan de Pineda,[18] who is inclined to give some credence to this opinion.

The basis and conjectures on which they endeavor to found their opinion are these: first, the authority of Admiral Christopher Columbus, discoverer of this New World, of whom Peter Martyr tells in Book 1 of his *Decades* that the Admiral used to say that he had discovered the land of Ophir; second, the similarity and relation between these two names, Ophir and Peru. It is usually explained in two ways. Some affirm that this province of Peru, and even all of America, was called Ophir in ancient times and little by little the natives have made changes and alterations in the letters of this word until it came to have its present form of Peru or Piru. They advance as proof of this the similarity in the number of letters that the two names have and in the pronunciation and sound of these two names Ophir and Piru, and they affirm that this land was named Ophir by the founder whom they give; they say that two brothers named Hevila and Ophir, sons of Jectan and nephews of Heber, occupied the East Indies after the Flood, and from there Ophir came to these Western Indies, and this land took the name of its founder, as is common in other parts of the world, which usually take their names from their founders.

Others, although they use this argument of the similarity and affinity of the two words, modify it a little, so that it seems very different. In order to derive the word Peru from Ophir, they give the latter word as many transformations as Ovid's poem, until it has the form Piru, which suits their purpose. They get this word, as they themselves say, from its original through the following steps. They state that, where our Vulgata latina was translated "Porro aurum erat probatissimum" (2 Paralipomenon, Chapter 3), the exact text in Hebrew is "aurum erat de loco Paruaim"; this latter word was retained in their translation by the Seventy Interpreters;[19] Paruaim is the plural of this name Ophir, whose singular is Paru or Peru; the Holy Book used this name in the plural in order to signify and include both parts of America, South America and North

America; but of these forms now only the first is preserved in the name Peru. And in order to confirm this argument, they cite the names of many other provinces and places of this land, such as Paria, Paraguay, Piura, Pariacaca, and other similar ones; and because of the convenience and the similarity between the latter words and the word Paruaim, they feel that they have been derived from it.

The third conjecture that moves them to adopt this opinion is the abundance of gold, precious and exquisite woods, the many apes, peacocks, and other unusual and very valuable things that Solomon's ships brought from Ophir. The above-mentioned authors think that this land of the Indies abounds in the things those ships brought back more than any other land in the world, and for this reason only this land sent those riches back to Solomon.

The fourth and last reason is the long period of time that those ships took on the trip, which was three years; they do not think that such a long voyage could possibly be made unless it was to the most remote and distant regions that could be reached by sea toward the east or the west; although the voyage that the Portuguese make today to the East Indies is very lengthy, they do not take more than a year to reach there, and at the most, a year and a half.

Chapter 16: In which the proposed opinion is refuted

Through long years of practical experience, some of us have achieved a reasonable understanding of the nature and qualities of the land of this New World. With the speculation of many years, we have penetrated the secrets and the qualities and customs of its inhabitants. It comes to us as a great surprise to see grave men who are renowned scholars so bent on obstinately carrying forward their pretension to strengthen and attempt to make probable what they thought up out of their own heads, without any other valid evidence or even conjectures that would merit the attention of prudent men. It is particularly surprising that these men jump to conclusions at such a distance from what they have learned neither from experience nor from sight. In fact, hardly any of those who accept this view has set foot on this land; for this reason they make us suspect that they want to use this way to diminish the felicity of our times and lessen the glory that belongs to our nation for such a singular and heroic undertaking and feat as discovering a new world and enlarging the temporal dominions of our nation and the spiritual dominions of the Church of Christ, our savior. It may well be that in the minds of those ignorant about these Indies, their keen and ingenious discourses, so adorned with subtle interpretations, etymologies, and translations, may carry some weight; but they are so far from convincing the most experienced of us here that the most common solution that we usually give for all of these explanations and arguments is to say they clearly show by them that they have very little knowledge of the things of this land, and if they came here and explored it with diligence, no doubt they would change their minds.

How is it possible that no traces would have remained up to the present anywhere in these Indies of the Hebrew nation having business dealings here, in the same way as any of the other nations of this New World, if, as they say, the Hebrews had had such well-established commerce? And since I do not think there is a better argument for refuting the opposing opinion than the absolute lack of any indications that could give life to their position, with only this idea, somewhat expanded, I expect to prove my point. Before proceeding, I consider that a certain principle, which in similar controversies has been expounded in this work, must be accepted whenever the occasion arises, and it is that the course and order of human affairs has in all ages been one and the same. In accordance with this concept, unless there is evidence to the contrary, the qualities and intelligence of the men of the past centuries were the same as at the present time; and the appetite for glory that burned in them was no less vehement at that time than it is now; from this comes the solicitude and care taken by all nations, each one by the most suitable means at its disposal, in making known and endeavoring to perpetuate their glorious deeds.

With this taken for granted, I think that the following is a strong argument (and let it be the first one used to refute the opposing opinion): that navigation and commerce [by the Hebrews] have not continued up to the present time. On the contrary, in the one hundred and sixty years that have passed since our Spaniards found this land, they have not stopped sailing to it with such frequency that hardly a month passes during the whole year in which our ships do not cut through the sea. Although large flotillas make this trip only at specified times, nevertheless, since there are three or four main flotillas that arrive once each year at the ports of different kingdoms, such as New Spain, the islands of Barlovento, Tierra Firme, and Brazil, leaving Spain at different times and not all returning there together, my proposition is verified. This is particularly so if we add to the aforementioned flotillas other innumerable ships sailing alone, such as merchant ships sailing from Spain to the port of Buenos Aires, from the Canary Islands with wine to New Spain, and from Guinea bringing blacks to all of the principal ports of this land, as well as ordinary and special dispatch boats that at any time may be found crossing the wide sea that separates us from Spain. Therefore, this ocean road has come to be no less passable and frequented than the road between Seville and Madrid. Being, as I say, that these voyages are so common, and not finding any cause for them to cease in the future, because when our nation wishes to stop (which it will not), the other nations of Europe will continue making these voyages, for the way is known by all of them better than we would wish, due to the many pirate ships that overrun and infest these seas—why then should we believe that if this same route had been used in the past, its use would have been discontinued and abandoned to such an extent that no record or trace of it remains? Perchance were the men of that time of a different nature than those of today? In order to explain why that commerce and those voyages have not continued, we can say that it was either because the riches of this land were depleted or because man's greed disappeared; both of these conjectures would be sheer stupidity.

In the second place, since Christopher Columbus certainly did discover this New World, and owing to the fact that everybody was especially amazed by such an unusual and new undertaking, its fame spread and extended so fast that before long news of it was published with illustrations and drawings of the new-found lands; with this the memory of it became so firmly entrenched that even if all communications stopped today between the people of Europe and those of us who are here, it would be impossible, rationally speaking, that with time this New World could be buried and forgotten as completely as it was before the aforementioned discovery. In those centuries why did the fame of those renowned voyages not spread across the bordering nations to Palestine, if voyages had been made to such distant, rare, and singular regions? Or if word of the New World spread as now, what could have been the cause of it being so completely forgotten that no notice of it reached us through either history or tradition? In fact I do not believe that the men of that time were more careless than now or less ambitious for honor to the point that they would not make their deeds known and endeavor to be remembered for these deeds. The truth is that in the ancient histories we find no mention of these lands of the New World or of anyone having sailed to them.

Those who hold the opposing view attempt to prove that many men in ancient times wrote about this New World; they list such authors as Plato, Seneca, Lucian, Clement of Rome, Origen, and I do not know how many others. This is totally contrary to what the most outstanding philosophers and geographers believed about the nature, form, and position of the earth;[20] even those who were most accurate in affirming that the earth was spherical in shape and surrounded everywhere by the sky could not in the last analysis convince themselves that all of the regions and zones of the earth were habitable, nor even of the existence of men in the Southern Hemisphere opposite the Northern Hemisphere which they inhabited or in the lower part opposite the upper part of the same hemisphere. Concerning this point we find a notable variety of opinions which would have been forgotten with experience if the ancients had achieved such indisputable experience in the New World as we have. On the contrary, the opposite is clear; in describing the boundaries of the earth both in their written accounts and in their drawings and paintings, not only do they omit making mention of this large and important part of it, but they confess by word and deed that they did not even have complete knowledge of the edges and boundaries of the first three parts of the world about which they

knew. Thus, at the ends of the world known to them, they put
the city of Meroe toward the south, since they were unaware of
what lies beyond toward the equator; they put Borysthenes to the
north, not knowing what there was from there on to the North Pole;
toward the west, their information ended with the Fortunate Islands; and toward the east, it ended in Cattigara;²¹ these were the
boundaries of the habitable world known to the historians, poets,
and geographers; they divided the habitable world into seven zones.
From this it may be deduced that if they had had the information
about this New World that the opposition attributes to them, they
would not have put the end and boundaries of the world in the
places mentioned above, nor would they have been so constant in
their opinion that the western sea was unnavigable past the Fortunate Islands.

From what may be gathered out of that obscure mention found
in the authors cited above, I am of the opinion that they were not
speaking there of definite and specific lands known by them. Being
wise men, they were aware of the size, characteristics, and shape
of the terrestrial globe and that what they had discovered of it did
not include half of its circumference, so they considered it to be
very probable and reasonable that the waters of the sea would not
occupy the rest of the world about which they had no information;
rather, they thought that in some places there would be large lands
similar to those of that hemisphere where they lived. In the same
way, we now suspect that in what remains to be discovered of the
universe in the direction of the two poles, man will not fail to find
other lands no less extensive than those discovered up to now.

Chapter 17: Of another argument with which the same thing is proven as in the last chapter

The third thing that disproves the aforementioned opinion is that there is no place across which it is possible to sail to this New World from the other where it is not necessary to cross the ocean, going out into the open sea without being able to see anything but water and sky for many days; the only exception would be to take that route within sight of land along the coast of Asia, and it is clear to see how inconvenient and even impossible it would be for those who tried it. Apart from the innumerable inconveniences that would result from sailing along the coasts of such extensive regions with such a variety of geographical zones and weather conditions, the duration of the trip would be so long that the three years that they presume it took Solomon's ships would not be enough, nor would they find provisions that would last that long, especially since a considerable part of the trip would have to be made in the Torrid Zone, where the climate is such that if the ships are detained there for long, the food rots and spoils. And, thus, of the two routes that can be taken from Europe to these Western Indies, the one that ordinary voyagers take is to travel west, sailing across the broad sea that falls in between; this voyage takes at least twenty to thirty days before the first islands are sighted. By this route, which is the most common and widely traveled, it is impossible to come to the New World without going out into the open sea.

The second route is the contrary, sailing from Europe toward the east until putting into port in Asia or one of the nearby islands. This is the route that the Portuguese take through their demarcation[22] and Eastern Hemisphere to the ports of India, from where there is also a route through the demarcation of Castile to these Western Indies, which is the one that the armadas of New Spain take on their return from the Philippine Islands. Drifting along on this endless trip, it is certain that, even though the first part, which falls to the Portuguese, could be done within view of land along the coast, nevertheless, it cannot be done without going out to sea many leagues in some places; otherwise the trip would be extremely long and very dangerous. The second part of the trip, which belongs to the Castilians and goes from the end of the first on to America, is also by open sea and involves no less work and effort than the other; this voyage in no way can be made within the sight of land. Although within the Torrid Zone breezes and winds usually blow which are favorable for westward travel, these same winds are so contrary for those who travel from the west toward the east that they cannot take the same route until they pass the tropics so they go either north or south toward the poles in search of favorable winds for their trip. In accordance with this, for two reasons it is impossible to make the aforementioned voyage from the farthermost coasts of Asia to these Indies without losing sight of land, even though, as we have already said above, a continuous stretch of coast does extend from there to here. In the first place, this coastal voyage is hindered in the southern part along the coast of New Guinea, which is within the Torrid Zone and so close to the equator; the contrary winds blow there that we mentioned above as hindering the eastern route to America. In the second place, if this voyage is taken in the direction that experience has shown to those who frequently travel from the Philippines to New Spain, passing the Tropic of Cancer and going north thirty degrees and more to the final edge of Asia, which is the coast of Tartary, the land falls back so much toward the North Pole that it is not possible to continue sailing within sight of the coast until reaching America, whose northern coast also falls off a lot toward the North Pole; and for this reason, those who sail across there go out in the open sea so far that they spend three or four months without seeing land.

The conclusions I draw from this line of reasoning are, first of all, that it is impossible to sail from Europe or from the Red Sea to these Western Indies without going so far out to sea that sight of land is lost for a long time; and second (and this is inferred from the first conclusion), that it is not possible to make this trip without the most important nautical instrument, called the compass. Since the ancients had no knowledge of the compass, they were never accustomed to sailing far out to sea as we do now. In accordance with this, I say that Solomon's ships could not have come over here from the Red Sea, sailing all the way around East India and going out across the broad expanses of the South Sea [Pacific Ocean] until reaching the coasts of New Spain or Peru; and they are taken along this course by the inventors of this voyage.

We have taken two things for granted as certain and beyond doubt that require more proof than would be permitted by the brevity I wish to maintain here: first, that it is impossible to navigate on the open sea without a compass, and, second, that the ancients

had no compass. Experience is sufficient proof of the former state-
ment, and no more proof is necessary. To believe that a ship so
far out on the high seas that land cannot be sighted anywhere could
be navigated and make trips without a compass to replace other
guides makes as little sense as asking a blind man to point out and
indicate with his finger the things around him. I do not deny that
for a brief time and while the weather is calm, the moon and the
stars at night and the sun during the day can serve as guides, as
well as some of the most steady and common winds that usually
blow in several seas at certain times, but these guides, as I say,
are not very dependable except for crossing some bay or stretch of
sea; this would be when the weather was good and the seas calm,
but not out on the high seas, making a long trip; no man is so daring
that he would tackle such a foolhardy venture. How could the stars
be of any use on a dark night or the sun on a cloudy day, or when
it becomes so overcast with thick clouds and the visibility is so
poor that the men on the stern section of the ship cannot see those
on the bow? Who would not become exasperated, no matter how
skilled and well-trained a pilot he may be, when a hurricane comes
up so furious that in an instant it completely changes the direction of all the winds? What would become of the distressed naviga-
tors if in such a troubled and difficult situation they find themselves
without the consolation and guide of the compass? No matter how
rough the sea gets, how much the winds change, how furious they
get, how they come together, shaking the troubled ship and twirl-
ing it around like a weather vane, the compass remains peaceful
and quiet, pointing always toward the North Pole with such seren-
ity and stability that because of it we overcome the turbulence
and disturbance of the sea and wind. For this reason, I am of the
opinion that the ancients did not, for lack of this instrument, venture out into the middle of the ocean. Moreover, the men of today
will not even dare to roam along the shores of the ocean because of
the evident danger of being thrown out to sea by some storm or
by the sea currents; and without the aid of the compass, they would
be hard pressed to find the coast from whence they came. And our
view is strengthened not just a little by the discovery in our times
of the unpopulated islands mentioned in Chapter 12 of this book;
in my opinion these islands were unknown to the ancients because
they never navigated on the high seas far from land, and if they
had known of them, they would not have hesitated to populate
them just as the Portuguese did right after they found them.

The second point (and what I have just said is based on this), is made by many modern authors such as Francisco Lopez de Gomara, Volume I, Chapter 10, of the *Historia de las Indias*; Father Joseph de Acosta, Book I, Chapters 16 and 17, of the *Historia de Indias*; Father Juan de Mariana, Book I, Chapter 22, of the *Cosas de España*; and many others quoted by Father Juan de Pineda, Book 4, Chapter 15, of *De Rebus Salomonis*. They all agree that the compass is a modern invention and that it was discovered not more than about three hundred years ago. This is very clearly inferred to have happened as they say on the testimony of the ancient authors; whether it be in treating of navigational instruments or the qualities of the lodestone, the ancients never mention the compass or the marvelous power and efficacy that the aforesaid lodestone has on touching the iron needle to make it point toward the North Pole.

Those of the opposing opinion usually reply to this argument by mentioning some of the long voyages that ancient historians say were made in the past; from this it is inferred that the ocean was navigated then as it is now and, therefore, that it would not have been so impossible as we say for Solomon's ships to make the voyage to this land. Herodotus, in Book 4, section on Africa,[23] mentions three of these voyages. The first is the one made on the orders of Necos [Necho], the king of Egypt; it is said that he sent certain Phoenicians in boats from that kingdom to explore the coasts of Africa and that these men, leaving from the Red Sea, sailed along the coast all along the southern side of Africa, going around the Cape of Good Hope until reaching the Strait of Gibraltar; up to this point they had taken two years. Then, making a complete circle, they returned to the place where they had set sail three years before; and this is said to be the first time that the coast and shores of Africa were explored.

The second such voyage, he says, was made by Sataspes, although in the opposite direction. After leaving Egypt by the Mediterranean Sea, he reached the Strait of Gibraltar, and, going through the Atlantic Ocean, he made the same circle as the first men, finishing his journey in the Red Sea on the coast of Egypt.

The third voyage is the one made on the orders of King Darius; it was accomplished by sailing along the coasts of East India from the mouth of the Indus River up to the coast of Egypt. The authors who disagree with me also cite Pliny, Book 2, Chapter 67, who makes mention of other voyages like the last ones. One of these was made by Hanno, a brave captain of the Carthaginians, during the time when that republic flourished; he navigated from Cadiz along the coast of Africa itself up to the far corner of Arabia. Another voyage is also related by Pliny himself, and he got it from Cornelius Nepos, a serious author who tells of another man of his time named Eudoxus who made the same trip; fleeing from the king of the Lathyrus, he set out from the heart of Arabia and, emerging on the ocean, sailed around the coast of Africa until he stopped at the Strait of Gibraltar. Suidas, treating the exploits of Semiramis, tells how he had ships navigate the ocean and sail along the coasts of Africa.

But these histories that the opponents alleged to be in their favor, are (in my view) so far from confirming their opinion that actually they are very fitting to support mine. First (if they are true), they show a great contradiction among the ancient historians themselves, which is easy to see for this reason. Those who traveled from Spain to the Red Sea or vice versa, sailing along the southern side of Africa, could not help but cross the Torrid Zone and the Equator; thus, those who told of these explorations would also tell of the places and geographic zones they visited. Since all during ancient times the Torrid Zone was held to be uninhabitable or inaccessible, those men should have corrected that false assumption they had held up until then, and the news would have spread throughout all the nations receiving information about the aforesaid voyages that the Torrid Zone was navigable and inhabited by many people who were found on those trips by those who sailed around the coast of Africa. This is exactly what has happened in our times owing to the news that has been given to us from the modern voyages.

How can what has just been discussed not be in opposition to the widely accepted and documented opinion, held by all the ancients, that the Torrid Zone was inaccessible and uninhabitable, as is stated in all the histories? This view was held before and after those voyages around Africa, and it was passed from person to person and was universally accepted until the experience of our times proved it to be false. Among the most reliable authors who expressed it in their writings are the prince of philosophy, Aristotle, in Chapter 5 of Book 2 of the *Meteorologia*, and the prince of eloquence, Cicero, in the fragment, Book 6 of *De Republica*, as well as Pliny (*Natural History*, Book 2, Chapter 68), Macrobius, and many other of the greatest authors celebrated by antiquity. Of them all, the one who surprises me the most is Pliny; on the one hand, he himself recounts those navigations made below the Torrid Zone, of which he confesses having news, but on the other hand, he affirms that this same Torrid Zone is uninhabitable and inaccessible. When he describes the five zones or regions into which the surface of the land and water is divided, he says that three of them are uninhabitable; the two most distant because they are always frozen, and the one in between because of the excessive heat that is sent down on it by the rays of the sun which shine on it directly and scorch it continuously; thus, only the two remaining zones can be inhabited, and since they fall between the Frozen Zones and the Torrid Zone, they are temperate. From this he concludes that heaven has taken three parts of the earth from us, and of the two that were conceded to us for our habitation, he even denies that it is possible to travel from the northern zone to the southern zone, because this is impeded by the fires of the middle zone. Certainly, with his discourse this author gives us plenty to think about; either he had some reservations about what the historians said about those voyages, or, if he accepted their stories, he casts doubt on his own reliability and reputation because of the disparity and contradiction that he exhibits in his own views. If he believed that the southern part of Africa had been explored, how is it that he felt that the Torrid Zone was uninhabitable and for that reason there could be no communication between the two Temperate Zones on either side? He should know the contrary from those voyages, since they could not be made any other way except going across the whole breadth of the Torrid Zone and going from the northern Temperate Zone to the corresponding zone in the south, in order to be able to sail around the southern part of Africa, which enters well into the Temperate Zone of this Antarctic Hemisphere along the Cape of Good Hope. This testimony of Pliny leaves us in doubt, and we find that the testimony of the other authors that I have cited causes us to have the same doubt; this is also true for other authors who hold this view. For this reason, we must confess that they did not have news of these voyages, or if they did, they did not believe in them as much as the modern authors do who allege their validity for their argument. It is easy to see the difficulty of reconciling testimonies and views that are so diametrically opposed. For this reason, it seems to me that the way they can most easily be reconciled is by saying that the opinion of all antiquity in feeling that the Torrid Zone was uninhabitable was so universally accepted and firmly held in the minds of the wisest men of those times that they would not change their opinion with less certainty and experience to the contrary than we have now; so, although they had some news from men who had sailed those seas, since those voyages were very few in number, not customary, and occurring by chance or due to the misfortune of the ones who undertook them, the ancients did not accept the full validity of the authors of the reports, and therefore the evidence was insufficient to make them change their minds.

Now I want to take advantage of the history of the aforesaid voyages to confirm my opinion, since carefully examined, it supports my view more than that of the opposition. First of all, if the ancient authors made a record of these voyages with such diligence and admiration, they would have also kept a record of the much more arduous and admirable trip of the Hebrews to the New World, if they had traveled to it during the time of Solomon or before or after. In the second place, it follows from the aforesaid history that at that time the ocean was not navigated with such frequency that the route along the coast of Africa was considered as well-traveled as any of the routes to the overseas regions are at present; this I surmise because of the admiration and circumstances with which the aforementioned authors tell about those voyages, making it clear by their way of speaking that the voyages were unusual and not customary. If this were not the case, why then did they mention the exact number of them, the names of those who took them, and the reasons that moved them to take such an arduous resolution? Today we speak in a very different way about the many voyages that our Spaniards make along the route to the Indies, and thus we show how frequent and usual this trip is. Finally, I think that on the basis of those voyages there is no proof that it is possible to navigate on the high seas without a compass; in fact, the ones who write about those voyages also show that the route taken was close to land along the shores of the ocean, never far out to sea.

78

Chapter 18: The same thing is proven with other evidence

Up to this point all we have done is cut off the passage of Solomon's ships on the route by which the opposition attempted to direct them to this land; now it is time for us to start searching here and picking up more evidence that will strengthen our position and weaken theirs. In the first place, taking for granted the great barbarity and rudeness of the people of this New World, which I understand has been the same all the time, we find ourselves faced with a difficulty derived from this. If Solomon's ships were able to put into port here without hindrance or resistance, how could the Hebrews deal with these Indians in trading and commerce? Logically it seems that they would proceed just as we did, founding some colonies of their people among the Indians and subjugating some part of this land for their own security and to keep the barbarous furor of the inhabitants of this land within bounds; by other means, it would not have been possible to carry on commerce with these people, for they were very savage and not the least bit in need of foreign merchandise. They needed no more to sustain themselves than the fruits of their land, nor did they care to dress and adorn themselves with our precious silks or delicate woolen and linen cloth; the majority were satisfied to use the suit and uniform in which they were born. By experience we see that the biggest volume of trade carried on generally by our Spaniards with the Indians that have not been pacified, and the trading they carried on at first with the Indians that are now pacified before they were friendly, consisted of very insignificant bartering and trading, exchanging for gold the baubles and trifles which the Indians like the most, such as small bells, mirrors, needles, knives, and little things of this sort. But the gold that the Spaniards got from them with this kind of commerce was very limited in comparison with the great wealth of this metal and of silver that the Spaniards themselves are extracting now from the mines, after seizing them and working them on their own. This is true because the Indians were satisfied with very limited use of these playthings and because they were accustomed to taking only small quantities of gold and silver from the mines. From this, it can be inferred that if Solomon's ships had navigated to these Indies, the Jews could not have established and protected their commerce with the Indians in any other way than that the Spaniards have established and maintained; therefore, the Jews would have built some towns, forts, and garrisons in the style of their nation, and in everything else, they would have proceeded like us.

This being the case, we would find extensive signs in this land of their stay here; if they had really come here, it would be impossible to erase so thoroughly all memory of them that not even any trace remained of the names and ruins of their colonies and settlements. It is impossible (humanly speaking) that the ruins of our stay here would be totally eliminated, even if all of us who are here from Spain returned to our nation now. In my opinion, it would be impossible to extinguish and erase, from now until eternity, even the memory of just the names of the provinces and towns that we have founded in this New World. The conquistadores and settlers have been naming these places in honor of our nation and in memory of their provinces there or for other reasons and motives, always with the objective of making eternal the fame of our people in these new lands.

For this reason, there is hardly a kingdom in Spain whose name has not been taken by now to this land and applied to the provinces that have been pacified and settled. In commemoration of our nation, those who conquered and settled it gave the name of Española [Hispaniola] to the island that was called Hayti by its inhabitants; and in memory of our country, the name of New Spain was given to the Mexican Empire by those who pacified it; and if we go roaming about the rest of these Indies, we will find that many other places here have the same names as various provinces of Spain, so that the description of this great Spanish colony matches its counterpart exactly. The Kingdom of Tierra Firme was named Castilla del Oro in memory of Castilla [Castile]; and out of respect for the same name, the Marques Francisco Pizarro gave half of this Kingdom of Peru the name New Castile, and, as for the other half in which the city of Cuzco is located, His Majesty ordered that it be named the New Kingdom of Toledo, although both parts are now included in the name New Castile. There are also provinces named New Andalusia, the New Kingdom of Granada, New Vizcaya, New Galicia, and the New Kingdom of Leon. Other lands have been named in other ways, either because of some similarity with those they were named after or out of devotion to some mystery of our holy faith, or for some patron saints, or in memory of their founders, taking their last names; and other places have been given other names that are meaningful in our language, owing to some characteristic of that province or in memory of its discovery and foundation or for other similar reasons.

In imitation of Venecia [Venice] they gave the name Veneçuela to the province of Caracas; out of reverence for the Santisima Trinidad, they gave this title to the island of that name; out of devotion to the saints, the island of Boriquen was given the title of San Juan, but it is commonly called Puerto Rico; Jamayca was named Santiago, and innumerable other islands were named after saints. Out of devotion to the Santa Cruz [Holy Cross], they named the province of Santa Cruz de la Sierra, which is one of the provinces of Peru; and in honor and memory of the glorious resurrection of Christ our Redeemer and of the Pascua Florida [Easter] when it is celebrated, they gave the name that it has to the province of Florida. Some meaningful names have also been given, such as the one for the province of Honduras [depths], that of Tierra Firme [terra firma, or the mainland], Buenos Ayres [good winds], and Verapaz [true peace].

This same pattern has been followed in naming the towns that have been newly founded; now there are so many names of places in Spain in this land that it seems as if that whole kingdom had been brought here. I will mention here the ones that come to mind, and I do not think that very many will escape me. To start with my home, Andalucia, since it is the closest to these Indies—the following towns were named after towns in Andalucia: two after Granada, three after Cordoba, three others named Seuilla, two Xerez, two others with the name of El Villar; and the following have one named after them: Jaen, Baeça, Ecija, Alcala la Real, Antequera, Archidona, Velez, La Palma, Medina, Gibraltar, Puerto Real, and Guadalcaçar. From places in other provinces of Spain, these are named: there are three named Trugillo, two named Guadalajara, two named Merida, two Oropesa, one each named Cuenca, Ciudad Real, Caceres, Llerena, La Serena, Ocaña, Guadalupe, Cartagena, Cañete, Valuerde, Agreda, Aranjuez, Talavera, Avila, Portillo, Carrion, Becerril, Arnedo, Salinas, La Rioja, Nieua, Almaguer, Madrigal; four towns with the name of Valladolid, two with that of Zamora, three with that of Leon, two named Segovia, and two more called Salamanca and Villa de Mancera.

Apart from these names of places in Castile, there are also others that fall in other provinces of Spain such as Compostela, Durango, Lagos, Pamplona, Zaragoza, Valencia. Even towns outside of

Spain have given names to others; including Antioquia, Cartago, Londres, Esquilache, and Tenerife.

No less in number are those named for the titles of some of the mysteries of our holy faith and for some angels and saints and others from Spanish words. In honor of the divine faith upon which is founded our sacred religion there are three towns with the name Santa Fe; two with the sovereign name of our Lord God (Gracias a Dios and Nombre de Dios); four named after the Santisima Trinidad [Holy Trinity]; five with the name of Espiritu Santo [Holy Spirit]; one named Altagracia [High Grace]; sixteen with the name of Cristo Salvador [Christ the Savior], taken from the various mysteries that our mother the Church celebrates during the course of the year; five of them have the name San Salvador; one has the name Cristo, called Monte Cristo; for devotion to his holy birth, the port of Puerto de Navidad was given its name; and in memory of the most holy name of Jesus one city has this name; for the name of the mystery of the Epiphany and the Adoration of the Reyes Magos [Wise Men] three towns are called Los Reyes; in memory of his Holy Passion and death on the Cruz [Cross], four towns take the title of Santa Cruz, and one that of Ascension.

Not less in this respect have been the demonstrations of devotion that our nation has made to the Holy Mother the Virgin Maria; in her honor sixteen towns are named with the titles of her holy mysteries; for her sweet name three are named; for the same, with other attributes, such as de los Remedios [Remedies], de la Paz [Peace], de la Vitoria [Victory], de las Nieues [Snows], and de la Guardia [Guardian], five; out of devotion for her Inmaculada Concepcion [Immaculate Conception] six are named; one after the title of her Purificacion Santisima [Most Holy Purification] and another with the title of her glorious Asuncion [Assumption].

In honor of the holy angels they named Puebla de los Angeles; and owing to the great devotion the Spaniards have for the archangel San Miguel, this name has been given to ten towns; after the name of San Rafael an island is named. But, in order to appreciate the high regard, esteem, and filial love that we the Spanish nations have for the Patron of Spain, it should be known that we give nineteen towns of these Indies the title of Santiago; in honor of San Juan we give sixteen towns his name; two have that of San Pedro and one that of San Pablo; there are four with the name San Felipe; two with that of San Bartolome; and of the rest of the Apostles, there is one town named after each of the following: San Andres, Santo

Tome, San Lucas, San Marcos, San Felipe, and Santiago. With the name of San Sebastian there are four towns; with that of San Cristoual, three; seven with that of San Francisco; two with that of San Martin; and two others with that of San Luis. There are many others, one each with the name of the following saints: San Joseph, San Lorenço, San Esteuan, San Vicente, San Jorge, San Antonio, San Augustin, San Jeronimo, San Gregorio, San Bernardo, Santo Domingo, Santo Tomas, San Amaro, San Ignacio, Santa Ana, Santa Maria, Santa Catalina, Santa Barbara, Las Virgenes [The Virgins], and two with the name of Todos los Santos [All the Saints].

The following towns have the last name of their founder: Mendoça, Castro, Leyua, Pedraça, Salazar, Garcimendoza, Arias, Castro Virreyna, Loyola, Ibarra, and Montesclaros. In memory of the kings during whose time they were pacified and settled, some provinces and towns also get their names; in honor of King Ferdinand, by whose order Columbus discovered this New World, the island of Cuba is given the title Fernandina; and as a tribute to his wife, Queen Isabel, the first Spanish town that was founded in this New World on the island of Hispaniola was named the Villa de la Isabela, which was changed to another place shortly afterward, and now it is called the city of Santo Domingo. In memory of the Emperor and King of Spain Charles V, they gave the name Villa Imperial de Potosi; in honor of King Philip II, the Philippine Islands were named; and out of respect for King Philip III, the town of Oruro was given the name of Saint Philip of Austria, and in this same way other places have been named.

The following take their names from Spanish words because of their meaning: Villa Hermosa [Beautiful Town], La Frontera [The Border], Villareal [Royal Town], Puerto Viejo [Old Port], Puerto del Principe [Prince's Port], Puerto Seguro [Safe Port], Realejo [Hand Organ], Monte de Plata [Hill of Silver], La Grita [Clamor], Pueblo Nueuo [New Town], Buena Ventura [Good Luck], and the city of La Plata [Silver].

Apart from those places mentioned, which are all Spanish colonies that have been founded recently, almost all of the towns of the Indians within the Spanish dominions have been named by us. We have given Christian names to almost all of the Indian towns within the Spanish dominions, giving the majority the titles of saints; and we have given many others the names of our towns in Spain; some examples are Toledo, Cordoba, Oropesa, Salamanca, and many others like these. For this reason there are a great many Indian towns that have no names other than the ones we have given them, and these names are used not only by the Spaniards but also by the Indians themselves. I will not mention the innumerable names from our language that our Spaniards have given to hills, valleys, mountains, rivers, lakes, islands, ports, bays, and innumerable other things, since to enumerate them would be an infinite task.

Chapter 19: *The same subject is continued*

I have mentioned all of this with the object of proving that the memory of our nation is so deeply rooted in this land that even if we left it now, it would not be possible to erase this memory from the minds of the natives of this land succeeding those who are alive today. There would perpetually be very evident traces from such a multitude of words, and I hold that it would be impossible to erase the memory of the above-mentioned words. I consider even more impossible that the signs and vestiges remaining of the things referred to by those words would come to be erased and concealed; consider the durability of so many towns built according to our pattern, so many magnificent buildings of masonry, all the many stones carved with the skill and art used in Europe in the form of columns, bases, and many different types of designs and moldings, the many magnificent tombs, the many vaults, ditches, and bridges of stone masonry, and the bricks, tiles, chinaware, and glass, of which the Indians had no knowledge at all before, and finally, what of the deep foundations of the temples, castles, walls, cutwaters, and other durable structures, and the signs, inscriptions, and epitaphs carved on slabs of marble and on sheets of bronze which adorn many buildings with innumerable coats of arms of stone and metal? What reason can there be that the duration of these things would not run parallel with that of time itself?

Let us add to these indications the ones that would perpetually be given by the animals and plants brought to these Indies by the Spaniards; reference is made here to the animals and plants not present in the Indies previously, which are treated in the book before this one,[24] and the indications of the things of this sort that have been transported to Europe from here. Furthermore, we must mention all our arts and the instruments and tools that accompany them; the Indians have learned these arts and practice them with no less perfection than the Spaniards whom they learned them from. There are the customs that the Indians have picked up from us regarding their clothing and their way of life, including the words from our language that they have incorporated into their speech; there are not a few towns that have adopted Spanish so fully that the Indians have completely forgotten their native tongue and speak only our Castilian language. Finally, the people here have become so accustomed to using our alphabet and writing that, judging by how much they esteem it and by the eagerness with which they learn it, these Indians will never forget how to write. Thus, from this line of reasoning I draw the obvious conclusion that the Hebrews never had any commerce in this land, nor did they set foot on it. Although they might not have established themselves here as firmly as our nation has, it would be inevitable that at least from the majority of the aforesaid indications, if not from all of them, many vestiges would remain today. They would not have refrained from making some buildings modeled after those of their land or from bringing here, in so many trips (as are mentioned by those who are of the opinion that the Hebrews came with their fleets) the things necessary for the sustenance and service of men, things that were lacking in this land, such as the ones that our Spaniards brought at first; nor would they have neglected taking to their country some of the plants and animals of this New World; these would have spread throughout the other regions of the globe, just as the ones the Spaniards brought have dispersed and spread after being taken back; neither would the Hebrews have neglected to improve the customs, practices, and respect for law and order of the natives of the provinces where they traded with most frequency.

There is no vestige or memory of any of this anywhere; in the many ruins of the very ancient structures that we see here, we have not found so much as a single stone cut in the European style. I have seen and examined for myself many times, and with more than average diligence, the ruins of the most magnificent and ancient buildings of this Kingdom of Peru, such as those at Cuzco, Guamanga [Ayacucho], Vilcas, Tiaguanaco, Pachacama, and others, to see if in some of the unusual slabs and stones that are taken from them I could find signs of letters, characters, or some workmanship similar to that of our structures, and nowhere have I found anything like that, no stones cut for arches in the form of bases, capitals, columns, or other forms of rocks commonly used in the art of architecture. Nor have I found any trace of it in the principal towns of New Spain such as Mexico, Tezcuco [Texcoco], Tacuba, Guajocingo, and Cholula. Nor do I have any information that anything like this has been found in any other part of these Indies. Nor have any signs been found of the mixture of lime and sand, except for that which the Mexicans used mixing lime and crushed teçonte, or any construction of plaster or of brick; in fact, not even a broken piece of brick or tile has been found, nor is there any memory among these people of there ever having been any of these things here.

Traces of the most antiquity are normally found in graves, but

all of the graves that we have discovered in this land are uniform
in each province, and the custom of burying the dead is the same.
Nowhere do we see any notable difference, not in the materials
of these graves, nor in their arrangement and appearance, nor in
the things that are usually taken from them, which are those things
that the Indians customarily bury with their dead. The jewels and
arms that are dug up from these graves are of the same style; no
type of arms or other instruments of iron have been discovered,
nor is there any memory of the use of this metal among these people. In fact, if the ships of Solomon had sailed frequently to this
land and traded here, would the Hebrews not have left some trace
of these things? Even to bury those who died here while they were
trading, would they not have made graves according to their customary style? Since we do not find the dwellings that they used
while they were alive, some vestiges and traces of their graves could
not help but remain. And were they so careless of their own comfort that, at least to be more at ease, they did not bring animals
to ride and to transport from the mines to the ports the valuable
metals that they came to seek from such distant lands, since they
did not care for the other things?

Nor is it reasonable to attempt to explain away all these difficulties by saying that during their trading and navigation they
brought to this land the same things that the Spaniards have brought,
but that, with the passage of time, these things finally disappeared.
The plants and animals that our people brought have multiplied so
much in this New World that in many places so many of them were
born that when the people wanted to do away with them, even
though they used all their intelligence and effort, they failed; but
moved by their own interest and the usefulness that results from
such things, how much more would the animals multiply, if the
people took care of them? In conclusion, we see no difference from
one region to another, since they all lack any signs of the Hebrews.
This is another strong argument in our favor, because without a
doubt in some of the places where the ships came most frequently
to trade, more signs and evidence of them would have remained
than in other places, and in these places, from their communication and dealings with the Hebrews, the natives would have assim-
ilated something, but that does not happen to be the case, since
the natives are all the same, whether they be from rich lands or
poor lands, whether they live on the seacoast or inland. And these
arguments apply equally to those who would presume to answer

that when Solomon's ships sailed to this land, it was not populated with other people, but that then the Hebrews started to settle these Indies. Finally, these arguments also apply if it is conceded that this land was already populated with Indians.

Chapter 20: *In which the arguments of the opposing opinion are answered and the location of Ophir is established*

If we examine the explanations and arguments on which the opposition base their opinion, I hold that they have very little substance for determining so much. Concerning the first argument that they get from Admiral Christopher Columbus, I say that it is not a good idea to pay much attention to the names with which new lands are proclaimed and praised by their discoverers. Great caution must be exercised in order to extrapolate from these names the thread of truth that is sought in making an investigation of some mystery. Ordinarily these names are given by chance, based on the situation that presents itself to the discoverers, who may even be influenced by the common need to augment their accomplishments. This is particularly true with regard to discoveries and conquests of unknown lands, as we are shown by experience. In fact, there is hardly a man who, on returning from some discovery, does not exaggerate and praise to high heaven with extravagant hyperboles the excellence of the land found by him, preferring it to all other lands of the world for its goodness and wealth. This may be the case even though manifestly the new land may be the poorest and most miserable place on earth. And in order to give such discoveries a greater reputation and fame among the people, they usually give them illustrious titles and appellations that will serve to proclaim the excellence of the new lands. We have a good example of this (leaving aside many others) in the islands of the south; their discoverers named them the Solomon Islands with no other reason than to make them famous in the world with such an honorable and noble name; and another example is found in the provinces where the Marañon River[25] flows; these provinces were named El Dorado for the same reason, although they are quite despicable, as many have found out, to their regret and personal loss.

To the second argument, so cleverly conceived, I answer that those who thought it up would have saved themselves the trouble of seeking out and making so many deductions from the original Hebrew if they only knew the real name of this Kingdom of Peru, which is not Peru, as they think, nor was this name applied to any part of these Indies in other times. This Kingdom of New Castile, which we call Peru now, was called by its natives Tahuantinsuyu. The name Peru is new, given by the first Spaniards who attempted to pacify and conquer it; the word Peru was never known or used by the Indians. Those who in fact conquered and won it gave it the name New Castile, although the name Peru has prevailed, and we use it more frequently. If the matter is carefully analyzed, it is a very superficial conjecture which is based on the similarity that we find between names of lands, such as Paraguay, Paria, and others mentioned in Chapter 14, and that name "Paruaim." If we were to be guided by the correlation and affinity in the pronunciation and material sound of words, each one of the European nations, and even the others in the rest of the world, could allege the same right and show that the natives of this land have proceeded from them by finding many words in their languages that are similar to those of the Indians in the material sound, that is to say, similar in the letters and number and amount of syllables; but the main substance, which is the meaning and soul of the aforementioned words, is very different from what they mean in other languages. At least in the languages of the Indians of this Kingdom of Peru, we find many words whose sound is the same as words from our Spanish language, and even the same as some words from Latin, and I believe that any of the other European nations could find this same correlation with names and words from their language.

Nor does the third argument seem to me to have any substance to it; although as a matter of fact there is an abundance of gold in these Indies, still the amount produced here is not so great that it would overshadow the fame of the riches of other regions of the world praised for producing gold by the ancient authors. Actually, before Solomon's ships traded in Ophir, the Divine Scriptures praised the great abundance of gold which the province of Palestine obtained from the surrounding provinces. In the first chapter of Deuteronomy, it is told that in the time of Moses there was a great abundance of gold on the other side of the Jordan River, within the borders of Moab, between Thophel and Haseroth; and in many other places the Holy Scriptures mention other lands in the areas surrounding Palestine where an abundance of gold was found; and especially, King David is said to have amassed much gold from the plundering of the Syrians, Edomites, and Ammonites, whom he defeated by force of arms, as is stated in Chapter 22 of the First Book of the Paralipomenon. Who does not know how valuable the wealth of that land of Hevilath[26] was? Gold abounded in this place, and according to many wise men, it was not far from Judea; nevertheless, others put it in East India, along the shores of the Ganges River.

The rich and very famous gold and silver mines of our Spain are well known to anyone versed in ancient history. Thus, the following is not consistent: In Peru an abundance of gold is produced; therefore, the gold that was taken to Solomon was from there, regardless of whether there was gold in many other parts of the universe. To this is added another very good reason for refuting the aforesaid opinion—many of the things that Solomon's ships took from Ophir were never present in these Indies, nor were they ever heard of here; some examples are ivory, peacocks, and apes. There are no elephants here, and the *pavos* or peacocks[27] found here are not those colorful birds with the beautiful feathers that this name is correctly used for, but *pavos* here are another fowl, very different, that we call "chickens of the land"; we call them *pavos* because they are somewhat similar to the real ones. It is true that there are many different kinds of *micos* or monkeys here, but they are all different from the apes of Africa which have no tails; the *micos* of this land have very long tails. Nor do I think that the very valuable and highly esteemed wood that was brought from Ophir is found in this land; although many trees are found here that have hard, fragrant, and medicinal woods, nevertheless, they are not worthy of that praise with which the Holy Scriptures speak of the woods brought from Ophir. Nor is there present here the abundance and quality of precious stones that East India has.

To the fourth conjecture, which holds that Solomon's ships took such a long time on that voyage to Ophir, I say that the Sacred Scriptures do not state that they took three years, but that they took the voyage once every three years, and even if they did take all that time on the voyages, it does not follow that they came to this New World; rather it implies that they went far away to distant lands. For those times and even for our own time, it is a very long journey to any of the coastal lands of East India, where I believe the region of Ophir was located; this is stated by Josephus, Book 8, Chapter 2, of the *Antiquities of the Jews*, and by Saint Jerome, Theodoret, Procopius, Rabanus, the Abulensis, and many others that are cited by Father Juan de Pineda, in Chapter 16 of *De Rebus Salomonis*.[28] The port of Asiongaber is located on the Red Sea, and from there the ships of Solomon left, as is stated in Chapter 9 of the Third Book of Kings and in the Second Book of the Paralipomenon, Chapter 8. It was easy to sail from there to East India, going along the coasts of Arabia and Persia, without going far from land. It would not be appropriate to make the objections to this voyage that we made above to the trip that the opponents thought the aforementioned ships could take along that route to these regions of America; on the contrary, during all the centuries of the past, it has been very common to make that voyage along the coasts of the Red Sea to the Orient, bringing from there the spices, medicines, and all the riches of the Orient to the ports of Egypt. For this very reason the city of Alexandria has always been so rich and famous; it was like a well-stocked emporium and marketplace that supplied the regions of Europe and the other regions surrounding the Mediterranean Sea with the precious objects and wealth of East India.

BOOK II

Chapter 1: Of the former inhabitants of Peru before the Incas reigned

Since the Indians had no writing, the information we find among them concerning their antiquities is very meager. Although it is true that the Peruvians used certain strings or cords to preserve a record of their deeds (as we shall see), nothing was kept on these records except what occurred from the time that the Inca Empire started its conquests and within the provinces that the Incas subdued during their rule. And even this they kept with such a lack of clarity that from their account it has not even been possible to infer the number of years each king reigned. They give some information concerning the state of the land when the Incas started to rule, probably about four hundred years ago, but upon moving from there back, everything is confusion and darkness, in which hardly any trace or vestige can be perceived that would guide us on an inquiry into earlier times.[1]

One thing cannot be denied, on the basis of the Indians' tradition, as well as indications and relics that still remain up to the present time, and it is that there have been giants in this land.[2] Where they came from, how they may have gotten here, and how long they stayed is not certain. Vestiges of them have been encountered both inland and by the sea. The first Spanish conquistadores of this kingdom, in the area of Santa Elena Point, Diocese of Quito, found human bones of such enormous size that clearly they were from a giant—some from the limbs were four spans in length. Many other bones of similar proportions have been discovered here in other parts of that same province and in the province of Trujillo; also bones just as large have been seen inland, such as in the provinces of Tucuman and Tarija; in the latter an entire body was found at the bottom of a ravine, on a riverbank where the water, washing away the earth, had uncovered it. This body was so enormous that its grave occupied a very large space, and the skull was of such unusual size that some Spaniards, thrusting a sword through its eye socket, barely touched the nape of the neck with the tip of it. In the province of Santa Cruz de la Sierra a very truthful Christian gentleman named Lorenzo Suarez de Figueroa was governor; he founded the city of San Lorenzo, capital of that province, and he had taken part in the conquest of Tucuman. This gentleman used to say that, during that conquest, an ossuary was found, which apparently had over one hundred human bodies in it, and all the bones were from giants of unusually large proportions; the governor himself thrust his sword into one of the skulls, and the whole sword was buried in the cavity of the skull. This was told to me by an old priest of our Society; while he was staying in the province of Santa Cruz, Don Lorenzo himself told him the story.

I was unable to find out if that body with such a large head was the same one that was found in Tarija or a different one; since these two provinces of Tucuman and Tarija are contiguous, it could have been the same one. From the vicinity of the same part of Tucuman and Tarija, some years ago a large quantity of giants' bones were brought to the town of Potosi; all the bones were in pieces; not a bone was intact except for some molar teeth, but the unusual size of them proved that they were from enormous bodies. The molars were each as big as a fist; one of them was put on a scale, and it weighed eleven ounces; I found this out from the same person who weighed it, and he was a reliable man. I do not know if it was some of these same bones that were shown to me in this city of Lima; among them was a molar, and it was of the size that I have stated. Although it is true that it had the exact form of a molar, due to the fact that it was very ancient, it looked more like a rock than a bone.

This is notably supported by the antiquity of some buildings in ruins that we see in this kingdom; they are made of very large, well-worked stones such as those used in the building at Tiaguanaco, the one that is located underground two leagues away from Guamanga, and others. More important than the buildings are the statues of stone that have been uncovered near the building at Tiaguanaco; these statues are so large that I measured the head of one of them myself across the forehead and temples, and it was twelve spans around. Not only in the size, shape, and features of the face do they prove to be figures of giants, but the fact that their garments, headdresses, and hair are of a very different style from those of the Indians is no small indication that these statues were made by other people. If the statues had been done by Indians, they would have had the Indians' stature and dress, as do many other statues that we find in other places.

Added to this is the account that the Indians themselves give, particularly those along the coast by Puerto Viejo, who say that giants had come there from the south in large rafts, but since they had not brought women with them, they died out. It can be presumed that they came from the Strait of Magellan, since to this day men of more than ordinary stature live in that land. Not only in Peru but also in New Spain, there are vestiges of giants, which is an argument in favor of there having been giants throughout America. And although we cannot determine the time when they lived, it is certain that they did not reach the time of the Incas; rather I think that several centuries passed from the time that the giants died out until the beginning of the reign of the Incas. And this concludes the inquiry regarding the fame and vestiges that we find of there having been giants in these Indies in the past.

The people who possessed this Kingdom of Peru when the Incas started to rule it are the same as those that inhabit it now. Although they still conserve their own particular languages that were spoken in diverse provinces, in other respects their way of living was changed much with the domination and authority of the Incas; according to what the Indians of Cuzco say, formerly the inhabitants of this kingdom were extremely barbarous and savage, like the ones that we previously classified as the first type of barbarians.[3] They lived with no chief, no order or respect for law, spread out in small villages and collections of huts, with hardly any more indications of reason and understanding than brutes, to which they were very similar in their savage customs; actually the majority ate human flesh, and not a few took as wives their own sisters and mothers; they were all very addicted to the devil, whom they venerated and served with diligence.

These barbarians would wage continuous war on one another for the slightest reason, capturing and killing each other with unusual cruelty. The most frequent causes of these fights and quarrels were water and land, which they would take from each other. In order to defend themselves against their rivals, the least powerful made their dwellings and towns on high strongholds in the manner of castles and fortresses, where they would take refuge when they were attacked by their enemies. Today we see the ruin of many such forts on hills and high places. Although they lived like beasts, some gave themselves over very much to the religion of their false gods, adoring many, as we will see;[4] this gave rise to the building of many temples, where they went to pray and offer their sacrifices.

Living, then, in this barbarity as the people of this kingdom were, in several places those who surpassed the others in ability and vigor started to seize power over their villages. These are the ones that we call caciques, who with cunning and force came to tyrannize the provinces, each one endeavoring to enlarge his dominion by the means that his fortune offered. This ambition and desire to command caused them great calamities. Because these caciques waged bloody *guazauaras* [battles] on each other and made continuous attacks in which they robbed and killed, with the ruin and destruction of some, others grew greatly in power and expanded the limits of their states; this happened in the case of some caciques of the Colla and others along the coast of the sea. Being very powerful, for a long time they resisted the Incas, who were in the process of founding their empire.

Chapter 2: Of the efforts that have been made several times to ascertain the true history of the Incas and the rites and customs of their republic

Writing in this and the two books that follow[5] about the republic, government, religion, and customs of the Incas, former kings of Peru, I felt it advisable, in order to give greater credence and authority to what is stated, to put in this chapter the fundamentals upon which the facts of this history are based. In case anyone tries to contradict it, moved by the word of some old Indian or by not finding the memory very vivid now of many of the things that are treated here, or for any other reason, it should be borne in mind that everything written here was preceded by a very careful inquiry and study over a long period of time and with such persons that it certainly is true. What moves me to draw attention to this is that I have obtained some reports and papers[6] of inquiring men who consider themselves experts in the ancient times of the Indians, and their ideas about this subject are different from what is accepted by all of the authors who have published works about it. These experts principally aim to persuade us, first of all, that the Inca kings started to rule much earlier than the historians state and that the Incas were much more numerous; and second, that the Incas did not worship nearly as many gods as we indicate.

Before all else, it is advisable to point out one very substantial thing about this business, which is that not all the Indians knew how or were able to give explanations about these subjects at first and much less now, because to ask common people such as *mitayos* and *yanaconas* to inform us about the Inca kings would be as if someone wanted to ask in Sayago about the laws and *fueros* of Spain, or as if someone were to discuss the statutes of a city with the average citizens, since very few of them would know how to give an account or explanation except concerning that which they deal in; and out of every ten with whom one talked, that many different opinions would be forthcoming. Therefore, since all those who were concerned with government and religion resided in the city of Cuzco, only they were able to understand and give explanations about what they were asked concerning this, and the rest, for this purpose, are totally incompetent, because they had very little to do with anything other than carrying out orders. It is stated that very few of the common people understood the purpose of the tasks in which the Incas kept them occupied, nor did they even have permission to ask about it. This is true to such a degree that I have had personal experience with this situation numerous times, and anyone who has had such experience will find this to be true: If we ask about anything of this sort now of an Indian of the *hatun-runas*, who are, so to speak, the country people, they do not know how to answer, nor do they even know if there were Inca kings in this land; but upon asking the same thing of any of those of the lineage of the Incas who live in Cuzco, at once he will give a complete explanation of everything, of the number of Inca kings that reigned, of their ancestry and conquests, and of the families and lineages from them that have survived; therefore, attention should be paid only to the reports that have been made on this subject in the city of Cuzco. I will follow these reports in all of this writing, especially the one made on the orders of Viceroy Andres Hurtado de Mendoza, Marques de Cañete, and the first Archbishop of Lima, Fray Jeronimo de Loyasa, by Licentiate Polo de Ondegardo in the year 1559, while he was the corregidor of Cuzco; to this end Polo de Ondegardo brought together all of the old Indians who had survived from the pagan era, including the Inca rulers as well as the priests and *quipo camayos*, or Inca historians. They could not be ignorant of matters pertaining to the government, rites, and customs of their own people, owing to the fact that they actually lived at the time of the Inca kings, held office then, and were questioned about their own experiences; the validity of their testimony is borne out by the record of their *quipos* and their paintings which were still intact.

Of particular importance is the painting that they had in a temple of the sun, next to the city of Cuzco, where portraits were painted showing the lives of each one of their kings with the lands that he conquered. This history, in my opinion, must have been taken from one that I saw in that city outlined on a tapestry of *cumbe*, no less detailed and carefully represented than if it were on fine royal fabric. For these reasons, the report, based on the inquiry at that meeting, that was made by Licentiate Polo has always been considered authoritative; in the provincial councils that have been held in this kingdom, everything in it was adopted. It was used for the instruction that is given to the priests assigned to Indians

concerning their ancient rites and superstitions so that the utmost
diligence and care could be taken in eradicating these practices,
as well as for resolving the doubts and difficulties that often came
up in the beginning concerning the marriages of those who were
converted over to our Holy Faith. I have this report in my possession; it is the same one that, with his own signature, Licentiate
Polo sent to Archbishop Jeronimo de Loyasa.

Some years later, Viceroy Francisco de Toledo took great care
in obtaining a true history of the origin and form of government
of the Inca kings, and to this end, since he was in the city of Cuzco
himself, he ordered all the old Indians who remained from the time
of the Inca kings to be brought together. To insure that the proceedings were conducted with less danger of misunderstanding in an
undertaking whose ascertainment was so much desired, each Indian
was interrogated separately; they were not allowed to communicate
with each other. The person entrusted by the viceroy to make this
inquiry, who was one of those working under him on the general
inspection, made the same careful inquiry with all the old Incas
he found in the provinces of Charcas and Arequipa, and with former
Spanish conquistadores who were in this land, not a few of whom
still lived at that time.

And a little later, another general meeting of all the old Indians
that had lived during the reign of the Inca Guayna Capac was held
in the city of Cuzco itself by Cristobal de Molina, a parish priest
at the hospital of the natives in the Parish of Nuestra Señora de
los Remedios; this meeting was ordered by Bishop Sebastian de Lar-
taun and confirmed the same things as the previous meetings; the
result was a copious account of the rites and fables that the Peruvian
Indians practiced in pagan times. This information is substantially
the same as that of Licentiate Polo and that of the report that was
made by order of Francisco de Toledo. Both Toledo's report and the
account by Molina have come into my possession, and it appears
that they were followed by Father Joseph de Acosta in what he wrote
about the government of the Incas and their idolatry in Books 5
and 6 of his *Historia de Indias*. Recently, Garcilaso de la Vega Inca,
in the first part that he published on the republic of the Incas, hardly
deviates at all from these reports.[7]

I certainly could follow in the footsteps of such grave and reliable authors without trying to make a new inquiry on this subject,
but since I have resided in the city of Cuzco for some time, and
this is very close to the reign of the Inca kings, I have known a
number of Indians who took part in the Inca government, and many

of them were descendants of the Inca kings. I found that their memory concerning these things was very vivid. Taking advantage of this opportunity, I obtained all the information I desired from them concerning this matter, and I found nothing contrary to what was reported by Licentiate Polo. In confirming this, first I met and conversed at length with a high-ranking Indian of Inca lineage, who, on the orders of the viceroy, had made a report about his ancestry, which he read to me himself, and I found the same order and number of Inca kings that Licentiate Polo puts in his report.

Besides this, during my residence in Cuzco, the city celebrated the beatification of our father Saint Ignatius with public and extraordinary festivals in the year 1610; among other inventions and displays of joy that the Indians came up with, one was the representation of their former kings in a great and splendid display, which included the eleven Inca kings of Cuzco, looking very majestic on their litters, which were highly decorated with feathers of diverse colors and carried by Indians on their shoulders. The kings were wearing the same mantles and adornments that the kings themselves used to use; dressed in fine *cumbe*, which was their brocade and finest cloth, holding a scepter, each one had his royal insignia and attendants dressed according to their custom and an officer by his side who carried a sunshade of attractive feathers. They represented each king, his descendants, and his nearest kinsmen. The kings, accompanied by the infantry, which must have numbered over a thousand Indians, were spaced out in chronological order, the last one being the first Inca king and the first, Guayna Capac. In charge of the whole squadron and parade was Alonso Tupa Atau, paternal grandson of Guayna Capac and uncle of Melchor Inca, who died in Spain. Alonso was carried in the middle of the group by four prominent capitans, and he surpassed everyone in being the most elegant and splendid. With the number of kings that the Indians brought out in this spectacle, it is sufficiently confirmed that there were no more than eleven kings who reigned in Peru; later Alonso enumerated these kings to me in their order and succession, with the families and lineages that issued from each king.

The other point, which pertains to the former rites and religion of the Indians, which those I mentioned above have tried to disprove, is no less confirmed than the last one about the number of Incas, since the authority of the authors who ascertained the facts in both cases is one and the same, and it is not reasonable to give them less credence in one case than in the other.

This is all the more so since even if nothing had been written about it, this matter is more vividly remembered by the Indians themselves than those of us would like who desire that all vestiges of their paganism finally be uprooted from their minds. It is certainly true that those who are new to the Christian faith frequently slip back to the superstitions and rites of the cult of their false gods (which are not a few in number). Though they would not invent new idolatries, they would go back to those of their progenitors; these are the same practices taught to them by the superstitious old practitioners and sorcerers (some of whom still remain among them). The ones which they usually fall into today are the same as those that are recorded in the aforementioned reports as having been practiced in past times. Why should these reports, which were made with so much work, diligence, and exactness, be considered false?

Chapter 3: Of the legendary origin of the Incas, former kings

of Peru The Peruvian Indians tell of the origin and beginning of their kings, the Incas, but this involves such a great confusion and variety of folly that on the basis of what they report it is not possible to ascertain anything certain. Some confuse their origin with the descent of man, considering the Incas to have been the first inhabitants of the world. Others tell that since all men perished in the Universal Deluge, only the Incas were saved and restored the universe; in this vein they report a world of nonsense, and they support it with arguments as weak as these opinions themselves. But leaving now for its proper place what they had to say about the Flood and the population of the world,[8] I will tell here only three or four fables, the most widely accepted of all, of the origin of the Inca kings.

The first one goes this way: From Lake Titicaca up to Pacarictambo, a place seven leagues from Cuzco [southeast], there came certain Indians called Incas, men of prudence and valor, dressed in clothing very different from that used by those of the Cuzco region; these Incas had their ears pierced and wore gold plugs in them. Their leader, whom they called Manco Capac, had two thin and polished sheets of silver made. He put one of them on his chest and the other on his back, and he put a diadem of the same material on his head. Setting out with this adornment for the Valley of Cuzco, he sent his messengers ahead to tell the inhabitants of it that his father was the Sun, and if they wanted proof of it, they should come out to see him, for he would show himself to them from one of the high hills that surround the Valley of Cuzco. There he was seen by the natives of the region at the top of a mountain, and since the rays of the sun reverberated on the sheets of silver and the diadem that covered his head, he appeared to be so radiant that no other argument was necessary to convince the Indians, for they were simple people and believed that the word he had spread about himself was certainly true and that they should revere and obey him as the son of the Sun and a divine being. With this enchantment he came to reign in that valley, and from there he started to conquer the surrounding towns.

Another fable no less ridiculous than this last one tells that after the Universal Deluge in which all men died, there came forth from a cave—in the aforementioned site of Tampu or Tambo, called Pacarictampu, through a stone window, which is the mouth or air hole of this cave—four brothers called Manco Capac, Ayar Cache, Ayar Uchu, and Ayamanco; and with them four sisters of theirs, who were called Mama Huaco, Mama Ocllo, Mama Ragua and Mama Cura. Concerning their origin they are not in agreement. Some of them pretend that they came out of themselves. Others say that from Lake Titicaca, where they escaped the Flood, the Creator of the world brought them through the caverns of the earth up to where they came out at that cave of Pacarictampu. With the seeds of maize and other foods that the Creator gave them, they set off on the road to the Valley of Cuzco, the one guiding the rest. And they had agreed that wherever he stopped, they would make their settlement and home. They came to a high hill called Huanacauri (which afterward was a famous place of worship among the Indians because this fable took place there), and from there the eldest brother marked the land, and, hurling four slingstones toward the four corners of the earth, he took possession of it. At this point the Indians disagree, telling a thousand foolish tales. Some say that one of the brothers returned to Pacarictampu, entered the cave which he had left, and remained there without ever appearing again; of the three that remained, two of them turned themselves into stones; one of them became the hill of Huanacauri itself, and the other remained not far from there; thus only Manco Capac arrived with his four sisters at the site where the city of Cuzco is located now. There Manco Capac made friends little by little with the natives of the region, who were few in number and lived spread out over that valley like savages without order or harmony. With the industry and help of his sisters, who called him the son of the Sun and spoke to him with great respect and reverence, especially because he was a peaceful, very prudent and humane man, he came to be respected and obeyed by all.

Others tell this story another way. All eight brothers and sisters arrived at the site of Cuzco, and the one who traveled ahead to guide the others, upon arriving at the place where the Temple of the Sun was built later, seated himself, and there he was transformed into stone. For this reason the rest of the brothers and sisters, in accordance with an agreement they had made, stopped there and made their home on that same site; and this was the beginning of the city of Cuzco.

Another foolish tale is that when the Creator of the world (who has two names in their language, which are Ticciviracocha and

Pachayachachic) made all things in Tiaguanaco, where they pretend that he resided, he ordered the Sun, Moon, and Stars to go to the Island of Titicaca, which is located in the lake of this same name, and that from there they should go up to the sky. When the Sun was ready to leave in the form of a brightly shining man, he called the Incas, and the Sun himself spoke like an older brother to Manco Capac in the following way: "You and your descendants will subjugate many lands and peoples, and you will be great rulers. Always regard me as your father, and pride yourselves on being my sons, without ever forgetting to venerate me as such." And after he finished saying this, the Sun gave Manco Capac the royal insignia that he and his successors used from then on. And then the Sun went up to the sky with the Moon and Stars, where each one assumed its habitual place. And at once, by order of the Creator, the Inca brothers made their way beneath the earth and emerged at the cave of Pacarictampu.

This same tale is told by others in another way. They say that the Sun took pity on the miserable state of the world, and he sent to it a son and daughter of his own so that they could teach men about the Sun, persuading them to venerate the Sun as God and to pay him the honors that he deserved as such, and also so that they could teach them to live like men of reason in a disciplined and orderly fashion, establishing laws by which peace and justice could be maintained. And they were put in Lake Titicaca by their father the Sun, who ordered them to take whatever route they pleased as long as they thrust into the ground, wherever they might stop to eat and take rest, a small golden staff about one cubit long which he had given to them. In the place where the staff would sink into the ground with the first blow, it was his will that there they should stop and make their settlement and dwelling place; and they should subjugate the peoples of the surrounding area and, after subjugating them, govern them on the basis of reason and justice, with fatherly love and mercy, after the example of the Sun; and he constituted them as kings and rulers of whatever they should conquer by dint of industry and force.

And after bidding farewell to the Sun their father, they walked toward Cuzco, trying to thrust the golden staff into the ground wherever they stopped; and they arrived at the Valley of Yucay, and going a little farther down along the bank of the river that runs through this valley, they made a stop at Pacarictampu, which means "inn (or rest house) of the dawn"; from here they left as the sun came up, which is the reason they gave that name to the place.

They set out for the Valley of Cuzco, which at that time was uncultivated, covered with brush and weeds, and poorly populated by
a few barbaric Indians. Upon arriving at the hill of Huanacauri, they
tried to thrust the golden staff into the ground, and at the first
blow it sank in and they saw it no more; for this reason they knew
that they had reached the end of the pilgrimage and they knew that
was the place where the Sun their father wanted them to live. They
divided up in that valley, the prince on the one hand and the
princess on the other, in order to call together its inhabitants and
win them over with reasoning and benefits. The prince and the
princess let it be known that they were children of the Sun, sent to
provide the people with instruction and benefits. The barbarians,
who saw how well dressed and adorned they were, with clothing so
different from their own, started to respect them, and on the advice
and orders of these children of the Sun, the barbarians called one
another together; and with the skills that the Incas gave them, they
built houses on the site where the city stands today, and it was
divided into two barrios: one with the people who were attracted by
the prince, and the other with those who were brought together by
the princess; the former was called Hanan Cuzco and the latter
Hurin Cuzco, meaning "Upper Cuzco" and "Lower Cuzco"; and
this was the feeble beginning of the city of Cuzco and of the empire
of the Incas.

Another fable of the origin of the Incas is very similar to this
one, except that it affirms that the first Incas were born, in the
aforementioned island, of a woman called Titicaca, from whom the
island and lake took the name that they have today. In memory of
that woman, who was the Inca's mother, her descendants had a gold
and silver statue or idol in the form of a woman located in a solemn
temple that they built on that island.

In this fashion they tell a thousand other foolish tales and
stories, and trying to write them all down here would be a never-
ending task. The ones that I have just told will suffice to show how
uncertain and obscure the beginning and origin of the Incas is. But it
is customary for true histories to be filled with such fictitious
stories, and all those on this subject that the Indians commonly tell
point to certain facts, such as agreement on the name of the first
Inca, called Manco Capac, and mention of Pacarictampu. And on the
basis of other conjectures and indications that I have been able to
trace, I am convinced that the first Inca, Manco Capac, who marks
the initial memory that we find of these kings of Peru, must have

been from the Valley of Tampu or from some place close by and, either alone or accompanied by some of his kinsmen, probably came to live in the Valley of Cuzco; and, surpassing its inhabitants in ability, ingenuity, and valor, he must have contrived so well to win their friendship and bring himself into their favor and good graces, making up some fantastic idea upon which the Indians must have based the fables mentioned above, that they ended up by yielding their obedience to him and allowing themselves to be governed by him.

Moreover, besides what is contained in the aforementioned fables, I consider it to be no small indication in favor of my view that the Incas had founded a town on the site of Pacarictampu, and that they built on it, in order to make it famous, a magnificent royal palace with a splendid temple. The ruins of this palace and temple remain even today, and in them some stone idols and statues are seen. At the entrance of that famous cave of Pacarictampu there is a carefully cut stone window in memory of the time when Manco Capac left through it. To this is added the fact that, apart from the language of Cuzco, which is the general language that the Incas introduced throughout their empire and was the one they used in speaking to their subjects, they knew a different one, which they used only among themselves when they dealt and conversed with those of their own lineage. Alonso Tupa Atau, grandson of Guayna Capac, assured me that this language peculiar to the Incas is the same one spoken by the Indians of the Valley of Tampu, but with the changes that have occurred in this kingdom with the new rule of the Spaniards, now the descendants of the Incas have forgotten this language, although they still remember some words from it. For me this last bit of information is the main argument supporting the idea that the first Inca was native to the Valley of Tampu.

108

Chapter 4: Of Manco Capac, the first king of the Incas

Once the Inca Manco Capac was in command of that small community and republic of barbarians, he treated them in a humane and familiar manner, more like brothers than with the authority of a superior. He employed all of his ingenuity in striving for the welfare and increase of his subjects. The first thing he did was to divide the population of Cuzco into the two groups of Hanan Cuzco and Hurin Cuzco mentioned above. He put matters pertaining to religion in order, designating the gods that they had to worship and teaching them the way that these gods were to be venerated and invoked, especially his father the Sun. He built temples and appointed ministers and priests for the service and rituals of the temples; he established the ceremonies, rituals, and sacrifices with which the gods should be venerated. He had all the leaders brought together who lived in the Valley of Cuzco from Carmenga up to the narrow passage they called Ancoyapuncu [Acoya Puncu], which were the borders of their domain, in order to parcel out the lands of the valley. In the first place he designated the lands to be used for himself and for all the *guacas*, temples, and places of worship; this was for their service as well as to support the ones who engaged in this ministry; and he distributed the rest of the land among the members of the community, and with this he made them very happy.

The king set himself to teach the men all of the tasks that are theirs, such as the work in the fields, how to make ditches from the rivers in order to irrigate, and the proper times for sowing and harvesting their crops. He instructed them in the use of clothes and footwear of the type they used thereafter and the majority still use today. The Coya, or Queen, took care to teach the women to spin and weave wool and cotton, as well as other tasks and occupations of their profession.

With such good works as the Inca performed for his subjects, they came to like him better each day; and in order to enjoy the same benefits, strangers willingly submitted to his rule. Thus he came to rule over the whole Valley of Cuzco and the sierras that surround it, and in this district he founded many towns. Although they were small at first, they grew steadily as time passed. The Inca made useful laws to teach his vassals praiseworthy customs and to increase the size and ensure the success of his state.

Before the Inca went into Cuzco, his wife, Mama Huaco, bore him a son in a town called Matagua, which was one league from Cuzco; he named his son Cinchi Roca, and he raised him with great care, as the one who would succeed him as ruler of the kingdom he founded. So that this son would be acknowledged as his heir and be respected, the Inca commanded his most important subjects to gather together on a certain day in the same town of Matagua to celebrate the Rutuchico, a new ceremony never held before; the Inca invented it on this occasion to celebrate his son's first hair cutting; from then on it was an accepted practice.

This fiesta was held with stately display before a large gathering of nobles who came forward in sequence according to their rank within the nobility; each one cut part of the prince's hair, offering him at the same time magnificent gifts of fine clothing and jewels of gold and silver, and venerating him as the grandchild of the Sun himself, whom they worshiped for their god. In order to make this fiesta more solemn, new music, songs, and dances were invented; and between the music and the eating and drinking, the festivities lasted ten days.

It was with no less a royal, stately, and solemn display that they celebrated on the day that the young Inca Cinchi Roca was knighted and given the insignia of the nobility. For this fiesta, which was held in the aforementioned town of Matagua, a much larger group of people was gathered together than for the previous fiesta; the road from Cuzco to Matagua was adorned with meticulously constructed floral arches; and diverse inventions of dances and festivities were performed on this day. The assemblage included the young Inca, very richly dressed, and the king and queen, his parents, and along with them the priest who was to knight the young Inca; these four rode in litters and the rest went on foot. Upon arriving at the designated place, first the priest delivered a brief discourse which he had prepared for the prince; then the priest dressed him in the royal clothing and gave him the other insignia that from then on were used by the successors to the throne. When the prince was old enough to perpetuate the lineage of the Incas, children of the Sun, his father tried to persuade him to marry. In the Valley of Cuzco itself lived a worthy and valiant gentleman named Sutic Guaman who was the lord of a town called Sañoc, and he had a daughter named Mama Chura. The Inca arranged for his son to marry this girl, and the father of the bride willingly agreed. The wedding was held, and it made all the vassals joyful and happy.

After this Manco Capac lived in great peace and tranquillity,

without anybody bothering him, because he was much loved by his
subjects and reputed to be more than a man. In accordance with
the conviction, which was firmly set in the minds of those barbarians, that the Inca was the child of the Sun, sent from heaven to
the world in order to govern it, and in order to better establish
this deception, the Inca took special care to erect a temple for his
father the Sun. He selected for this a very spacious and prominent
site, and on it he started to build the great temple of Coricancha;
it was not such a magnificent edifice as it later became, but of humble and crude workmanship with adobe walls. This is because in
that unrefined period the technique of stonework that their successors achieved later had not been seen or used. Thus, this Inca only
began the magnificent temple of the Coricancha (which means
"golden house"), and the other kings who succeeded him raised
it up to the magnificence and loftiness it had attained when the
Spaniards found it. Finally, this first Inca established the kingdom
by winning the good will of those who approached him and by showing himself to be humane, affable, and very religious and well informed with regard to things pertaining to the divine rituals and
understanding the gods, especially his father the Sun, whose worship Manco Capac and his successors established throughout their
kingdom.

Having reached old age, when he felt the approach of death,
the Inca ordered his most important subjects to gather together before him, and he told them that it was time for him to return to
the sky; his father the Sun was calling for him to come there. The
most important thing that he entrusted to them in that hour, for
the love that he had shown to them, was to keep peace and harmony
among themselves and to be as obedient and faithful to his eldest
son, Cinchi Roca, as they had been to him. Having said this, he
died. His subjects were visibly stricken with grief, for they loved
him as a father, and in order to dignify the funeral rites of their
king, they invented the style of weeping and ceremonies that they
have used since that time in the burial of their other kings.

All the kings of Peru, who were descended from Manco Capac,
the same as this first king, were called Incas, in the manner of the
Roman emperors, who had the name of Caesars; this family name
Inca was held not only by those who possessed the royal scepter
and crown, but also by all those of his lineage and royal blood,
whether they were descended in the male line or the female line.
And to this day, although their reign has already ended, the Inca
descendants who remain are proud of this name and ancestry, and

they conserve it with great respect; and the rest of the Indians consider it to be so honorable that when one Indian calls to another, he usually gives him this title, as an honor, saying "Inca" to him, in place of the terms *señor* or *caballero* that we use. All the Incas, from the first one, in order to be obeyed and respected by their vassals and in order to give more authority to their laws and commands and make as many innovations as they wanted, gave their subjects to understand that whatever they commanded or ordered was ordered by their father the Sun, with whom they communicated and consulted concerning all the matters that they arranged in their kingdom; in this way, besides their being held and venerated by the people as children of the Sun and more than men, there was no opposition to anything that they ordered because all of their commands were held to be divine oracles.

According to tradition, it is considered that from Manco Capac came the two tribal groups of Hanan Cuzco and Hurin Cuzco, into which all of the Incas were divided. It was customary among all of these kings for each one to found his own lineage and family in the following way: Not counting the prince who succeeded his father as ruler, his brothers and sisters were considered to belong to a single lineage originated by their father the king; the crown prince did not belong to this group and family because, as the future king, he was to be the head and initiator of another new family, and every lineage of these had its own name. Furthermore, upon the death of the king, the prince did not inherit his house and treasure, but it was handed over along with the body of the deceased king to the family that he had founded. This entire treasure was used for the cult of his body and the sustenance of his family. After having the body of their father the king embalmed, they kept it with all of his dishes and jewelry; the king's family and all of his descendants adored the body as a god. The body was handed down to the most prominent members of the family, and they did not make use of the dead king's dishes, except when the town or place where the body was deposited held an important fiesta. And the successor to the crown set up his house anew, accumulating for it a treasure to leave to those of his *ayllo* and lineage. Since the Incas felt sure that they all descended from Manco Capac, his body and idol were adored by all of the families and *ayllos*, and with more veneration than the others, as a universal *guaca* whom they acknowledged to be the second cause of their generation and birth.

From this first king came the *ayllo* and family called Chima Panaca, which adored no human body other than that of Manco

Capac, while the other families and lineages adored this one and the bodies of their founders. When Licentiate Polo Ondegardo, with unusual diligence and cunning, found the bodies of the Inca kings and their idols and took them out of the hands of their families in the year 1559 (which was a major factor in eliminating many idolatries and superstitions), he was unable to discover the body of Manco Capac because (or so it seems) his descendants never had it, rather they believed that it turned into stone, and they said that it was a stone that Licentiate Polo himself found, all dressed and properly adorned, in a town near Cuzco that was called Membilla. The tribal group of Chima Panaca regularly held great fiestas with many ceremonies and sacrifices in honor of this stone. The insignia and emblems of this first king, the ones used by his tribal group and lineage, are some round plumage called *purupuru* by the Indians, symbolizing the whole world and that this first Inca had conquered it.

Chapter 5: Of the second Inca, named Cinchi Roca

After the death of Manco Capac, his eldest son Cinchi Roca was obeyed as the king; he was already a man twenty years old. He was so well trained by his father with regard to matters pertaining to the government and republic, and he conducted himself with such great prudence and treated his subjects so well that he came to be loved by all no less than his father. At the beginning of his reign, he visited the places and towns of the Valley of Cuzco, which were already much expanded and enlarged with buildings and people, and on this visit he commanded that everyone should cultivate the lands that they needed for sowing *papas* [potatoes]; thus their lands were extended to a place called Cinga, which is a hill that is opposite Cuzco, because up to this time they had not wanted to enter into distant lands. As a result of this order, they expanded to the hills surrounding Cuzco, and he gave permission for all those who desired to take up residence in the aforementioned lands; this included both the Indians born there and newcomers; he did this because it already seemed to him that it was advisable to expand the boundaries of his kingdom and move ahead, particularly after the birth of his first son, to whom he gave the name Lloque Yupanqui. He also discussed the matter with his mother, Coya Mama Huaco, who was very old, but she told him that it was not advisable to try to enlarge his state then, since all of the neighbors who populated the area surrounding Cuzco were his friends and they had also been friends of his father, and that, until his children were older, he should not try anything new.

The death of Mama Huaco came, and there was much mourning for her, because her funeral rites lasted for two months. First they were held in Cuzco for a period of ten days, and later the king went with his court to every town and place throughout the whole Valley of Cuzco, doing his mourning in each one. For many years the Inca did nothing but teach his son Lloque Yupanqui how he should govern his vassals. He trained him also in the use of arms and the manner in which he should increase his dominions. Cinchi Roca was a man of such valor and good counsel that he got people to come to see his son from some provinces far from Cuzco, and he gave jewels and very valuable clothing to all of the lords and leaders, which pleased them very much. He was also able to name caciques to govern in some towns, when he knew that they had no natural lord or no one who could administer them; in order to accomplish this he said that the Sun his father had given power to him and his descendants; having seen this, some leaders came to ask him for the right to rule the town where they were born, either by way of a favor or confirmation of the *cacicazgo* that they already possessed.

By this time the fame of the Incas had spread everywhere; they were known to be children of the Sun and to have power and valor; for these reasons it was surmised that the Incas were going to rule all the land, and the Indians of many provinces sought their friendship and alliance, and in order to attain it, they sent them many presents of gold, silver, and clothing. Cinchi Roca tried with wile and cunning to win the friendship of everyone, and to this end he sent them presents of jewels and other valuable things. This Inca invented the *sunturpaucar* of colored plumage. He sought to have his son marry, for he wanted him to remain with a legitimate wife so that there would be legitimate children according to their laws, but the youth did not accept the marriage that his father arranged; this caused Cinchi Roca much grief, and being old and very honored, he came to the end of his days. His death was deeply felt and mourned with some new kinds of ceremonies because his great goodness had made him loved by his subjects.

From this Inca came the *ayllo* and family called Rauraua Panaca. He left a stone idol in the form of a fish that was named Huanachiri Amaro, and he was adored through it the same as the other Incas from the first one on, and these stone idols were kept and venerated as gods. Cinchi Roca's body was found in the town of Membilla when the bodies of the rest of the Incas were discovered. It was between some copper bars and sewed with *cabuya*, but it was already consumed. His idol was next to the body, and this idol was much venerated and had servants and a *chacara*.

Chapter 6: Of Lloque Yupanqui, the third Inca

After the third king of Peru, Lloque Yupanqui, started to govern, he discussed the matter of how to be the lord of all the towns in the area surrounding Cuzco, and he appointed some important men to help him in this as captains and officers in the armies that he had. In their fables the Indians tell that during his sacrifices and prayers, which followed the custom of the Incas his fathers, the Sun appeared to him in the figure of the Inca Manco Capac, his grandfather, and the Sun told him that what he had arranged with his subjects had seemed very good to him, and he, the Sun, would help him as a father in whatever he undertook, that he should not fear, but immediately set to work on what he had started; after saying these and other things, he disappeared. This left the Inca with more courage and vigor than he had had up until then, and at once he informed the members of his household about this vision.

He endeavored with cunning and ingenuity to have the Indians come to see him and for them to yield obedience to him as the principal lord of all that land, and as a matter of fact, they came to visit him from many provinces and nations that had never been seen during the time of his father or grandfather. The first ones to do this were from the Valley of Guaro, six leagues from Cuzco; it had many people, and the lords of the valley were very powerful at that time. The most important ones were called Guama Samo and Pachachulla Viracocha. These were followed by the Ayarmacas of Tambocunca and the Quilliscaches with their caciques; since they had seen the greatness of the Inca and his court and how he commanded so much authority, they yielded obedience to him, and they swore allegiance to him as their lord; this took place in the temple of Coricancha, before the Sun and the Moon and the priest who was there, and the power of the Sun and the Incas was represented by this priest. These Indians promised that they would be obedient to his commands forever and ever. Already having the Valley of Guaro under his control with no more than his good planning and counsel, and at no material loss whatever to the Inca, he dwelled in peace and tranquillity for many years. Nevertheless, in many parts of the land there were wars between opposing caciques; the Inca would send his ambassadors to keep the peace, and he would advise the caciques not to wage war, because the Sun his father was angry and if they did not set aside their arms he would make war on them and take away their states. Because of the respect they held for him as the child of the Sun, the lords took his advice willingly and endeavored to make amends and live in peace.

Since he had no legitimate wife or a son who, according to their laws, could be his heir, those of his council implored him to try to marry, even though he was getting old, so that a legitimate lord would remain for them; although he had many women, none of them was considered to be legitimate. Being persuaded by his men, the Inca made up his mind to marry, and to this end, he had Pachachulla Viracocha called; he was one of the lords from Guaro who had yielded obedience to him, and the Inca commanded that he go to the town of Oma, little more than two leagues away from Cuzco, and that he ask for the daughter of the lord of that town to be his wife. Upon receiving this message, the lord of Oma was very happy about it, and on the advice of the other lords, they gave her to him.

This lady was called Mama Cachua, and they say that she was so beautiful that her father had not wanted to marry her to anyone; he felt that no one deserved her. But, once the leaders of Oma realized that she was being asked for by the Inca, a child of the Sun, they held this marriage to be very fortunate. They sent her to Cuzco with a large escort, and all along the road where they had to pass, many flowers were scattered, archways were erected, and magnificent cloth was hung. It took her four days to get to Cuzco because the Inca had commanded that she rest every half league and be entertained and given a feast. When they were drawing near, the king with all the nobles of his court came out to meet her, and many new songs and dances were performed.

Very big fiestas were held for the wedding because all the lords under the Inca attended. As a result, within a year the Inca had a son whom he named Mayta Capac, and his birthday was celebrated with every indication of happiness and pleasure by everyone in his kingdom, for they were very glad to see the successor. The Inca commanded that many rich garments be distributed, and he did many favors for the lords who came to the fiestas. A few days after that he died; but before he died, since Mayta Capac was still very young, he had two Indians called. They were sons of Cinchi Roca, the king's father; their names were Apu Condemayta and Tacachuincay; to them he entrusted the government of the kingdom and the rearing of the young Inca until the boy was of age. They did it with as much care as if they were parents of the prince. Lloque Yupanqui founded the lineage called Ahuani Ayllu, which was spread out in the towns of Cayucache, Membilla, and the area surrounding Cacra. He had an idol that was discovered with his body in the same manner as the rest, and it was much venerated by those of this *ayllo*, and they had the same fiestas and sacrifices for it as for the others.

Chapter 7: Of Mayta Capac, fourth king of the Incas

The governors reared the prince with more comfort and liberty than the children of the kings before him had had; for this reason Mayta Capac turned out to be a mischievous and impudent young man, but aside from this, he was brave and courageous by nature. Before he got out of his tutelage, while playing one day with some other boys of his age, there was one who told him to look out for himself and mend his ways, because if he did not, his mischief would be the cause of his ruin; this was due to the fact that the sons of some of the leaders of the town were offended and insulted because he did not treat them in accordance with their position. While they were involved in this discussion, the Inca saw that many Indians were coming to where he was with weapons and that they were determined to cause some trouble. He came out to meet them without fear, and he recognized that they were Alcayviczas, sons of an important lineage of Cuzco, who showed that they wanted to quarrel with him. He took up his arms, which his servants brought to him immediately; he had a dart and a round shield, and attacking his opponents boldly, he killed some of them so quickly that he did not take time to hear any explanations from them. The noise brought some people out of the Inca's house to see what it was, and realizing that someone had wanted to kill their lord, they helped him against the traitors until they put them to flight.

Since some of the most important men of the court saw that the Inca had gotten so angry that he had killed their children, they tried to rebel against him and join forces with the Alcayviczas in order to put him to death; they thought that since he was a youth he would not know how to defend himself. Once Mayta Capac and his two uncles knew about this rebellion, they got ready as best they could and were on the alert to find out what the Alcayviczas and their confederates sought to do; actually their intention was to kill all the Incas and leave no trace of them. These Alcayviczas were natives of Cuzco; the Inca Manco Capac had seized power over their ancestors, as has been stated before. Along with their friends and supporters, they discussed the way to conduct this affair in order to accomplish their goal, which was, as has been stated, to kill the Inca and his uncles along with all of their lineage; as a matter of fact, according to everyone, they decided to perform this act of treachery. Their proposal was not hidden from the Inca Mayta

Capac because one of the important men who found out about it revealed the plan to the Inca and told him how those of the tribal group of the Alcayviczas were withdrawn inside their houses, where they were gathering arms and friends with whom they had their alliance.

The Inca, without any visible signs of annoyance, rather with a happy and serene look on his face, said to the person who gave him the information: "Well, friend, you who know this, go to the Alcayviczas and tell them that I command that they come immediately to accompany me, that I want to go hunting, and come back at once with their answer." While that servant of the prince went with the message, the Inca gave word of what was happening to his two uncles and his councilors, who immediately began getting ready as best they could, and concealing their true feelings, they awaited the messenger's return. The answer that he brought was that the Alcayviczas said that they recognized no lord or Inca, that they were at home in their lands and that the Inca was to stay on his own land. Upon hearing this answer, the Inca, in agreement with the rest of the people, decided that it was not good to hide his feelings any longer about those who so insolently put him to shame and refused to obey him; thus, with his uncles and about fifty men who were with him, he attacked the house of his opponents, who were all together, so suddenly that he did not give them any time at all to get ready. Shortly the enemies were defeated, and many of them were killed. Those who escaped, seeing that their cause was lost, surrendered to the Inca. This was the first dispute in which the Incas killed a large number of men, and it was a matter of great consequence for their reputation and for the wars that occurred later. The Inca celebrated this victory with many sacrifices that he offered to his father the Sun in the temple of Coricancha.

When the prince came of age, he took the fringe[9] and the government of the kingdom, and he married a lady named Mama Tancaray Yacchi, daughter of the cacique from Collaguas; and for this reason, the Indians of that province, as a service to this king and queen, made a house all of copper in which to accommodate them when they went to visit the queen's kinsmen. Some of this copper was found due to the diligence of the Franciscan friars who teach in that province; from it they made four large bells. The Indians said that the rest of the copper that was missing had been given to Gonzalo Pizarro and his army during the time of the civil wars.

Mayta Capac started to become a greater lord than his predecessors; this was seen in the royal pomp of his house, where he was served on dishes of gold and silver, as well as in his power and authority. By this time the dominion of Cuzco was already so populated with so many different nations that its name filled all the land with terror; this was because the people were convinced that the Sun and Moon communicated with the Incas, whose sons and grandsons were already very numerous, and because they distinguished themselves from among the other nations by virtue of their valor and knowledge. The lords of many provinces of the land sent their sons to the Inca Mayta Capac so that they could help out in the court and serve the Inca; each of these lords boasted of having a son who was performing this service. This king had two sons by his legitimate wife; their names were Capac Yupanqui and Tarco Huaman; by other wives of his, not counting the legitimate one, he had many other children, to whom he gave the posts and offices of governors in charge of the tribal territories and places controlled by Cuzco. He lived many years, and he left the *ayllo* and tribal groups called Usca Mayta, of which the greater part lived in Cayucache. The body of this Inca was taken from his family and the idol that he left of himself was also taken; the same veneration and sacrifices were performed for this body as for the rest.

Chapter 8: Of the Inca Capac Yupanqui, fifth king of Peru

The Inca Capac Yupanqui succeeded his father Mayta Capac in the kingdom; he had other brothers who were illegitimate and bastards whom his father had placed as governors of the towns of the Cuzco region. After the death of their father, these brothers tried to ask their brother the king for some privileges in order to command more authority and dominion than they had before in their posts and offices, but the Inca Capac Yupanqui was so prudent and farsighted that he penetrated the thoughts of those who came to negotiate and seek favors from him, and on this occasion he was able to understand the intentions of his brothers, who had secretly agreed among themselves to take the crown away from him and give it to his brother Tarco Huaman, whom they considered to be more valiant and discreet and a man of better counsel. After the Inca heard his brothers' request, it became clear to him where their efforts were being directed from some indications that he had concerning the agreement that his brothers were making. In order to remedy the situation and to avert the damages that could befall him, he employed this expedient: He commanded all of the nobles and lords of his court to assemble on a certain day because he had informed them about a serious matter concerning the service to their Inca and lord. When that day arrived, all his brothers and the other lords and important men assembled. The Inca made a speech in which he praised and honored them with such skill that he caused them to change their attitude, converting their hatred for him into love, and they were so happy and satisfied, that, in order to indicate the obligation under which he had brought them by the great honor he had bestowed on them, they stood up in the presence of all and once again swore allegiance to their brother Capac Yupanqui, holding him as their king and lord, and they persuaded the others to do the same. In this way the Inca won the affections of his brothers, and from then on he had them so firmly on his side that they helped him much on important occasions that came up, both in times of peace and in war. This assembly ended with rejoicing and great fiestas held by order of the Inca because his brothers had sworn allegiance to him as their king for the second time.

After some time, it happened that the Inca made a request of the lord of the province of Cuyos, in the Andes, for him to send certain birds that are found in that land, to be kept in cages; paying no attention to the message from the Inca, for his answer he sent word to the Inca that in his land they had no birds or other animals for their use. The Inca decided to castigate that cacique for his disrespect, and to this end he ordered his brothers to raise some men and name captains, and, in a short time, a good army was formed. The Inca himself left with it for the province of Cuyos; he found that the residents of this province were off guard, and he attacked them so suddenly that they were not able to react in time to take up arms and resist. The Inca seized power over those towns and made prisoners of the caciques and leaders with their women and children; they were all taken to Cuzco, where justice was brought to the principal cacique and the rest of the culprits involved in making the reply to the Inca's messenger who went to get the birds. The Inca put his brother Tarco Huaman in charge of the government of that province, and as a sign of gratitude for this favor, he sent a thousand cages of birds from the Andes and the puna, and many strange animals; this pleased the Inca, and he presented to his brother a large quantity of fine clothing and many women, besides the ones his brother had taken from Cuzco when he went to his governorship. This Inca also subdued the province of Condesuyo; he went in person on this conquest, and he had a hard-fought battle with the Condesuyos, in which many of them died and the Inca was victorious.

Capac Yupanqui married a lady who, because of her extreme beauty, was called Cori Ilpaycahua, which means "golden jewel"; she was the daughter of a nobleman from Cuzco, who was highly respected by the previous Incas. The Inca had two sons by her, Inca Roca Inca, who succeeded him in the kingdom, and Apo Mayta, who turned out to be very brave, not to mention other children that he had by women who were not legitimate wives; actually the Inca kings normally had between fifty and one hundred wives, and the last ones, who were the most powerful, had from two hundred to three hundred wives. The Coya was so loved by her husband that, during their many years of married life, he always entertained her with festivities, and every day there was a fiesta with new inventions and new kinds of rejoicing. Forests with many shade trees were planted in the plaza, and there they put lions, tigers, bears, deer, and other wild animals and a thousand different kinds of birds. Having governed prosperously for many years, Capac Yupanqui died, leaving as heir his eldest son, Inca Roca. His death was deeply felt and mourned, and in order to show greater sadness,

his wife ordered the forest and shade trees that were in the plaza
to be removed, and much of it was planted in the place called Puma-
chupan, below which now is the convent of Santo Domingo; the
forest lasted up to the arrival of the Spaniards.

From this Inca descends the tribal group and *ayllo* of Apuamay-
ta, and the idol that he left had the same name as the *ayllo*. His
body and idol were found in one of the towns located near Cuzco
before the Christian settlement. Except for Manco Capac, who, as
the head and trunk of both tribal groups of Hanan Cuzco and Hurin
Cuzco, was not counted in their division, some of the other kings
were from the Hanan Cuzco group and others were from the Hurin
Cuzco group. The first four successors of Manco Capac, whom we
have already described, are counted by the Indians as members of
the tribal group of Hurin Cuzco. During this time, their dominions
were extended only a little; for this reason at that time there were
caciques in Peru as powerful as the Incas, such as those from Chucuito,[10] Hatuncolla,[11] Chincha, and others of the coastal provinces
of the llanos. I find no explanation among the Indians as to why
the following kings belong to the tribal group of Hanan Cuzco and
the four previous ones belonged to the other one of Hurin Cuzco.
Although the Incas who live today in Cuzco have a clear notion
and account of the kings who belonged to each tribal group, they
cannot give the reason for this distinction; not even Alonso could
remove the doubts I had on this point; he was the grandson of Guayna Capac and the son of Paullu Inca, and we conversed at length
about the affairs of the Incas and other antiquities. What they are
certain about is that the last six kings were from the tribal group
of Hanan Cuzco, which became very enlightened and ennobled, because from it came the most powerful Incas, who enlarged the empire and achieved the greatness which it had when the Spaniards
found it.

Chapter 9: Of the sixth king of Peru, named Inca Roca

The sixth king of this land was Inca Roca, and the Indians say that he started the tribal group of Hanan Cuzco. But inasmuch as that division of the city of Cuzco into the two tribal groups called Hanan Cuzco and Hurin Cuzco was made from the time of Manco Capac, the division of Hanan Cuzco could not have been begun by this Inca. The reason for making him the head and origin of it was perhaps because he was the first of the Inca kings to be counted in the ranks of that tribal group and because the crown never left his lineage. Inca Roca married a lady named Mama Michay, cacica of the town of Guayllacan, and, before he married, it happened that the priest of the temple of the Sun told him that he should marry because his father the Sun had commanded that he tell him this, because it was advisable to do so, and that very soon he would have many battles and he would be lord of many provinces. The Indians tell that after the fiestas of this marriage were over, the Coya noticed that the Valley of Cuzco lacked sufficient water to irrigate the *chacaras* of maize so she had the majority of the water brought in that it has to this day, and in memory of this service which she performed for the region, the family and lineage which issued from her remained in charge of the distribution of the water used to irrigate the valley. This Inca had three legitimate sons. The first one was Yahuar Huacac, who succeeded him in the kingdom, and the other two, who turned out to be very brave, were named Vicaquirao and Apo Mayta.

This Inca subdued many provinces, conquering some by force of arms and others by peaceful means. He sent his sons with an army to conquer the towns along the road through Collasuyu. They started their conquest with the Valley of Moyna, which is four leagues from Cuzco and was not under the Inca's domination. They entered into battle with the lords of this place, and although those lords did their duty, the sons of the Inca were victorious. They captured the cacique named Moina along with another lord of that place named Caytomarca. Another cacique, Guaman Tupa by name, fled from the battle, and he did not appear any more either alive or dead. It was understood that to avoid combat with the Incas, he jumped into the lake that is located in that valley. This time the Inca's sons conquered up to Quiquijana, another six leagues past Moyna, and from there they returned victorious to Cuzco, which pleased the king their father very much. A little later, the king waged war on the Indians of the Chanca nation, native to the Valley of Andaguaylas, thirty-four leagues from Cuzco. These Chancas were so brave that by their efforts they had won many lands and dominions, but by attacking them suddenly with a large army, the Inca left them no time to assemble their forces and resist him; and so, with great despair and unable to do otherwise, they surrendered to him, but not without the hope of promptly shaking such a heavy yoke off their shoulders. The king himself was present in person during this war; and besides the men that he raised for it in the towns of his dominions, he requested help from his neighbors the Canas and the Canches, who still were not under his domination; from them he took some companies of salaried men.

With this victory won, the Inca sent his son the prince Yahuar Huacac to make war on the provinces of the Andes; he conquered Paucartambo along with the surrounding towns, and he did not proceed any further because of the dense growth of vegetation and underbrush of those woodlands and *arcabucos*. With these new conquests Inca Roca left his kingdom quite enlarged and he encouraged his successors not to desist from trying to augment it. He founded the family of Vicaquirao. His body was found well adorned and with much authority in a small town of the Cuzco region called Rarapa, along with a stone idol that represented him, of the same name as his *ayllo*, Vicaquirao, and this body was much honored by those of the aforesaid *ayllo* and family; in addition to the ordinary adoration and sacrifices made for it, when there was a need for water for the cultivated fields, they usually brought out his body, richly dressed, with his face covered, carrying it in a procession through the fields and punas, and they were convinced that this was largely responsible for bringing rain.

Chapter 10: Of Yahuar Huacac Inca Yupanqui, the seventh

king Inca Roca was succeeded in the kingdom by his eldest son, Yahuar Huacac, "he who weeps blood"; and it is said that he had been given this name because once, having been defeated and imprisoned by his enemies, he wept blood out of sheer grief and suffering to see himself in such a miserable state. His vassals had a very poor opinion of him, because he had the reputation of being a coward, and this opinion was confirmed by the predictions that the augurs drew from his name, that he was to be unhappy and unfortunate; and the Inca himself, fearful of these predictions, did not dare go to war in person; thus in the account that is made of his life in the histories and songs of the Indians, after he was crowned king, no record is found of his leaving Cuzco on any conquests. When he was in the process of selecting a legitimate wife, his private counselors advised him to marry one of the concubines who had already borne him children; but he did not agree to this. When he found out that in the town of Ayarmaca there was an important lady who, owing to her valor and beauty, deserved to be his wife, he commanded that she be brought to him immediately. In view of the king's decision, the great nobles and important men sent an embassy to the lady, who was called Mama Choque Chicllayupay, letting her know the will of the Inca. Since she was favorably impressed by such great favor and good will, she prepared herself immediately to go to Cuzco, where she was received as a queen, and the wedding was held with a large assembly of important personages and public merriment. The Inca had many sons by her; the eldest, who, as we will explain later, took the name of Viracocha, succeeded him in the kingdom.

Since Yahuar Huacac realized that his eldest son was harsh and arrogant and that he had sunk below the kind and gentle condition of his Inca forefathers, and fearing that he would destroy the kingdom if he took the scepter, the Inca attempted to discipline him by every possible means, but when he saw that his son did not mend his ways, he forced him to leave, sending him as an exile to a cold bleak place called Chita, two leagues away from Cuzco, and he commanded that his son live in the company of the shepherds who looked after the livestock of the Sun; and in order to show more disfavor, he took as his companion in the government another, younger son, whom he gave authority and command equal to his own. During the exile of the prince, the Chanca Indians rebelled; actually they had never surrendered to the Inca; rather they surrendered to the necessity of adapting themselves to the times. They killed the governors appointed by the Inca, and with an army of thirty thousand men they marched around Cuzco, intending to destroy it. On considering the danger to himself and how that rebellion had taken him by surprise, the Inca did not dare to confront his enemies; rather, on receiving the news that they were close to the city, he abandoned the place, leaving it, along with the majority of its residents, who, imitating their king, took refuge in secure places.

When this news reached the ears of the exiled prince, he decided to come out to meet this challenge and oppose the enemy. He went into the city to defend it along with the few residents who had remained, and while he was leading those he was able to assemble, the ones who had abandoned the city joined him along with many others. The prince, with the object of establishing a good reputation among his subjects and gaining acceptance as their rightful king, made up a story that was the beginning of his fortune, good luck, and name. He told his subjects that while he was in exile, resting one day in the shade of a large rock, the god Viracocha appeared to him in a dream in the figure and dress of a bearded white man with clothing that reached down to his feet. This god complained to him, saying that although he was the universal lord and creator of everything—the sky, the sun, the earth, and men— and although everything was under his command, the Indians did not honor and venerate him as they should; rather they worshiped him with the same reverence that they showed to the Sun, Thunder, Earth, and other created things that by themselves had no other power than that which he gave them; and he let the young man know that in the sky, where he lived, he was called Viracocha Yachachic, which means "universal creator." So that those people would believe in the creator Viracocha, the young prince, although alone and out of favor with the king his father, should raise men in the name of Viracocha. Although the Chancas were numerous and enjoyed victory, with his favor and help the Inca would defeat them and Viracocha would make him lord of the land, because, at the time of going into battle, he would send the prince invisible reinforcements that would help him against his enemies; and in memory of this favor that he did for him, from then on the prince's name would be Viracocha. This revelation or fable that he told the

Indians was of great importance for the purposes of this prince, because the priests, as great augurs, accepting the fable, exhorted and persuaded the people to obey Prince Viracocha and to follow him in this undertaking against the Chancas.

The Inca Viracocha assembled an army of thirty thousand combatants and left Cuzco in search of his opponents, for whom he waited on a plain that is called Guazauara today, one league from the city, where men from the surrounding towns did not cease to come to his aid, and so his forces increased continuously. The Chancas arrived at the same spot; they came determined to take possession of Cuzco or die in the attempt. The two armies met with great fury and shouting; the battle was very hard-fought and relentless, but while the fighting was going on, bands of Indians from places nearby came to Virachocha's side, and thus the Chancas started to lose courage, and the army of Viracocha ended the battle with victory, slaughtering and destroying the enemies. Since much blood was spilled in this battle, that field was named Yahuarpampa, which means "meadow (or plain) of blood."

The Inca Viracocha based a fable on this defeat of the Chancas; he said that victory was achieved not so much because of the fighting done by the men of his army as because of the help and assistance from the god Viracocha, who had sent a considerable number of bearded men with bows and arrows; these men had fought so well that they cut the throats of the majority of the Chancas who were killed in the battle; and the Inca Viracocha had seen these men, and he was the only person permitted to see them. The story turned out to be very suitable for his purposes; although at first he must not have gotten very far with this fantasy, eventually he became well known for it, which furthered his intentions, and thus he came to be well reputed among his soldiers. His enemies helped him considerably by their credulity and lack of firmness, and also by one thing that is natural and common to all, which is to look for some way to excuse ourselves when we are defeated, and when something turns out worse than we would like and it seems that we could be blamed. It happened in this way: this report started to spread throughout the provinces of the kingdom, and when it reached the ears of the Chancas, they were pleased to hear it, and they confirmed this belief, declaring that without this help they could not be defeated by the Inca; they strengthened their opinion with explanations that our own inclination in such cases teaches us; and they themselves gave the name *pururaucas* (which means "hidden thieves") to these reinforcements sent by the god Viracocha. Upon seeing the effects produced by this nonsense, the Inca decided to make it more credible by saying that the *pururaucas* had turned into stones with which he was familiar. He pointed them out and commanded that they be worshiped and that sacrifices be offered to them. Having achieved this victory, he took possession of the kingdom without much opposition and dispossessed his father and brother of it; and thus ended the reign of Yahuar Huacac, whose body—along with the idol that he had designated when he was alive—was found in a town called Paullu, in the direction of Calca; and it was highly respected and worshiped by the lineage and *ayllo* that issued from him, which is the one named Aucayllo Panaca.

Chapter 11: Of Viracocha Inca, eighth king

The Inca Viracocha, eighth king of Cuzco, put on the fringe, which was the same as crowning himself king; and he showed great promise of being a valiant prince in times of peace as well as war; he was loved and respected by his vassals and feared by his enemies, for fame of his wisdom and valor soon reached the most distant provinces. Since his father had not been a warrior, nor had he tried to conquer new lands, Viracocha found the military to be very disheartened and held in low esteem; so the first thing that he endeavored to do was to restore its importance by offering great honors and awards to those who wanted to enlist; and since it is normal in all nations that the subjects readily accept that which is seen to interest their prince, as Viracocha started to raise men and name captains and officers of war, the satisfaction and delight with which they took up arms was something to see; for this reason very soon a splendid army was assembled in the city of Cuzco. When the grandees and lords of the court saw that he was so heartened and resolute in undertaking new conquests and that he wanted to go on them in person, they advised him that before starting them, it would be wise for him to marry in order to assure succession in the kingdom. To this proposition the Inca answered that he did not want to do it; the reason he gave was that no man of repute should try to take a woman until he had achieved illustrious deeds in war, because it was plain to see that those who gave themselves over to women become cowards and effeminate and held matters of honor in low esteem. From his earliest years Viracocha Inca showed himself to be so warlike that when he was in exile and disgraced by his father, it was his custom to speak often of matters pertaining to war, showing with disparaging words how he felt about seeing that his father was so far from being a soldier that he did not try to undertake anything memorable, and Viracocha would add in these conversations that the people should not regret his father's failings because Viracocha expected that upon seeing himself with the scepter of the kingdom, he would conquer half the world.

The lords and caciques of the towns near Cuzco were not under the domination of the Incas, but from ancient times they had lived in peace and confederation; in order not to break the loyalty and trust with which they were united, Viracocha's predecessors had not dared to wage a war to subjugate them, especially since they gave no cause for it. Therefore, although the dominions of the Incas extended at that time to provinces many leagues away from Cuzco, the caciques who were their neighbors still did not consider themselves to be under the vassalage of the Incas. But now, either because they had given him some cause to break the peace or because the Inca himself had sought one, moved by the ambition to subjugate them, Viracocha Inca waged such a cruel war on them that he brought all of them under his obedience. Among the Indians there is the recollection that Viracocha made war on these lords because they were unhappy about what he had done to his father when he took the kingdom away from him, and they were also unhappy that he had made changes in matters pertaining to their religion by commanding that the god Viracocha be given preference over the Sun and the rest of the gods, and they complained about it. Whatever the case may have been, the fact is that the Inca subjugated them by force of arms, starting with the lord of the Valley of Calca, four leagues from Cuzco, and the others of that vicinity, who lived along the banks of the Yucay River and everything that is included in the Marquesado[12] today.

After he had won these victories, the grandees implored him once again to marry, and he yielded to their will. They looked throughout the kingdom for a maiden who possessed the qualities and gifts of nobility, purity, and beauty that would make her worthy of the honor and title of Coya, or Queen. This good fortune befell the daughter of the lord of Anta, a town three leagues away from Cuzco. Her name was Mama Roncay; she was carried in a litter to the court with a large accompaniment of the most important lords of Anta; they passed through a series of floral archways covered with fine cloth that were placed all along the road; the happy procession was accompanied by songs and dances.

Since Viracocha was not content with the subjugation of the aforementioned caciques, after his marriage he tried to continue the war, a thing greatly desired by his soldiers because they prospered so much in the wars with the sacking and plundering of the towns. He got his army ready without letting his captains know the task that they were undertaking (which was the style used by this Inca, ordering his army to go about one or two leagues away from the city and announcing his plans there). He went himself in person on this expedition, as he had done in the past, and he headed for the provinces of the Canas and Canches, who, although they defended themselves well at first, were defeated at last and put under his obedience. These provinces of the Canas and Canches were always held in high esteem by the Inca Viracocha and his successors, who granted them special insignia of honor, because from the time that they yielded obedience to this Inca, they helped and served the Incas with notable effort and fidelity in all the wars and conquests that they undertook. In the province of Cana near the town of Cacha, ten leagues away from Cuzco, the Inca Viracocha built a magnificent temple, and in it he placed a statue of Ticci-viracocha. The ruins and thick walls of this temple are seen today; it is an extraordinarily large structure with very high walls, made of adobe, because at the time of this king stones were not yet used for building.

Fame of the exploits of Viracocha spread everywhere, and moved by it and principally by the fear of being devastated if the Inca made war on them, many provinces sent him ambassadors and presents, asking for his friendship and offering to obey him; therefore, he ended up by expanding his kingdom greatly and becoming richer than his elders. He had large dishes of gold and silver, and during his time the name of the Incas became much more famous and esteemed than before in foreign provinces. He founded the *ayllo* and tribal group called Socsoc Panaca, and he left an idol named Inca Amaro, which he designated as his brother and which was much revered by his tribal group. The body of this king was deposited in Jaquijaguana, and having some information and indications of its whereabouts, Gonzalo Pizarro searched a long time for it in order to get the great treasure that was widely thought to be buried with it; in order to discover it, he burned some Indians, men and women. At last he found it and a large amount of wealth was given to him by the Indians who looked after it. Pizarro had the body burned, but the Indians of the Inca's *ayllo* collected the ashes, and, with a certain concoction, they put them in a very small earthenware jar along with the idol, which, since it was a stone, was left by Gonzalo Pizarro's men, who paid no attention to it. Later, at the time when Licentiate Polo was in the process of discovering the bodies and idols of the Incas, he got word of the ashes and idol of Viracocha; so the Indians moved it from where it was before, hiding it in many places because, after Gonzalo Pizarro burned it, they held it in higher esteem than before. Finally, so much care was taken in searching that it was found and taken from the possession of the Inca's descendants.

Chapter 12: Of Pachacutic Inca Yupanqui, ninth king

Viracocha Inca left four sons by his principal wife; they were called Pachacutic Inca Yupanqui, Inca Roca, Tupa Yupanqui, and Capac Yupanqui. The first one succeeded him in the kingdom, and concerning the rest, although they were lords and grandees, nothing is said. Pachacutic married a lady named Mama Anahuarque, native to the town of Choco, near Cuzco, and he founded a family that they call Iñaca Panaca. This king was the most valiant and warlike, wise and statesmanlike of all the Incas, because he organized the republic with the harmony, laws, and statutes that it maintained from that time until the arrival of the Spaniards. He injected order and reason into everything; eliminated and added rites and ceremonies; made the religious cult more extensive; established the sacrifices and the solemnity with which the gods were to be venerated, enlarged and embellished the temples with magnificent structures, income, and a great number of priests and ministers; reformed the calendar; divided the year into twelve months, giving each one its name; and designated the solemn fiestas and sacrifices to be held each month. He composed many elegant prayers with which the gods were to be invoked, and he ordered that these prayers be recited at the same time that the sacrifices were offered. He was no less careful and diligent in matters pertaining to the temporal welfare of the republic; he gave his vassals a method of working the fields and taking advantage of the lands that were so rough and uneven as to be useless and unfruitful; he ordered that rough hillsides be terraced and that ditches be made from the rivers to irrigate them. In short, nothing was overlooked by him in which he did not impose all good order and harmony; for this reason he was given the name of Pachacutic, which means "change of time or of the world"; this is because as a result of his excellent government things improved to such an extent that times seemed to have changed and the world seemed to have turned around; thus, his memory was very celebrated among the Indians, and he was given more honor in their songs and poems than any of the other kings that either preceded him or came after him.

It is said of this Inca that before he became king, he went once to visit his father Viracocha, who was in Jaquijaguana, five leagues from Cuzco, and as he reached a spring called Susurpuquiu, he saw a crystal tablet fall into it; within this tablet there appeared to him

the figure of an Indian dressed in this way: around his head he had
a *llauto* like the headdress of the Incas; three brightly shining rays,
like those of the sun, sprang from the top of his head; some snakes
were coiled around his arms at the shoulder joints; his ears were
pierced and he wore large earplugs in them; his clothing was of
the same design as that of the Incas; the head of a lion jutted out
from between his legs and he had another lion on his back with
its paws around his shoulders; and there was a kind of snake that
stretched from the top to the bottom of his back. Upon seeing this
image, Pachacutic became so terrified that he started to flee, but
the image spoke to him from inside the spring, saying to him: "Come
here, my child; have no fear, for I am your father the Sun; I know
that you will subjugate many nations and take great care to honor
me and remember me in your sacrifices"; and, having said these
words, the vision disappeared, but the crystal tablet remained in
the spring. The Inca took the tablet and kept it; it is said that after
this it served him as a mirror in which he saw anything he wanted,
and in memory of this vision, when he was king, he had a statue
made of the Sun, which was none other than the image he had seen
in the crystal, and he built a temple of the Sun called Coricancha,
with the magnificence and richness that it had at the time when
the Spaniards came, because before it was a small and humble structure. Moreover, he ordered that solemn temples dedicated to the
Sun be built throughout all the lands that he subjugated under his
empire, and he endowed them with great incomes, ordering that
all his subjects worship and revere the Sun.

After having shown himself to be so devoted to the Sun and
having taken the care just mentioned that all worship him in the
same way that his ancestors had done, one day Pachacutic began
to wonder how it was possible that a thing could be god if it was
so subject to movement as the Sun, that it never stops or rests
for a moment since it turns around the world every day; and he
inferred from this meditation that the Sun must not be more than
a messenger sent by the Creator to visit the universe; besides, if
he were God, it would not be possible for a few clouds to get in
front of him and obscure his splendor and rays so that he could
not shine; and if he were the universal Creator and lord of all things,
sometimes he would rest and from his place of rest he would il-
luminate all the world and command whatever he wished; and thus,
there had to be another more powerful lord who ruled and governed
the Sun; and no doubt this was Pachayachachic. He communicated
this thought to the members of his council, and in agreement with

them, he decided that Pachayachachic was to be preferred to the
Sun, and within the city of Cuzco, he built the Creator his own
temple which he called Quishuarcancha, and in it he put the image
of the Creator of the world, Viracocha Pachayachachic; it was made
of gold, the size of a ten-year-old boy, the shape of a shining man
standing upright with his right arm raised, his hand almost closed,
and his thumb and first finger held up, like a person who is giving
a command. In spite of the fact that from the beginning the Incas
had had some notions about a Creator of all things and had revered
him and made sacrifices to him, nevertheless, he had not been venerated so much as he was from the time of the Inca Viracocha and
his son.

Pachacutic's great wisdom was accompanied by a great heart
and a courageous spirit, with which he achieved illustrious victories; so he was equally fortunate in war and peace. He enlarged
his kingdom much with the many big provinces that he and his
captains conquered. He began his conquests with the provinces of
Viticos and Vilcabamba, a very difficult land to subjugate because
it is so rough and covered with dense jungle and many *arcabucos*.
The Inca left Cuzco with the bravest and most carefully chosen men
he had; he passed through the Valley of Yucay and continued down
the river to Tambo; he came to the Valley of Ambaybamba, and
there he got word that it would be impossible to continue ahead,
since there was no bridge across the river; his adversaries had removed the bridge of Chuquichaca (which means "golden bridge");
confident that the Inca would not be able to cross the river, they
had made up their minds to try to resist him. But the power of the
Inca was so great that not only did he make that bridge in the place
where it was before but he made many others in places where the
river was narrow, and those of Vilcabamba were so astonished and
fearful that they confessed that only the power of the Sun's offspring
could accomplish those great deeds.

Upon finishing the bridges, the Inca ordered his men to proceed
in a very orderly fashion, so that the enemy would not be able to
harm them; and when he arrived at Cocospata, about twenty-five
leagues from Cuzco, ambassadors came to him from the caciques
of Viticos and Vilcabamba, and they told him that since that was
rough land with brambles and forests and very unhealthy, his Highness might fall sick if he insisted on pressing ahead, and as soon
as he talked over what he wanted with the lords of that land, they
would have whatever orders he sent to them carried out. The Inca
refused to accept this offer, and the answer he sent the ambassadors

back to tell their caciques was that he swore by the god his father
that if they did not have the roads leveled and in good repair, the
Inca would sacrifice them to the Sun himself. The ambassadors returned very sadly with the threat, and they warned the cacique's
warriors that were in convenient places along the roads to withdraw
to the interior, saying that the power of the Inca was so great that
he would destroy the whole province right then.

When their ambassadors returned, the caciques of Vilcabamba
were in the llanos of Pampacona, which is before the woodland
starts; and once they were informed of the great power of the Inca
and warned by their spies that he was marching with his army
and that the sappers that he brought with him were opening up the
road, they lost courage, judging that if the Inca attacked them, they
would be destroyed. In order to avoid the danger that they feared,
they used a cruel trick; with a false pretense they had their captains
come before them, and when they appeared, they cut off their heads;
and some days later they went with the heads to the Inca, and they
told him that they were coming with peaceful intentions, and their
will had been none other than to obey him, but, against their will,
their captains had taken up arms and advanced in order to block
his passage; for this reason, as a punishment for their disobedience
and disrespect for his Highness, their heads had been cut off, and
they were bringing the heads to offer along with their own, so that
if they were guilty in any way, his Highness could do whatever
he saw fit with them. After seeing the heads of the dead captains
and the good intentions and fidelity that the caciques showed him,
the Inca received them with pleasure, praised what they had done,
and told them that the Sun his father and he would pardon them
and accept them under their protection and obedience. The Inca did
not go beyond the llanos of Pampacona; the rest of the lords of the
land came there to pay homage to him, bringing him a great many
provisions and gifts for the army.

The caciques, in order to please the Inca more and gain his good
graces, told him that they wanted to give him a mountain filled
with fine silver and some rich gold mines. The Inca was very pleased
with this offer, so he sent some of his men to see if this was true
and bring back some samples of gold and silver. They went quickly,
and they found that the wealth of the mine was much greater than
what had been described to the Inca, to whom they brought many
loads of gold and silver; this made him exceedingly happy. He stayed
on there longer, having a large amount of gold and silver taken
out for himself. (At that time these mines of Vilcabamba started

to be worked on the orders of Pachacutic, and his successors continued this work; with the silver and gold that they took out of them, they accumulated in Cuzco the wealth that the Spaniards found.] The Inca left Vilcabamba by the same road he had used to come there, and upon arriving in Cuzco, he ordered that this expedition and the discovery of the mines be celebrated with public fiestas which lasted for two months.

When these fiestas were over, Pachacutic was informed that one of his illegitimate brothers, named Inca Urco, was secretly trying to rebel against him and tyrannize the kingdom. Without investigating any further, the Inca had his brother called and, on the pretext of honoring him, put him in charge of a certain war; secretly he ordered another of his captains to kill Inca Urco in the heat of the battle; this was carried out as ordered; and when the news of the death of his brother reached the king, he pretended to feel very sad about it, and he ordered solemn funeral rites to be held, and public weeping.

He went on another expedition in which he finally pacified the Chancas, who were still uneasy and did not stop trying new strategies and revolts in order to free themselves from the domination of the Incas; this is because the Chancas were natural leaders, and they resented taking orders from others. After trying everything they could in order to gain their freedom, and failing in the attempt, they lost all hope of being lords as they were before, and, with unusual rage and desperation, they took as their leader a brave Indian named Anco Ayllo; many of them left their country, and getting aboard rafts on a tributary of the Marañon River, they disappeared into the Andes Mountains that lie to the east of that province, and nothing was ever heard of them again.

Chapter 13: Of the rest of Pachacutic's victories

Pachacutic moved ahead with his banners along the road through Chinchaysuyu, and he subjugated the province of Vilcas and those of the Soras and the Lucanas with little effort, owing to the powerful army he brought, which no nation had sufficient forces to resist. But, when he arrived at Guamanga [Ayacucho], he found the natives of the region armed and ready to defend themselves, because they were a very warlike and unruly people, and they had confidence not so much in the number of their combatants, which was inferior to that of the Inca, as in a naturally well defended fortress on a rocky hill, where they had taken refuge. The Inca laid siege on them, and he kept them under great pressure for a long time, for he was very desirous of gaining dominion over such a rich and fertile province, and especially so as not to lose one bit of the reputation he had earned on his past undertakings.

The besieged experienced great difficulties in this war; to avoid losing their freedom, they constantly suffered extreme hunger and a thousand other misfortunes; at last, unable to do anything else, they were forced to surrender and yield obedience to the Inca, who, having subjugated this province, got no resistance from surrounding towns such as those of the Chocorbo, Angará, and Parinacocha. But the nation of the Huanca, native to the Valley of Juaja, defended themselves at first bravely; and although there were more than thirty thousand of them, in the end they were defeated and subjugated. With such a fortunate series of victories, Pachacutic did not put aside his arms, nor did he stop until he reached the province of Tumibamba, which marked the farthermost limits and boundaries of his empire after he had incorporated into it all the provinces that come before there on the road through the sierra, such as Guarochiri, Canta, Tarama, Chinchacocha, Cajatambo, Bonbon, Conchucos, Cajamarca, and others.

The Inca did not let much time pass before he set out on another expedition on the road through Condesuyo, in order to conquer the provinces of the seacoast bordering on those that he had won in the sierra. The Inca went himself up to the edge of the llanos, and, without descending to the hot land of the seacoast, he sent one of his brothers as commander with thirty thousand soldiers, and he kept another thirty thousand with him in reserve, so he could exchange them every two months, because the coastal lands were unhealthy for the people of the sierra.

Many valleys of the coast gave up peacefully, but it was necessary to make war on others; soon along the coast all of the provinces were conquered that are included today in the Diocese of Arequipa from Tarapacá up to Hacarí, which is close to two hundred leagues of coast. As the Inca's troops entered what is now this Archbishopric of Lima, peace was offered to him by the valleys of Nasca, Ica, and Pisco, with the Indians of Chunchanga and Humay; but the Indians of Chincha, who were numerous, took up arms, and they fought many times with the people of the Inca, by whom they were defeated. No less brave in their defense than their neighbors the Chincha were the Indians of Huarco and Lunaguana, because they continued to make war with vigor and steadfastness for many months, during which time notable things were done by both sides. Finally, the Inca reduced them to such a state that they were forced to submit to him. Once the Inca had achieved this victory, the Indians peacefully yielded obedience to him throughout the valleys of Mala, Chilca, Pachacama, Limac, Chancay, Guaura, and La Barranca, along with all the rest up to the Valley of Chimo. The cacique of this last one was very powerful, and he refused to surrender to the Inca before fighting and being defeated, as he was. Having won so many and such illustrious victories, which took some years, the king returned to his court, which was rich with plunder and much more honored and respected, leaving fortresses constructed in appropriate places and sufficient soldiers garrisoned in them to defend what had been won.

The fiestas that were held in Cuzco to honor his triumph on this last expedition were hardly over when the Inca made another one on the road to Collasuyu, for his spirit was restless and uneasy unless he was occupied in enlarging his empire. He sent a brave and experienced captain named Apu Condemayta, and the Inca ordered him to stop and wait in Lurucache, which was the edge of his dominions and the border of the provinces of Collao; the cacique of these provinces was very powerful, and his state started from the sierra of Vilcanota, from where, up to the town of Hatuncolla, where he resided, it is more than twenty-five leagues. Having organized things in Cuzco, the Inca set out with the rest of his army, and upon arriving at Lurucache, without halting there, he proceeded on to quarter his troops at the foot of the Vilcanota, within the confines of Collasuyu. Once the cacique or king of Collao found out about the Inca's arrival, he came out to meet him with all of his power, determined to make war on him, and he waited for him in the town of Ayavire, ten leagues from the Inca's camp. Pleased with the news that the enemy had stationed his troops so close, the Inca moved his squadrons and proceeded through those extensive meadows and savannas which are found on the other side of the sierra of Vilcanota; and as he neared Ayavire, the Colla Indians came out to meet him in battle array, inciting the Inca to make war. The two military camps attacked each other with equal courage, and both sides fought with much fury and persistence. But, owing to their lack of experience, the enemy started to weaken; sensing this, the Inca's men began a victory chant. Seeing that the majority of their men were dead, the Colla Indians lost courage, retreated with as many men as possible, and repaired to Pucará. The Inca destroyed the town of Ayavire, and on his orders, all the people his men could lay hands on were beheaded. Without stopping to rest after the battle, the Inca went looking for Colla Capac, as the king of Collao was called. The Inca fought with him for the second time at Pucará, and he defeated him there also. A great many Colla Indians died in both battles; those who escaped ran away at first, but later they came back and turned themselves over to the Inca. The cacique of the nation of the Lupaca Indians, who resided in Chucuito, was just as powerful as the cacique of Collao, but he took sounder advice, because he received the Inca in peace and turned over his state to him. Thus, the Inca honored him very much and in order to show him more favor, he stayed in Chucuito for a few days.

On this expedition the Inca subjugated all the towns and nations surrounding the great Lake Titicaca, which on the one side includes the provinces of the Lupaca and Pacasa Indians, and on the other side the provinces of Paucarcolla, Asangaro, and Omasuyo, along with the islands of the aforesaid lake, which were densely populated at that time. Some of the towns defended themselves bravely, and they had many clashes with the Inca before they were subjugated. The Inca subjected many of them to a relentless siege, and they built forts in order to defend themselves, such as those at Caquingora and the one we see on a high hill near the town of Juli, which has five dry stone walls, one inside the other, where the natives took refuge and fought for a long time in defending themselves; more by cunning and deceit than by force of arms, the Inca made them surrender. Also for a few days the Pacasa Indians defended the bridge over the outlet [Desaguadero] of Lake Titicaca

or Chucuito, and in order to win it from them, the Inca sent part
of his army to look for a ford eight leagues downstream.

Pachacutic saw the magnificent buildings of Tiaguanaco, and
the stonework of these structures amazed him because he had never
seen that type of building before; and he commanded that his men
should carefully observe and take note of that building method,
because he wanted the construction projects in Cuzco to be of that
same type of workmanship. From there he went to Copacabana and
on to see the sanctuary of the Island of Titicaca, and finally, crossing the Strait of Tiquina by raft, he passed through Omasuyo, and
on to the city of Cuzco, where he entered as a victor with great
authority and a large escort.

Having enlarged his empire with so many and such vast provinces, during the remainder of his life this king devoted himself
to improving the provinces by building in the major towns of each
one magnificent temples and palaces and some strong castles, all
according to the model of the buildings that he had seen at Tiaguanaco; such are the buildings of Vilcas, Huarco, Limatambo [west
of Cuzco], and the great fortress at Cuzco. In short, the most magnificent structures that there were in this kingdom, whose ruins endure to this day, were built by King Pachacutic, according to the
traditions of the Indians. This king had a large golden idol called
Inti Illapa, which, during all his lifetime and afterward up to the
arrival of the Spaniards, was greatly venerated. He had it placed
on a very valuable golden platform, and, according to reports, the
idol and platform were broken into pieces and taken to Cajamarca
for the ransom of the Inca Atauhualpa; in addition, much more of
the treasure left by Pachacutic was used for the same purpose. This
king's body was entombed by those of his tribal group in Patallacta,
from where it was moved later to Totocache, and there it was found
by Licentiate Polo; the body was kept with great care, and it was
so well preserved with a certain bitumen and concoction that it
appeared to be alive. Its eyes were made of a thin golden cloth;
its hair was grey, and it was entirely preserved, as if he had died
that same day. The body was very well dressed with five or six
magnificent mantles, the royal fringe, and some well-made *llautos*.
On the orders of Viceroy Andres Hurtado de Mendoza, Marques de
Cañete, this body was brought to Lima along with others that were
found whole and well preserved.

Chapter 14: Of Tupa Inca Yupanqui, the tenth king

Pachacutic was succeeded by his eldest son, Tupa Inca Yupanqui, who started to govern during the lifetime of his father; when Pachacutic realized that he was too old and disabled to administer such a large kingdom, with the consent of his vassals, he renounced the crown in favor of his son Tupa Inca Yupanqui. It is said that he had two brothers, called Amaro Tupa Inca and Tupa Inca, and that they were rich and esteemed lords. This king broke the inviolable custom that existed among the Incas, strengthened by a general and very ancient prohibition of marriage within the closest degree of blood relationship. In spite of the aforesaid custom and prohibition that had lasted without being questioned up to his time, he took as his wife Mama Ocllo, his sister on both the paternal and maternal sides; and according to what was shown by the *quipos* and records of the time of this Inca and according to the elders who kept these records, Tupa Inca made a law to the effect that only the kings could marry their full sisters by the father and the mother, as he did. At the time of his death he left orders that his two children Guayna Capac and Coya Cusirimay, who were brother and sister by father and mother, should marry; he based this order on certain dreams he said he had had, and he explained that it was advisable that the one who was to become Inca should have no mixture of other blood and that procreation through a sister was true succession. From this king came the lineage and *ayllo* that is called Capac Ayllo. Upon being crowned king, he decided to continue with the conquests of his father, and since he found the military so well prepared, because of the many captains and soldiers who were veterans that had seen service with his father, very little was necessary in order to put his desire into effect. The Inca decided to start the war in the direction of the Antisuyu road, which we call the Andes now, because his kingdom extended only a few leagues on that side; he went in person to this war with a very large army, and overcoming the difficulties of such rough roads as those are, he crossed the rugged, snow-covered cordillera and the thick jungles and *arcabucos* that separate the *yunca* provinces from those of the sierra. He fought with the Chuncho and Mojo Indians, extremely barbarous and inhumane people, and he won from them a considerable amount of their land.

While he was in this war, one of his captains, who was from
Collao, fled; after returning to his land, he made it known that
the Inca was dead in the Andes. Since the lords and caciques of
Collao were discontented with their subjugation by the Inca, this
was all it took to make them revolt. They killed the governors
appointed by the Inca, and they united their forces in order to gain
their liberty. Upon finding out about this turn of events, the governor who had remained in charge of the government in Cuzco sent
word to the Inca by means of the post service; as soon as he received
the news, the Inca took action to remedy the situation. He arranged
matters pertaining to the conquest the best he could; and, leaving
some of his captains there to proceed with that, he left for Paucartambo, and without going to Cuzco he headed for Collao, crossing
behind the Vilcanota mountains, and he came out at Chungará,
taking the army of the Colla Indians from behind. He fought with
them many times, and, coming out with victory, he played havoc
with those towns, punishing those who were guilty of starting the
rebellion with unusual rigor. He had the two main caciques skinned,
and he ordered two drums to be made from their hides. With these
drums and with the heads of the executed caciques placed on pikes,
and with many prisoners to be sacrificed to the Sun, the Inca returned in triumph to his court, where he celebrated his victories
with great sacrifices and fiestas.

Shortly afterward he made another expedition, this time to the
provinces of Chinchaysuyu. On it he took a powerful army with
many very skillful captains, and he did not stop until he reached
the edge of the Kingdom of Quito; and in a certain part of it he
ordered a stop so that his people could get reorganized and so they
could obtain the things they needed. Upon seeing that the son of
the Sun with his great captains was going to make war on him,
the lord of Quito was doubtful as to whether he should obey the
Inca or put up a defense; in order to take counsel on this matter,
he made the customary prayers and sacrifices to his gods, asking
them to tell him what he should do for the welfare of everyone.
His idols answered that he should not fear the power of the Inca,
but that he should go out to meet the Inca and fight with him and
defend the homeland, that the gods would support and help him so
that he would not be defeated by the Inca. The king of Quito was
pleased with this oracle, and so that his gods would be more favorable to him, he commanded his people to be prepared for a certain
day, because he had decided to make a solemn sacrifice to his gods
of human blood from boys and girls; and they did. In order to show

that he was especially religious, one important nobleman sacrificed his own children. But their confidence was vain, because in the battles and skirmishes that they had with the Inca, they always got the worst of it, and at last they were defeated, and their king was taken prisoner and killed.

The Inca decided to return to Cuzco by the road through the sierra, because he had made the first part of the trip by way of the llanos, and he wanted to pacify the Indian nations between Quito and Cuzco. As he arrived at the province of Cañares, many came out to greet him in peace and yield obedience to him; but he made war on others who were rebellious, and he devastated their lands, sending many thousands of them to Cuzco as *mitimaes*. He commanded that a great fortress be built in that province; there he put his governors and a presidio of soldiers and many *mitimaes*. From there he took the road leading east, and he entered into the provinces of the Chachapoya Indians, with whom he had hard-fought battles, because they defended themselves bravely; but fortune was always favorable to the Inca. He captured the caciques and captains of that land and ordered that they be brought along with the other prisoners, and the Inca entered the city of Cuzco with these prisoners, showing that he had triumphed over them.

After spending a few years organizing government affairs, he decided to make an expedition to Collasuyu. Before leaving, he made his customary sacrifices to the Sun his father and to the rest of the gods, promising them that, if they favored him, he would not return to his court before reaching the Ticcicocha, which is the same as the end of the world; he was convinced that there was no more to the world than the lands that he had heard about. He made a call for men, and with the largest army that he could assemble, he left Cuzco. As he was passing through the province of Chucuito, he was given a more solemn reception than his father Pachacutic had been given, and the lords of that province implored him not to continue on, but to make his court there and that they would go on the conquests, and they would win all the lands in the world. The Inca thanked them with kind words and promised to do them some favors for the good intentions they showed in offering to serve him. The Inca continued ahead, and on the way he went to visit the temple at Titicaca. The people of the province had many rafts ready for him to make the passage to that island, where he remained for a few days and ordered the construction of a magnificent palace and other royal buildings; and, having made sacrifices to the Sun, he continued on his way. He made a stop

in Tiaguanaco in order to look over that magnificent structure at
leisure; he tried to find out, by asking the natives of that town,
from where the stone for that structure had been brought and who
had been its builder. The Indians answered that they did not know
nor did they have any information about when it had been built.

After leaving Tiaguanaco, the Inca made a campaign through
the provinces of Carangas, Paria, Cochabamba, and Amparaes, along
with the other provinces that fall within the borders of Charcas.
Many Indians fled from these provinces, and in looking for secure
places where they could take refuge and defend themselves from
the Inca, by common agreement they entered through the valleys
of Oroncota, where they found a natural fortress formed by the
lay of the land, because it was a large hill, many leagues around,
walled in everywhere by sheer cliffs, and on top it had much farm-
land, water, and a wood. More than twenty thousand Indians, including women and children, made use of this place with the intention of spending their lives there and never coming down from those
cliffs.

The Inca had news of this retreat and that it was impossible to
conquer those Indians because the place was so well fortified and
because they had everything they needed to live there; the Inca
said that he had a scheme by which they would soon yield obedience
to him. He ordered that drawings of the fortress be made for him
showing the arrangement of the terrain. This was done, and he noticed that the cliff that enclosed the place had a crack or gap in
it. Thinking that it would be possible to enter through there, in
spite of the fact that the enemy had their sentries in that place,
the Inca ordered that a town be made at once in front of the gap
and that some soldiers be stationed there; this was accomplished
in an exceptionally brief time. Then he ordered men and women
to gather there every night to sing and dance; whoever participated
in the dance could freely select any of the women that he pleased,
and the women also enjoyed the privilege of selecting the men they
liked; therefore, they could freely give themselves over to their car-
nal delights without anybody bothering them. (This type of dance
was invented at that time by the Inca; it was called *cachua* by the
Indians, and it was used thereafter during their pagan times.) In
carrying out the royal command, men and women came out to do
these dances every night in view of the enemies, and after a few
days of this dancing, the women, instructed by the Inca, started
to call the guards and sentries of the stronghold with songs and
flirting inviting them to come down and take the pleasures that

everyone was permitted to enjoy. In a very short time, they won them over and obliged them to come down from their lookout and take part in the dance; and so this made it possible for ten thousand of the Inca's soldiers, who were set in ambush, to enter the stronghold and imprison all those who had taken refuge there.

Fame of the power and marvelous victories of the Inca had, at that time, reached the most remote provinces, and it had caused such great terror and panic among the caciques and lords that the majority of them sent their ambassadors to offer peace and request that they be accepted as the Inca's vassals. Those who voluntarily subjected themselves to him were received with gentleness and love, but the Inca waged a cruel war on those who resisted him. As he was pacifying the land of Charcas, messengers came to him from the remote provinces of Tucuman, sent by their lords, and in the name of their lords, they yielded obedience to the Inca, and he sent governors and *mitimaes* there to teach them the customs and language of his kingdom.

And since he knew of the great provinces of Chile, he had a road opened in that direction through the province of Lipes, which marked the edge of his kingdom; and he sent an army of over two hundred thousand soldiers to conquer those provinces; and the Inca returned to Cuzco. Although the Chilean Indians were stronger and more aggressive than the Peruvians, nevertheless, living as they did in *behetrias* without any headman or leader to govern and unite them, the Chileans were unable to resist the throngs of the Inca, and thus they were defeated by the Peruvians; so the Inca took the inhabitants of Guasco and Coquimbo, along with the other coastal valleys up to the Valley of Mapocho, where many thousands of Chileans were called together, among whom were found the brave Araucans, who, in answer to the call of the Mapocho Indians, had come to help them. These Chileans and the Peruvians engaged in a very bloody battle, and in the thick of the fighting, help arrived for the Inca's men, which caused the Chileans to lose courage, and the Inca's men ended the struggle with victory. The Araucans began to flee, and the Peruvian army went after them, catching and beheading many of them. Upon entering their land, the Araucans made a stronghold in a narrow passage, and the Inca's captains followed them, and since they did not know the land, without realizing it, they fell into danger. Finding themselves with the advantage, the Araucans turned on their enemies and fighting broke out; it was the hardest-fought and fiercest battle that the Peruvians had ever had; they were defeated, and their captain was killed, along with the majority of their soldiers. The rest retreated to the other side of the Maule River, which is forty leagues south of the city of Santiago and the Valley of Mapocho. On other occasions the Inca's captains tried to place their banners on the other side of the aforementioned river, but the valiant Araucans, united with their neighbors the Tucupel and the Puren, blocked their way and did not allow the Incas to possess one bit of land on the other side of the Maule. When the Inca found out what was happening and became aware of the vast number of Indians who lived in the provinces that fall to the south of Maule River and how bravely they defended themselves, he sent orders for his captains to fortify the northern bank of the Maule River and said that for the time being it would be the border for the Araucans and the edge of his empire; and the dominions of the Incas never passed that line then or after.

Chapter 15: Of the rest of the events in the life of Tupa Inca

Yupanqui Among the women of this Inca there was one of the Guayro nation, a woman of great beauty, whom the Inca loved and favored more than his legitimate wife; and he had by her a son whom he loved as much as the boy's mother; and there was never a fiesta or joyful gathering where the Inca did not take mother and son with him. It was plain to see that this woman was the one that the king esteemed the most and that she was on the most intimate terms with him; all of his vassals endeavored to please and serve her, owing to the joy and pleasure that this gave the king. It happened once while the Inca was enjoying himself in the Valley of Yucay that along with certain lords he began to play a game of Pichca, which is a kind of dice game; and having won almost the entire game, the Inca needed only one more point, which was the ace, and if he did not throw it he would not win anything, and by throwing it he would win and end the game. At that point he said to Lady Guayro, who was present, "Sister, I need one point in order to win the game. What shall we do? If you want to start over again, so be it, and if not, let the next play be in your name, if it pleases you." Although she saw that the gem in play was very valuable, she answered him, "Come on, my lord, cast the die in my name, and say 'Guayro,' for Guayro will be the ace." The Inca said, "Well, win or lose, it will go in your name." And as the king was casting the die, all those present shouted, "Guayro, Guayro." And as luck would have it, the ace turned up, which was all that was needed. The Inca, as well as everyone else, was very pleased, and the lady was happier yet, for the Inca gave the jewel he had won to her. And from the time of this game, the Inca commanded that the number one be called Guayro throughout all the land, in memory of the luck he had had and the winnings that he had made in the name of this lady, and thus to this very day, throughout most of the kingdom, the number one is called Guayro, in the same way that among us the term *ace* is used.

The great love that the Inca felt for this lady Guayro prompted him to seek a scheme by which he could leave her son well endowed. With this object in mind, when the youth had reached the age to be knighted, the Inca introduced among his lords the game of Ayllos, which was played only by the Collao nations before; and thus, when the time came for the Guarachico fiesta, in which his son was to be knighted along with other boys, all the sons of great lords, the Inca told those of his council that, in order to make the fiesta more solemn, he would like to have a contest with his son and award the winner some towns of his dominions. In order to please the Inca, they consented to what he requested, and they replied that his Highness was welcome to play all he pleased. Judges and sponsors for the games were appointed, and in order to give the fiesta more authority, the king gave permission for any lords who so wished to take part in the games; and the rule was that a bet be made of a very valuable jewel or gem, or a certain amount of gold or silver. When the date that had been set arrived, the lords of the court started the games, and the king and his son were the last ones to take part in them. Being very effective and skillful in this game, the king performed miracles with his *ayllos*, and the youth was never off guard; on the contrary, he played so skillfully that in a brief time he won the bet from his father, and he asked the judges to give him his award. The judges were astounded at this, and suspecting that it would not be prudent for the king to lose, they felt that the game should resume; but the king's son refused, unless he was given what he had won first. Seeing that he was right, the judges promised to give him what he wanted provided that the game continue. Father and son resumed play, and the son was so lucky that he won for the second time. The members of the council did not consent to let the play continue because the youth looked as if he was going to win the whole kingdom from his father. The judges asked him what he wanted for his winnings, and the youth asked for the province of Orcosuyo [southwest of Lake Titicaca], and in this way he was given the five towns of this province: Nuñoa, Oruro, Asillo, Asangaro, and Pucará; and these are the towns that are called Aylluscas in memory of this story.

A long time passed during which the Inca did not leave his court; he was occupied in improving it with large buildings; by his order, work was continued on the magnificent structure of the fortress that his father had left in its initial stages, and the palaces of Tambo were built, whose ruins still endure, and other houses of pleasure in the Cuzco region. Judging that it was advisable to go out to visit his vassals, the Inca arranged to depart, and accompanied by many lords and soldiers, he left Cuzco by the Chinchaysuyu road, taking with him his wife the Coya, who enjoyed seeing the kingdom in the company of the king her husband. When they had reached a place called Yanayacu, within the borders of Vilcas, the Inca named a brother of his called Apu Achache to be inspector general of the provinces of the seacoast; this brother was a man of great valor and wisdom, and he set out ahead to take charge of his assignment, while the Inca decided to go through the Valley of Jauja, at the request of the local caciques. When the inspector general reached Huarco, the lady in charge of it, who was a widow, tried to prevent him from making his inspection or from taking the census of her vassals, saying that she did not have to consent to the Inca ruling her state. The inspector general informed the Inca of what was happening, and he asked him what should be done in that case. As he received this news, the Inca laughed and said that women bothered him; the Coya asked him what women, and he answered, "You and this widow, because if it were not for you, I would take the wind out of her sails." Then the Coya asked the Inca to give her permission, that she preferred to subjugate that woman herself without the Inca losing a single soldier; the Inca answered her saying that, by all means, she could do whatever she wanted. The Coya took charge of this matter, and she sent off the inspector general, after explaining to him the way she planned to handle it; she ordered him to tell that cacica that he had news from the Inca and the Coya that they wanted to reserve that whole province for her, and they wanted the inspector to ask her to order a solemn fiesta to be held on the sea.

Believing that the information given to her by the inspector was true, the widow agreed to the request and ordered that everybody should put to sea in their rafts to honor her on a certain day that the inspector himself designated; all of this was accomplished, and while the Indians were out on the sea enjoying themselves with their musical instruments, two of the Inca's captains entered the town; they were very sure that the cunning and deceit of the inspector had worked, and they took possession of the town; upon seeing this from the sea, the cacica and her vassals had no other choice than to surrender. The captains captured the cacica and took her to be given to the Coya.

The Inca spent four years on this inspection. He ordered construction to be completed on the fortresses and palaces that were started in many places, and in other places he had new constructions erected. He reached the province of Quito, more than four hundred leagues from Cuzco; from Quito he returned to the court, leaving the northern part of his kingdom fifty leagues larger, and along the seacoast, he conquered all of the valleys up to Tumbez.

Since he had achieved such illustrious victories, this Inca became known as a great Inca: his people called him the great Tupa Inca, and the fact is that he deserved this title. He died in the city of Cuzco, and his body, embalmed and well preserved, was kept intact until his grandson Huascar Inca was imprisoned. At that time the body was burned by Atauhualpa's captains Quizquiz and Chalcochima. Tupa Inca had an idol named Cuxichuri which was much honored by the Indians, along with his ashes that they kept in a jar. This Inca was very rich, and the aforementioned captains of Atauhualpa took many valuables from him, and the rest remained in the possession of his *yanaconas*.

Chapter 16: Of Guayna Capac, the last king of the Incas

Tupa Yupanqui was succeeded by his first-born son, Guayna Capac, a name meaning "rich and excellent youth," which he earned by his illustrious deeds, because from adolescence on he was endowed with both wealth and excellence beyond that of any of his predecessors. He was much loved by his vassals and held to be valiant and firm. He achieved many and renowned victories; he broadened the borders of his empire with many provinces that he added to it. He showed himself to be as prudent in government as he was vigorous at arms, and thus he imposed strict order in all parts of his states. At the beginning of his reign, he took as his coadjutor, with the title of governor of Cuzco, one of his uncles, his father's brother, a man named Gualpaya. With the great influence that he had, this man tried to usurp the crown for one of his sons. When he had communicated his plan to his friends and allies, they designated a day in which they were to assemble in Cuzco and kill the king. In order to carry out the plan, people from out of town started to come into the city, putting hidden arms into baskets like those used for coca and *agi*. The conspirators had already put more than a thousand of these baskets in Cuzco when the conspiracy was discovered in the following way: some thieves in Limatambo stole a few of these baskets, thinking that they were full of coca and *agi*, and when the baskets were opened, they found them to be full of arms and military supplies. As soon as they found out about this, some of the residents of that town went to Cuzco, and in great secrecy they informed one of the king's uncles about the situation. This uncle, called Apu Achache, was the governor of Chinchaysuyu; and as a result of this warning, he confiscated all the baskets and found that they were full of arms. He took great care to inquire into the case; he tortured the owners of the baskets, who clearly revealed the conspiracy, naming the people who were involved in it. With this information, Apu Achache took the governor Gualpaya prisoner and communicated the matter to the Inca and those of his council. Gualpaya and the rest of his consorts were condemned to death.

After this the king's mother, Mama Ocllo, died, and he took her death very hard, ordering by means of the *chasques* and post service that all of the provinces of his kingdom be informed of his mother's death, so that she would be mourned and funeral rites would be held for her everywhere. The mourning that occurred in the court was extraordinary and sorrowful, and it lasted longer and with more solemnity than any mourning that had been done before. Mama Ocllo was a very fortunate and discreet lady; and while she lived, her son Guayna Capac followed her advice.

After the funeral rites for his mother were concluded, the Inca left in person to visit the Collao provinces; and upon arriving at the border where his kingdom ended in that region, he made some conquests anew and punished some of his cacique vassals who disrupted the peace and quiet of the land with uprising and rebellions; he fortified the presidios and supplied them with sufficient troops. After this and after sending men to help in the provinces of Tucuman and Chile, he returned to Cuzco with the object of making a great expedition to the borders of Chinchaysuyu.

He left an illegitimate brother of his in Cuzco, Apu Cinchi Roca by name, who was very brave and clever, and the Inca set out with a fine army for Chinchaysuyu, to travel through the northern quarter. Upon arriving at Jauja, he ordered that his father and mother be honored, and this was done by the caciques and lords of that province with such splendor that the Inca was very pleased, and he was amazed at the valor of those people, at the style and ceremonies with which they mourned, and at the generosity they showed in offering him a large amount of gold, silver, and fine clothing so well made that the Inca himself wore it. While he was occupied in this mourning, news arrived for him that the lords of the province of Chachapoyas had revolted and refused to obey him; at this he showed no signs of being troubled; rather he said with arrogance, "My captains are hungry, and they will have their fill on the Chachapoyas."

After the fiestas were over, the Inca left Jauja and traveled without stopping until he reached Chachapoyas. He found the whole land up in arms, and so proud and obstinate were the Chachapoya Indians that they paid no attention to him or his forces; but Guayna Capac managed so well that in a few days he subdued them and imposed an exemplary punishment on the culprits. He continued on to Cajamarca, where mourning and funeral rites were also held for his parents. He went on from there, visiting the rest of the provinces of the sierra as far as Quito, and everywhere he ordered the people to honor his parents with mourning. From Quito, he decided to return to Cuzco, and he ordered that the prisoners taken in the war be brought there, and he entered the city with them in solemn triumph. During his absence, his brother Apu Cinchi Roca had built the palace called Casana, a costly structure which pleased the king so much that he wanted to move in at once.

Shortly after his arrival at the court, the Inca went to rest and take his pleasure at the Valley of Yucay, which was like his Aranjuez, in another palace which had been constructed at the same time, and without staying there very long, he left for the second time to visit the provinces of Collasuyu, in order to settle some differences that the lords of that region had among themselves over the division of the grazing land and pastures; and when he arrived at the province of Chucuito, he remained there for some time because he liked the Lupaca Indians, the residents of this region; and since they were very loyal to the Incas, they deserved their unwavering favor. From there he continued on to Tiaguanaco without wishing to enter Titicaca, since he was reserving this visit for the return trip. He went into the Andes and into the provinces of the Mojo Indians in order to calm down those barbarians, who were all stirred up and plotting revolts; he sent his captains against the Chiriguana Indians and other Indian nations of those mountains and cordilleras, who, feeling secure because of the rough terrain, could not stand their servitude under the Inca. He left the Andes by way of Cochabamba, and, seeing how fertile and abundant with food the valleys of that province were, and that very few people inhabited them, he ordered that some families from the Collao region should go to reside in these valleys; and for this reason now almost all the inhabitants there are *mitimaes*.

From Cochabamba he went on to Pocona, to visit the border there. He gave orders for a fortress to be repaired; it was one that had been built on the orders of his father. The Inca also changed the governors, and, leaving orders as to how the people were to live and care for that land, he commanded his captains to make the return trip through the Collao region. On the way he visited the temple at Titicaca, where he remained for many days, fasting and praying. There he commanded that the prisoners that he had taken from among those who had revolted should be sacrificed to his father the Sun; the Inca refused to take them to Cuzco as a sign of his triumph because there were so few of them. Once the sacrifices were over, he left for the province of the Lupacas, and in the city of Chucuito he ordered that a review and general inspection be made of the troops that he brought in his army; he spread the news of the war and expedition that he wanted to make in the provinces of Quito, and he levied men for it throughout the Collao region, promising great prizes for those who went on it. He entered Cuzco

with only the people who served in his house, and the army went
on ahead outside of the city and set up camp at Cinga, awaiting
orders from the Inca there. After resting a few days, the Inca had
all the great lords assemble, and he told them how he wanted to
go in person to finish conquering the rest of the lands in the world,
which was on past Quito as far as the coast of the North Sea, since
the coasts of the South Sea were already part of his empire. He asked
those who desired to do so of their own will to follow him, because
it was not his intention to force or compel anyone to serve. In this
way he assembled a large number of outstanding and important
men; he named some of his brothers to be captains, and when everything was ready for the departure, he ordered them to set out on
the Chinchaysuyu road.

The Inca traveled with his army, not halting until he reached
Tumibamba; there he stopped for a few days, and since that land,
which he liked very much, seemed to him suitable to be made into
one of the capitals of the kingdom, he commanded that a magnificent palace be constructed for himself and a temple for his gods,
and in the temple he put a golden statue of his mother, a large
number of silver dishes, and servants, both men and women. The
Cañares Indians served the statue of Mama Ocllo willingly because
she had given birth in that place to Guayna Capac. At this time,
he had become such a powerful lord that he attempted to found a
kingdom in Quito similar to the one in Cuzco; the capital and court
would have been Tumibamba, and he would have made that town
equal to the city of Cuzco in splendor and wealth; and in order
to accomplish this, he commanded that this region be populated
by all the nations that were included in his army.

Before starting to conquer new lands, the Inca consulted with
his captains as to the place where they should start, and there were
different opinions on the matter, but the final decision was to undertake the conquest of Pasto and the rest of the provinces that extend
from there toward the New Kingdom of Granada. At once many
brave captains offered their services for this undertaking with the
desire of achieving honor, imploring the Inca not to bother going
in person, but to stay in Tumibamba and enjoy himself there, for
they had soldiers so brave and experienced in war that he could
certainly entrust them with that undertaking and greater ones than
that. The Inca easily agreed with what his captains asked; thus,
he turned this expedition over to four of the bravest ones; Mollo
Cauana, of the Lupaca nation, a native of the town of Hilaui; Mollo
Pucara, a native of Hatuncolla; and two others from the province

of Condesuyo who were called Apu Cauac Cauana and Apu Cunti Mullu. And besides the soldiers from various nations that were going to this war, he gave two thousand *orejones*, knights of Cuzco, and, as their captains, his brother Auquituma and Collatupa, a brave captain of the lineage of Viracocha Inca.

These captains set out on their conquest, and the Inca stayed in Tumibamba fasting and making sacrifices in the customary way, with the priests of the temple of the Sun for good fortune in the war. The army began conquering the towns of that province with such overwhelming success that in the first skirmishes with the enemy, it routed and defeated them, taking their cacique prisoner. After achieving victory, the Inca's captains became more careless than suits those who are in the midst of their enemies, because through their carelessness they gave the cacique a chance to break out of prison; and before being missed, he assembled many of his men and made a sudden attack on the Inca's troops, who were so unaware that the farthest thing from their minds was such an assault; and thus they were defeated so soundly that many were thrown into confusion and killed, and those who escaped the battle scene continued to flee.

When the Inca learned of this routing, he was very troubled, not so much because of the loss of those who died in it, as because of the risk to his reputation. The Inca prepared himself as quickly as possible to go in person and avenge this disgrace, and he entered into the lands of his enemies with powerful forces, devastating and burning whatever he encountered, and he played such havoc with them and slaughtered so many that the enemies themselves came very humbly to beg the Inca for peace. Leaving the land pacified and well supplied with guards, he returned to Tumibamba, where he was received in triumph with great fiestas.

Chapter 17: In which the deeds of Guayna Capac are continued

From Tumibamba the Inca sent his captains on diverse expeditions, and he went himself on others, in which he encountered many difficulties, because the Indians of those provinces were brave and warlike, and many times the troops of the Inca were defeated and routed, and not a few times the king himself fled. The Cayambes, particularly, being men of valor and courage, made it so difficult for the Inca Guayna Capac and his captains that in conquering them a great deal of time and blood were lost. The Inca undertook this conquest in person with a very powerful army, whose commander was Apu Cari, a lord from Chucuito; the Inca entered the land of the Cayambes, carrying the battle forward with fire and blood. Finding that their forces were not sufficient to face the Inca on an open battlefield, the Cayambes withdrew and made strongholds in a very large fortress that they had; the Inca ordered his men to lay siege to it and bombard it continuously; but the men inside resisted so bravely that they forced the Inca to raise the siege because he had lost many men in the assaults on the fortress. Sensing that the opposition was weakening, the Cayambes came out to meet them and they pressed the attack so much that the *orejones*, who were the backbone of the army, broke and fled, abandoning their king; in the confusion of his men, who were fleeing wildly, the king fell to the ground, and if the captains Cusi Tupa Yupanqui and Guayna Achache had not helped him and removed him from danger, he would have died at the hands of the enemies. The Inca ordered that, before combatting the castle again, his men should make war on the surrounding towns, so that, being deprived of the help coming from nearby, the besieged men would surrender; and, leaving captains to carry out his order, he returned to Tumibamba, where he refused to enter on his litter as he usually did, but entered on foot, in front of his army, with a dart in one hand and a round shield in the other.

In order to continue with the conquest of the Cayambes and their neighbors the Carangues, the Inca sent his brother Auquituma, a brave captain, with a large army composed of all nations, and he ordered that they take along with them the garrison soldiers that were on the borders, and that with all these men together they should combat the fortress. Upon arriving, they laid siege to it,

and they made fierce combat; the *orejones* always got the best of
the enemy; since the Inca's soldiers were embarrassed and degraded
by their past retreat, they endeavored to regain the fame lost there.
They won in four places, taking the stronghold in each one, and
during combat at the last place, the commander, Auquituma, died
fighting like a brave soldier. This was such a hard-fought war and
so many men from both sides died in it that there were great heaps
of dead bodies stacked up next to the wall. When the Inca's men saw
that their commander was dead, they started to retreat, and, not
missing this chance, the Cayambes came out, continuing after them
up to a big river that could not be forded, and the Cayambes slit
the throats of as many men as they could get their hands on. Confused because the river blocked their flight, the Inca's men jumped
into it to avoid falling into the hands of their enemies, and many
of them drowned. Those who by great good fortune escaped, stopped
on the other side of the river, and the Cayambes returned victorious
to their fortress with the spoils of their dead enemies.

Although the Inca was much saddened by this loss, he acted as
if it did not bother him, saying that men were the food of war,
and he only ordered mourning for his brother's death; and a few days
after that, he ordered all necessary preparations to be made for the
king to go in person on this undertaking. Many men had come to
his aid from Cuzco and from the rest of the highland provinces;
with these men and with those that he had before, the Inca formed
a powerful army, and he divided it into three parts in the following
way: the regiment of the *orejones* was entrusted to the commander
Apu Mihi, and the Inca ordered him to go quietly past the fortress
of the Cayambes on one side without being seen by the enemies
and to continue on ahead a few leagues; the regiment of Chinchaysuyu was to go past on the other side in the same way, continuing
on a few leagues also; from there both groups of soldiers were to
swing back at a certain time, burning and destroying whatever they
encountered; and they were to come join forces with the Inca, who
stayed with the main body of the army to lay siege to the fortress;
all this was executed with great skill and speed. Thus, the Inca
finally attacked the fortress through the place that best suited his
purposes. The combat lasted a few days, and, according to the plan
that the Inca had made with his captains, he gave the signal for the
army to retreat, pretending to flee; when the besieged soldiers saw
this, they came out of the fortress, and, chanting victory, they went
after their enemies, thinking that the same thing would happen to
them as before; and when they were most intent on catching up,

the Inca turned to face them, and those who were lying in ambush attacked the fortress, and they entered it without resistance and set fire to it; upon seeing this, the Cayambes lost their courage and, throwing down their arms, made haste to take refuge in some clumps of rushes growing along the edge of a large lake nearby; in this place they hoped to be able to save their lives. The Inca's men surrounded them on all sides, and, assailing them with unusual furor, they slaughtered them in a cruel manner, for hardly a man was able to escape. The Inca ordered his men to cut the enemies' throats without pity as they caught them and to throw the bodies into the lake; as a result the water of the lake became so darkened with blood that it was given the name that it has today of Yahuarcocha, which means "lake of blood."

After this war was over, the Inca went down to the seacoast, and when he reached the Valley of Tumbez—along whose shore his empire ended—he encountered very great difficulties in expanding it because the land from there on was very rugged and covered with thick forests, rivers, and swamps; in spite of all this, with his invincible spirit, he endeavored to continue. He made war on the Island of Puná, whose lord was called Tumalá, and on the mainland border, which is the province of Guayaquil, and the war was very hard-fought and difficult; but the multitudes of the Inca's men overcame the islanders at that time, although shortly thereafter the Inca paid dearly, because when he returned to Tumbez, the men of Puná attacked the garrison that he had left, and all of the Inca's men were killed.

This incident angered the Inca; so he returned to the island with unusual fury, and he caused the islanders to undergo cruel punishments; but, considering that he was not gaining anything in that place, due to the harshness and barbarous cruelty of its inhabitants, he gave up that conquest and returned to the sierra, where he continued the war with more profit and less effort, because the land there was wholesome, firm, and even, without the difficulties that he had encountered along the seacoast. After completing the pacification of the provinces of Quito, which took him ten years, he had magnificent royal lodgings constructed in several places; and he become so fond of the goodness of that country that he refused to leave it again. He resided most of the time in Tumibamba, which is where the city of Cuenca is located now; the land there is so placid that, in mildness of climate, fertility, and beauty, no other place can compare with it in this whole kingdom.

While Guaya Capac was in his palaces at Tumibamba enjoying

himself, he received news of the arrival of the Spaniards at the coast and town of Tumbez; this was when Captain Francisco Pizarro with his thirteen companions was in the process of discovering the coast of this kingdom. The messengers, who were much alarmed and frightened as by something that they had never dreamed of, told the Inca how some strange people never seen before who preached new doctrines and laws had shown up on the beach of Tumbez; these men were so bold that they did not fear dangerous things; they were stuffed into their clothes, which covered them from head to foot; they were white and had beards and a ferocious appearance; and many other things were told about these strangers, all of which amazed the Inca; and when he asked from what part of the world they had come, he was told that the messengers only knew that the strangers traveled across the sea in large wooden houses, in which they came and went wherever they wished, moving them rapidly from one place to another, and at night they went out to sea and slept in their houses, and during the day they came on land; and by sign language they had asked about the lord of the land, and they had been told that he was far from there. As he heard these things, the Inca was astounded, and he started feeling so fearful and melancholy that he went into his chamber and did not leave it until it was almost night. Later other *chasques*, or runners, sent by the governors of the coast arrived, letting the Inca know how those people had entered into his royal houses and palaces and robbed them, taking all his treasures; and putting the strangers in the lion's den where the Inca kept his beasts had been to no avail for frightening them. Guayna Capac was astounded and beside himself as he heard such new and extraordinary things, and he ordered the messengers to tell him what was happening once again. They said, "Lord, the only thing to say is that the lions and wild animals that you have in your palaces cower before the strangers and wag their tails at them like tame animals." The Inca, very irritated, got up from his seat and, shaking his cape, said, "Signs and auguries, be gone, be gone; refrain from disturbing or upsetting my dominion and power." And sitting down again, but in a different seat, he told the ambassadors to tell the story over and over many times; due to its novelty and strangeness, he was still unable to believe the story.

Shortly after this first arrival of the Spaniards in this land, while the Inca was in the province of Quito, smallpox broke out among his subjects, and many of them died. Being fearful, the Inca went into seclusion to fast as was the custom in such times of hardship.

During this fast, they say that three Indians never seen before entered his chamber while no one was with him; these Indians were very small, like dwarfs, and they said, "Inca, we came to call you." Astonished with this vision, the Inca shouted out, calling his servants, and when his men entered in answer to his call, the dwarfs disappeared, without anybody seeing them except the king; so then he said to his men, "What has become of these dwarfs who came to call me?" They answered him saying that they had not seen them. Then the Inca said that he would die, and later he got smallpox. While he was very sick, his servants sent two relay teams to Pachacama to ask what should be done for the health of their lord. The sorcerers, who spoke with the devil, consulted the idol, which answered that the Inca should be taken out into the sun and then he would get well. This was done, but with the opposite result, for when the Inca was put into the sun, he died at once.

His death was deeply felt by all of his vassals. Funeral rites were held for him with much weeping and solemn sacrifices; a thousand persons were killed for his burial; they were to serve him in the other life (as they believed), and it is stated that he was held in such high esteem that these people were content to die, and besides those who were designated, many others offered themselves of their own free will. This is because (according to what could be ascertained) this Inca was adored as a god in his lifetime, differently than the others; and never for any of his predecessors were such ceremonies held as for him. He was married to his own sister, called Mama Cusirimay. He founded the family called Tumipampa. He had only one son by his sister; this son, named Ninan Cuyuchi, died before his father. He had numerous sons by his other wives; the two most important were Huascar, on the one hand, whose mother was called Rahua Ocllo, and Atauhualpa, on the other, whose mother had the name Tocto Ocllo. The heart of Guayna Capac was buried in Quito, and his body was taken to Cuzco. At first it was in the temple of the Sun, and later in Casana and other places. The Indians say of this king that he was very kind to the poor and that he ordered that they be very well cared for throughout all his kingdom; they also say that he was very affable with his subjects and that he drank more than three Indians together, without ever being seen unconscious; and when his favorites asked him how he could drink so much without getting drunk, he would say that it was because he drank for the poor people; and he looked after their sustenance a lot.

After the Spaniards entered this land, they made every effort to discover his body, and they even resorted to violence many times, because it was widely believed that he had a great treasure and that it would be buried with his body or in the places he frequented the most during his lifetime, since this was an ancient custom among them. At last, owing to the great diligence that was taken, it was found, at the same time as the bodies of the other Incas, on the road to the fortress, in a house where the body seems to have been taken the night before; since the Spaniards were on the right track and catching up with it, the Indians who took care of it would move it to many different places; and although they took it in such a rush, unexpectedly moving it from one place to another, they always took it in the company of five or six idols, for which they showed great veneration, because they were convinced that these idols helped guard the body of the Inca.

The main idol that he had when he was alive was called Guaraquinga; it was big and of pure gold, but it was not with his body, nor did it turn up. The Indians wept bitterly when the body was discovered; it was found covered with many fine blankets and a lot of cotton. The body was whole and well preserved. It was brought to this city of Lima with the others, and particularly with his mother's body, which was found at the same time, and it was held in great esteem by the Indians because her son had brought it into great veneration, and on his orders, frequent sacrifices were made for it, and it had many servants. The body of Guayna Capac was the best preserved of all, because he did not seem to be dead, and only his eyes were artificial, and they were so well made that they seemed natural.

Normally Guayna Capac is counted as the last king of the Incas; this is because, in the first place, he was the last one to possess the entire pacified kingdom and in the second place, because shortly after his death, the Spaniards entered into this land, conquering and taking possession of it. Although the Incas retained the title of kings for some time, this was merely a nominal title.

Chapter 18: Of the Inca brothers Huascar and Atauhualpa

The eldest son that Guayna Capac left was Huascar Inca; at first he was named Tupa Cusi Gualpa, and the name of Huascar was given to him for this occasion. In order to celebrate on the day of his birth, his father Guayna Capac had a golden chain made very thick and so long that the Indians could dance while holding on to it, instead of holding hands; and there was enough room for two hundred persons to dance with it, spread out like a wing. In memory of this marvelous chain or rope (called *huascar* in their language) the prince was given the name of Huascar. At the time when Guayna Capac died in Quito, Huascar Inca was in Cuzco; when the news of his father's death reached him, Huascar took the fringe and was crowned king and lord of all the provinces of the Empire.

Atauhualpa was the second-born brother on the father's side only; he was a noble youth, very prudent and sagacious and well received by those who associated with him, especially the old captains and soldiers. He was born in the city of Cuzco, from where his father had taken him at a tender age, and he had brought the boy with him during the wars. At the time of his father's death, he had already been the commander of a certain expedition, and while his father was ill with the sickness he died of, Atauhualpa was named governor and commander of some border areas; but this appointment did not go into effect because his father died thereafter, before Atauhualpa set out on his new occupation. Therefore, he had achieved more than average experience in matters of war, and the Inca's captains knew him and loved him much; it is said before Guayna Capac died, seeing that he was leaving such an extensive kingdom and that to the north and east other large areas still needed to be conquered, he appointed Atauhualpa lord of Quito and the lands conquered there, this with the consent of the heir Huascar. But others assert that Guayna Capac did not divide the empire, but rather it was done by his captains Chalcochima, Quizquiz, Inca Gualpa, Rumiñaui, and other military men held in high esteem by them; they were with Atauhualpa in Quito at that time, and they were the originators of this rebellion, moved by their own personal interests. Since they were doing very well in the province of Quito, and owing to the extensive riches they had acquired in the past wars and the important posts they held in the army, they were respected and honored by everyone and very favored by Atauhualpa; therefore, they thought that if they returned to Cuzco to serve Huascar, they would not have as good a position as the one which they had at that time; they considered that the Inca Huascar would have his favorites and friends whom he would accommodate with positions of honor; but if they acclaimed Atauhualpa as the king of Quito, it was certain that he would gratefully give them much sway in the government; and for these reasons, they decided to create a new Cuzco in that city and in the surrounding provinces, so that it would be a kingdom itself, separate from Cuzco, and they would raise up Atauhualpa as their lord; and he willingly agreed with these conversations. Whether it may have happened this way or the other way, they took action as they had planned, and Atauhualpa was acclaimed as king of Quito; this gave rise to the very bloody wars between the two brothers, which caused the downfall of them both.

Before the rebellion was declared, the two brothers made their demands and replies; since Huascar was advised by his council to send for his brother to keep him nearby, he did so; to this message Atauhualpa replied that since it was necessary to have an Inca in Quito as governor, Huascar should appoint him to the post. Huascar refused to approve his brother's demand because his relatives and favorites said that if he left Atauhualpa there, he would rebel; for this reason, he summoned him a second time, and his brother made the same reply as the first time. Huascar sent him a third message, warning him that if he did not come he would send and get him. Then his kinsmen and captains advised Atauhualpa not to go to Cuzco, because his brother would kill him; rather he should rise in rebellion and be lord; after all he was also the son of Guayna Capac like his brother Huascar; they would help him and keep the title of king for him; he knew how valiant the Indians of Quito were. Being convinced by this line of reasoning, and seeing that he had the support of the army, Atauhualpa took the title of king of Quito and Tumibamba.

The first to take up arms against the other was Huascar Inca, giving as justification that the entire empire belonged to him, just as his progenitors had possessed it, without it being broken up. On the other hand, since all of the military men that his father Guayna Capac had left him were at his orders, Atauhualpa was confident. Moreover, because of his own valor and military experience, he not only hoped to be able to maintain his position in the kingdom of Quito, but he even expected to dispossess his brother and throw him out of the whole kingdom. The two camps did battle at Tumibamba, where Atauhualpa was defeated and taken prisoner by Huascar's soldiers; and while they held him in a house with guards, and those of Cuzco celebrated his imprisonment with banquets and drinking bouts, he found a way to break out by drilling a hole in a wall with a silver bar given to him by an important lady, who was the only person allowed to go in and see him in jail. Atauhualpa fled to Quito, and, calling his men together, he made a wise explanation; he pretended that the Sun his father had performed a strange miracle on him. He said the Sun had converted him into a snake and had taken him out of prison through a small hole, promising at the same time to favor Atauhualpa in achieving victory, if he came out to fight Huascar. Atauhualpa described vividly the insults and bad treatment that he had received from his enemies while they held him prisoner, and he showed so much sentiment and pain as he spoke to them that everyone, sympathizing with him in his hardship, was moved to great anger and proposed to avenge the insults suffered by their king.

Atauhualpa formed a large army and went out to look for the enemy. The captain Atoco, who was in charge of Huascar's army, did not refuse to do battle. The two armies charged one another in Ambato [just south of Quito], and Huascar's army was defeated and routed with the death of its commander and a large portion of men. Atauhualpa left the Quito region with a much larger armed force and a greatly enhanced reputation, and as he entered into lands ruled by his brother, he endeavored to subjugate them, making war on some and attracting others through peaceful means; those who resisted him met a cruel death at his hands, so, some out of fear, and others won over with favors, they all started turning themselves over to him; he did favors for those who surrendered without war, and he gave them the plunder of his dead enemies. He sent his army ahead with captains Quizquiz and Chalcochima, and since the towns of Tumibamba and the surrounding area were on his side, and also since he had some news of the Spaniards who had reached the coast, in order to stop them from allying themselves with his enemy, he picked the town of Cajamarca as a place to stop, which he did with a large portion of his army.

Having found out about the routing of his men, Huascar sent one of his brothers named Guanca Auqui from Cuzco as the captain of a large army with the objective of opposing Atauhualpa's army. Except for the provinces of Quito, the rest of the kingdom was on Huascar's side; thus the men who came to him from everywhere were innumerable, but since they were inexperienced and joined together hurriedly and without order, and since the experienced captains and soldiers defended Atauhualpa's group, the latter went forward each day and the former lost ground. Nevertheless, some say that one reason why Atauhualpa's faction prevailed was that Huascar had lost the support of his vassals because he treated them harshly and not with the gentleness and love of the other kings. He seldom let himself be seen by his subjects; he did not go out to eat in public in the plaza, as was the custom among the Incas; he was lax in observing the veneration of the dead bodies of his ancestors and of the nobility that was to guard and serve these bodies; and for this reason his captains allowed themselves to be defeated by Atauhualpa and others came to Atauhualpa's side.

The two armies had many encounters and battles, and from all of them Atauhualpa's side came out victorious. Huascar's captains, with frequent reinforcements, waited for their opponents in strongholds, in order to give battle with the advantage; and in this way they fought with them in Bonbon and Jauja. And on the hillside of Vilcas they did what they could to cut them off, confident that with the many troops that had come to their aid and the strength of the place, they were in a better position; they had occupied the top of that slope and a stone fortress located there; but Atauhualpa's men attacked and Huascar's troops were routed and put to flight.

Huascar had frequent reports in Cuzco of all that was happening: the victorious army that was marching against him, the number and strength of his enemies, the places where they stayed, and the routs and havoc made with his men; and he did not cease to gather reinforcements quickly and send them to his men. With them, Captain Guanca Auqui, building up his army after the defeat at Vilcas, gave battle again to his opponents at Pincos and Andaguaylas, and again he was defeated; between Curaguaci and Auancay [Abancay, northwest of Cuzco], toward the puna of the Aymaraes, they had another encounter; it was very bloody, and many men died on both sides; but since fortune favored Atauhualpa, his men came out victorious. They had another battle next to Limatambo, in the sierra of Vilcaconga, seven leagues from Cuzco; it lasted a long time, and Huascar's men kept retreating and fighting at the same time for more than two leagues, up to Ichubamba, where they could no longer withstand the assault that the others were giving them; Huascar's men turned their backs and fled, giving complete victory to the other side.

Chapter 19: Of the rest of the things that happened in this war

Huascar still had such a powerful army with him that it was not inferior in numbers to that of his brother; nevertheless, in experience and valor Huascar's army was not equal to the other. He left Cuzco in person, bringing out the rest of his forces and stopping on the plain of Quipaypampa, about one league from the city. Men had come to his aid from the three *suyus* that were loyal to him: Collao, Contisuyu, and Antisuyu; and also from the provinces of Chuncho and Mojo that were under his domination there had come some companies of archers with plenty of poisonous plants to smear on their arrows. The commander of this large army was Guanca Auqui, brother of the two contenders; and Pascae Inca and Gualpa Roca served as field marshal and sergeant major; noticing the great fear that all of their men had of doing battle with the forces of Atauhualpa, for the latter were very valiant and fit for victory, Huascar's captains started to doubt that the outcome would be favorable, and in the interest of peace, they hoped that something could be done to settle those differences.

Atauhualpa's army was approaching at full speed; owing to the vigor and skill of their captains and the boldness that their past victories had given them, his men paid no attention to the host of soldiers opposing them, and with their eagerness to seize the great wealth of Cuzco, they could not wait for the moment to engage in combat. On the contrary, Huascar's men, at the sight of their enemies, became more disheartened than before; they remembered the many times that they had been routed and defeated.

The general of Atauhualpa's army was Quizquiz, a wise and valiant man who was very fond of his king and lord. This was not his true name, but he had taken it because of the many victories that he had achieved; and thus his men were instructed that, when he marched to his camp, to those that asked, "Who goes there?" they should answer that it was Captain Quizquiz, which is the same as to say Caesar or Cid; this was so that from fear of his great valor and the fame of the victories he had achieved, as soon as his enemies heard this name they would surrender. Chalcochima acted as the field marshal; and the sergeant major was a very aggressive captain, named for his fierceness Rumiñaui, which means "eyes of stone," because he would never open his eyes to be merciful.

After orders had been given to the forces of both sides to attack, but before giving the battle signal, Huascar spoke to his men in this way, "Confident in your loyalty and valor, my friends and relatives, and in the very evident justness of our cause, I hope that today we will achieve a glorious victory over our enemies and that we will give them the punishment that they deserve because these rebels are traitors to their king and natural lord; in failing to obey me, for I am the legitimate heir of the dominions of the Incas, my progenitors, they have accepted and supported the authority of the usurper; only through force and cruelty, without any other reason, he intends to take my kingdom from me and take your property, your rights, and your liberty. This is an occasion in which you must show the love you have for your prince and the fidelity with which you came to fight for him. If we are victorious in this battle, as I am confident we will be, from now on there will be no one who will upset and disturb our peace; but if we lose because of your failings and weakness, there will be no place in the whole kingdom where you can take refuge and save your lives; therefore, show with your weapons how much you esteem your liberty and the life of your king, for today it depends on the strength of your arms."

With these words the soldiers were somewhat encouraged, but not to the point where the fear they had come to feel toward their enemies was completely dispelled from their hearts. With the few words that Quizquiz said to his men before going into battle, the courage they had grew in such a way that, with no fear of the danger at hand, they started to do battle and inflict injuries on their enemies so bravely that during the first encounter they dispersed the main squadron; and breaking through the middle of them, General Quizquiz did not stop until he reached the Inca; and without much effort he took him prisoner. With the Inca captured, Quizquiz's men started to chant victory, and Huascar's men started fleeing to save their lives. Quizquiz had the Inca carefully guarded, and with all of his squadrons he followed in pursuit of the enemy until reaching Cuzco.

They pillaged the town without respect for the veneration in which it was held by all the people of Tahuantinsuyu (the name of the Peruvian Empire); they only saved the temple of the Sun and the house of the *mamaconas*, virgins dedicated to the Sun. The spoils that they got were very rich, because in that city, as the capital and court of the kingdom, there were innumerable valuables of gold and silver that the Incas had collected, not counting those that were hidden by the vanquished, which must have been a considerable amount. In memory of this battle in which the Inca Huascar was taken prisoner, the field in which it took place was named Guazauara.[13] Along with the Inca, his brothers Tito Atauchi and Tupa Atau, who did not leave his side, and many other important lords were also taken prisoner. Atauhualpa's captains had Huascar taken out of the jail where he was kept so he could witness a cruel spectacle; all of his brothers and sisters, children, and kinsmen who had been captured, along with all the Inca's personal house servants, were put to death in his presence. In spite of that, some of Huascar's brothers escaped this cruel act; dressed in the clothing of plebeians, they fled; also able to escape were some important women, daughters of great lords, who later became Christians; among them were Elvira Quechonay, Beatriz Caruay Mayba, Juana Tocto, Catalina Usoca, mother of Carlos Inca, and many others.

Quizquiz sent news by relay runners to his lord Atauhualpa of the victory he had achieved and of the imprisonment of his brother Huascar; the news reached him at Cajamarca, where he was still awaiting the outcome of the war and punishing those who had resisted him with exquisite cruelty. But our Lord God permitted that, while this Inca and his captains were involved in the human massacre that we have seen, punishment should come for his tyranny and cruelness, for he fell into the hands of the Spaniards, and he finally paid for every evil that he had committed.

The sorrow that was felt by the whole kingdom because of the imprisonment of their legitimate king Huascar Inca was very great, especially among the residents of Cuzco; in times of their greatest needs and hardships, it was their custom to resort to sacrifices, invoking help from those that they adored as gods; not being able to find for this occasion and conflict a means or scheme by which they could free their king, they agreed (and they even say that Huascar himself sent a request for this from his prison) to make a solemn sacrifice to their god Viracocha, imploring him that, heedful of their inability to free their lord from the hands of his enemies, he see fit to send help and men who would take Huascar out of the grips of those captains who had imprisoned him in the name of Atauhualpa. An account of the way they performed this sacrifice would be very long; let it suffice to say that they killed many children and llamas in various ways, and that a large quantity of clothing and other valuables were burned. While the Indians were still very confident of the value of this sacrifice, news reached Cuzco of how certain strange people who came by sea had defeated and imprisoned Atauhualpa in Cajamarca; the Indians held this event to be a mystery, because the Spaniards who took the Inca prisoner were so few in number and especially because this happened shortly after the Indians offered their sacrifice; therefore, they called the Spaniards *viracochas* (a name which is still used in this way) because they believed that the Spaniards were people sent by their god Viracocha; and that is how this name was introduced for those who came, owing to the above-mentioned cause, which is the reason why the Indians called us *viracochas*, giving us the most ancient and venerated name they had. And this name was given to us only by the residents of Cuzco and the followers of Huascar; the followers of Atauhualpa and the Indians of the seacoast called the first Spaniards that they saw "bearded men"; this lasted until the usage in Cuzco of the aforementioned name of *viracocha* became generally accepted.

Another explanation for this is also given by the Indians. They had a fable that in ancient times Viracocha sent three of his servants, called *viracochas*, and it is said that they had beards like the Spaniards and that the first one turned into a stone; they took the life of the second one, and for this reason a great pestilence came; the third, who was called Ticciviracocha, left by the sea at the end of the world; and when the Incas of Cuzco were informed of our clothing and appearance, they understood that, by means of their sacrifice, he who had left was returning with men to help Huascar Inca. Being imprisoned in Cajamarca by the Spaniards (as will be told in the second part of this history),[14] at first Atauhualpa was very doubtful and perplexed as to what he would do about his brother; this was because he was not at all sure he would be freed from the hands of the Spaniards, but when Francisco Pizarro started to discuss his ransom, promising him that he would be set free, Atauhualpa made up his mind to have his brother killed; and in accordance with this resolution he sent word to his captains to bring Huascar before him. When this order reached Cuzco, they left immediately with the prisoner; accompanying him came some of his most faithful servants carrying the dishes and jewels that had remained with the Inca; owing to the great love that they had for him, these servants refused to let him go alone into the hands of his enemies. On the orders that they received from their lord, Atauhualpa's captains who were transporting the prisoner Huascar killed him as they were leaving the *tambo* of Andamarca, thirty leagues short of Cajamarca and three leagues past a lake called Cochaconchuco. After Huascar's death, his servants turned back, fleeing with the wealth they were carrying, and fearing that they would be overtaken by Atauhualpa's men, and so that this Inca would not take advantage of their lord's treasure that they were carrying for his ransom, they threw it in the lake just mentioned.

Huascar was married to the Coya Choqueyupa, his sister; none of his children survived because, although he had many, they were all killed by Atauhualpa's captains, who burned the body of Huascar; some people from Cuzco gathered up his ashes, and back in that city the people held these ashes in the highest esteem, along with the other bodies of the Incas. The riches of this king were very great, although they disappeared with his death. It is said that at the time when Marques Francisco Pizarro was in Cuzco, an Indian came to one of his servants, who was named Maldonado, and the Indian told him that in a cave in the hill of Vilcaconga the Indians had hidden one thousand loads of gold sheets that Huascar had to cover his palace; and shortly thereafter this Indian disappeared without leaving a trace that could be found.

Not long after the death of Huascar, the Spaniards garroted Atauhualpa in the town of Cajamarca, and later they buried him with much honor, and they put a cross on top of him because he had become a Christian before his death, but his Indians dug him up secretly and took him to be buried in their *guacas*. Atauhualpa left successors; their grandchildren, called Diego Hilaquita, Francisco Hilaquita, and Juan Ninancoro, were living forty years ago when I was in the city of Cuzco.

Chapter 20: Of the rest of the Incas, sons of Guayna Capac who had the king's fringe

Guayna Capac had many children; but since Atauhualpa endeavored to extinguish the royal lineage, after the civil wars between the two brothers were over and both dead, as far as we know, no more than eleven remained, four women and seven men. The women were Ines Guaylas, who married Francisco Ampuero; Beatriz Quispiquipi, who was the wife of Diego Hernandez; another was the mother of Villacastin; and the fourth was the grandmother of Pedro de Soto, grandson of Hernando de Soto. All of these gentlemen were residents of Cuzco, except for the Ampueros and Pizarros who descended from the first daughter. The men were named Guamantico, Mayta Yupanqui, Tupa Gualpa, Manco Inca Yupanqui, Paullu Inca, and two others. The first three were present in Cajamarca when Atauhualpa was killed; orders were given to kill the first two by Atauhualpa himself; and when Marques Pizarro was informed that the third one was the only legitimate Inca successor to the kingdom, Pizarro gave him the fringe and crown in the name of the king of Castile; this made all the Indians very happy, but shortly thereafter the Inca died in Juaja.

When Governor Francisco Pizarro reached Cuzco, he found Manco Inca there, and the Inca came out to meet him in peace; Pizarro had the fringe and royal insignias given to him. At first this Inca showed himself to be a great friend of the Spaniards, although the friendship did not last long. It is said that the adelantado Diego de Almagro had Manco Inca's last two brothers killed in Cuzco in order to please Manco himself, who asked Almagro to do it. Manco Inca intended to kill all of his brothers because he had already planned what he did later, which was to rebel; so that none of his brothers would remain to oppose him and be named Inca by the Spaniards after he rebelled, Manco made every effort to get Diego de Almagro to kill those two, for at that time no others remained, except for Paullu, and since he was a boy, Manco Inca paid no attention to him. Almagro's reason for having these two sons of Guayna Capac killed was, it is said, to please Manco Inca and have him on his side, because it was Almagro's intention to take the city of Cuzco on the pretext that it fell within the confines of his grant of New Toledo; and he already had news that His Majesty had conceded that grant to him. And the occasion that Manco took to have the first one killed was as follows: Manco had made friends with a Spaniard named Simon Suarez, and one day the Inca told him that behind the fortress of Cuzco, on a plain, there was a large underground vault where more than four thousand loads of gold and silver were buried; the Spaniard gave an account of this to Almagro, and Almagro told Manco Inca about it; to this Manco responded, "Kill this brother of mine, for then I will show the treasure to you." And after the Indian was killed by Almagro, Manco acted as if he did not know anything, and he refused to give Almagro the information he had promised him. The other Inca who is said to have been killed on Almagro's orders, but at Manco's request, was called Octo Xopa; one night four Spaniards, who were sent by Almagro, stabbed him to death.

When Manco Inca saw the Spaniards divided as Almagro made his expedition to Chile, he revolted and made a cruel war on the Spaniards with the intention of putting an end to them or driving them out of the land. He laid siege to the cities of Cuzco and Lima, and he killed everyone he could lay hands on throughout the kingdom. But his plans did not turn out as well as he had thought they would because, upon the return of Almagro from Chile, the power of the Spaniards greatly increased with the men he brought; so right away Manco Inca realized how difficult a task he had taken on, and, doubtful of having success with it, he withdrew to the province of Vilcabamba with many thousands of Indians who followed him; there, owing to the ruggedness of the terrain, which is composed of rough mountains and thick jungles, he sustained a war against the Spaniards; this was kept up by his three sons, who succeeded him one after the other; Manco and his three sons lasted for a period of thirty-four years. During this time, Indian troops would come out of these mountains from many places to raid the land held by our people; the latter made war on the Indians at different times with varying degrees of success.

Marques Francisco Pizarro sent from Lima about two hundred Spaniards with many Indian friends to make war on the Inca; entering by way of Ruparupa on unused roads, they reached the provinces of the Andes. When Manco found out that Spaniards were coming to make war on him, he sent two valiant captains called Paucar Guaman and Yunco Callo to resist them; owing to the great valor of these captains, Manco had not wanted them to leave his side. They waited for the Christians in a difficult pass called Yuramayo, located behind the Valley of Jauja, and there they attacked the Spaniards, and they engaged in a hard-fought battle in which our men were defeated and almost all of them were killed; this happened because the Spaniards were tired from the rough roads and very hungry and almost without ammunition since their gunpowder had gotten wet in the forests. This victory made the Indians so arrogant that they sent word to their lord the Inca that they wanted to enter the city of Los Reyes [Lima] and take Marques Pizarro prisoner; and with this in mind some expeditions went out of the mountains, and one night they reached a small hill where eighteen Spaniards had escaped from the battle at Yuramayo. The Indians attacked them, but the Spaniards, encouraging each other on and realizing what a critical spot they were in, fought with such courage that they routed the Indians, killing many of them, including the captain Yunco Callo; because of his death, the Inca ordered prolonged mourning; and he was left so confused and gloomy by this routing of his men that he resolved never again to make war on the Spaniards except to defend himself when they came after him. In spite of this, his people did not stop overrunning the land; coming out on the roads in bands, they made the most frequent raids at Limatambo, Andaguaylas, and in the district of Guamanga. One night they came to Guamanga when its inhabitants were off guard, and having very quickly robbed what they could, they left without being harmed; our people came out after them and caught up with them and pursued them until they drove them into the mountains, which gave them protection. And the Indians did not come out of the mountains again grouped in an army during all the rest of Manco Inca's life. His death occurred in the following way.

Captain Diego Mendez was an important man and one of the closest friends of the Almagros, father and son; he had been one of those most directly responsible for the death of Marques Francisco Pizarro; he was taken prisoner in the battle of Chupas [near Guamanga], and, while awaiting punishment, he broke out of prison, and along with four other Spaniards he fled to Vilcabamba to avail himself of help from Manco Inca, who was pleased to see the Spaniards, and he thanked them for having sought his protection. He ordered that they be given all the Indian servants that they needed, and each day he did them great favors and gave them gifts, seating them at his table and making a habit of conversing with them. The Spaniards were very happy with such a good reception until news came to the Inca through his *chasques* and spies that Governor Vaca de Castro was going down from Cuzco to Lima because another governor was coming to the land; on hearing this news,

Diego Mendez and his companions were very pleased because they were fed up with living among the Indians and wanted to leave that province, but they waited for some good opportunity to have the Inca authorize it. It happened at this time that a certain cacique, vassal of Manco Inca, Carbayayco by name, lord of Cotamarca, tried to kill the Inca and occupy all that province. That rebellion was not kept a secret from the Inca, and he was much angered by it, and immediately he sent the men from his personal guard, a total of one thousand warrior-soldiers, in order to have Carbayayco captured and brought back securely. The Indians took more time on this expedition than they had been given, and during this absence, the Inca took it upon himself to have a solemn banquet in which, with good cheer and signs of affection, he drank many toasts to the Spaniards. After the dinner was over, they started a friendly game of ninepins; Diego Mendez won a gold piece from the Inca, and the Inca paid him at once; and as the game progressed, the Inca won back the gold piece; at this Diego Mendez became very upset, and noticing this, the Inca asked him why he was getting angry, saying that if he wanted that piece of gold and others like it, he would have them given to him. This got Diego Mendez all the more riled up, to the point where they had to stop the game. The Inca stepped aside with some of the Indians of his personal guard, and Diego Mendez took a long stroll with a Spaniard named Barba; at this time they presumably were scheming to kill the Inca, judging from what happened a little later. At this point a runner arrived with news that the Inca's captains were bringing Carbayayco as a prisoner, and hearing that they were to arrive the next day, Diego Mendez decided not to put off performing his act of treachery.

He came with his companions to ask the Inca about the news he had gotten from his captains; the Inca waited some time before answering, and he showed that he was angry about what had happened in the game. Seeing that the Inca was sad and annoyed, in order to cheer him up and make him laugh, the Spaniards started to joke around with each other; this made the Inca smile, but not at Diego Mendez, because the Inca frowned at him; this made Mendez even more indignant. The Inca called for drinks, and an Indian girl brought him two golden tumblers, and, taking one of them, he ordered that the other be given to one of the Spaniards who was playing the games. While the Inca and the Spaniard were both drinking at the same time, Diego attacked the Inca and stabbed him, finally leaving him for dead; none of the other Spaniards defended the Inca. The Indians who were present came to the aid of their lord, and some of the Spaniards were killed. After this cruel act was committed, it was just about nightfall, and the rest fled on their horses before the Indians who were in their houses found out what was happening. That night they traveled a considerable distance on their return to Cuzco; they crossed over a bridge, and on the other side they cut the bridge off in order to be more certain that the Indians could not follow them. But, as word spread of the incident among the Indians, they came from everywhere after the killers, and when the news reached the captains who were bringing the lord of Cotamarca as a prisoner, they turned him loose and went looking for the Spaniards, whom they overtook one night lodged in a *buhio*, and, attacking them suddenly, they killed all the Spaniards. Having avenged their lord, they went to the town where the evil occurred; it was Viticos, at that time a very restful place. They found the Inca alive, because he survived for five days after he was wounded, and they went in before him weeping so bitterly that they caused him to die more quickly. The Inca asked them where they came from, and they answered that they were coming from killing the Christians whom he had liked so much and treated so well that they took his life in payment for the good they had received from his hand. The Inca answered, "Do not be surprised that they have killed me in this corner; they killed my brother Atauhualpa while he was in possession of all his power and empire; for this reason we can infer that the power of the Christian God is greater than that of our god the Sun, and, therefore, do not be saddened by my death." He admonished them never to let Christians enter that land and that they should receive his eldest son Sayri Tupa; and since he was young, he left as his appointed governor one of the *orejones* from Cuzco who was present there, Ato Supa by name; after saying this, he died. The Indians embalmed his body, and after carrying it to Vilcabamba, they put it in the temple of the Sun, where it was found by the Spaniards who conquered that province during the time of Viceroy Francisco de Toledo. Manco Inca left three sons, who were called Sayri Tupa, Cusi Titu Yupanqui, and Tupa Amaro, and one daughter, who was called Cusi Huarcay.

After Manco Inca withdrew to Vilcabamba, out here the Spaniards gave the fringe and title of Inca to his brother Paullu, the youngest son of Guayna Capac; Paullu became a Christian during the time of Governor Vaca de Castro, and on his advice and urging he took the governor's name and called himself Cristoual [Cristóbal] Paullu Tupa. He was a great servant of His Majesty, and he always favored the side of the Spaniards against his brother Manco

Inca. The king confirmed this selection, and he granted the new Inca a coat of arms with the imperial eagle on it, and within one of its divisions, the fringe that the Inca kings used as an insignia and royal crown, and in another division, a tree with two crowned dragons or serpents, which were the heraldic devices and emblem of his elders. This Inca had two legitimate sons, called Carlos Inca and Felipe Manco Tupa. Carlos married a Spanish lady, and he had a son by her, Melchor Inca, who died in Spain. Cristoual Paullu Tupa also had two illegitimate sons called Fernando Puma Capi and Alonso Tupa Atau; I met this last one myself in Cuzco, and I conversed with him a lot; in talking about the descendants from the Inca line who have survived, he assured me that within Cuzco there were about four hundred males. Although Paulla Inca died a Christian and as such was given a church burial, nevertheless, the Indians made a small statue of him. On it they put some finger-nails and hair that they had secretly taken from him. This statue was venerated by them just as much as any of the bodies of their other Inca kings.

Chapter 21: Of the sons of Manco Inca who maintained the title of king in Vilcabamba

Sayri Tupa Inca remained in Vilcabamba with the fringe and the title of king, and since out here the civil wars of Gonzalo Pizarro ensued, no effort was made to subjugate the Inca or to make war on him until this land was pacified with the victory that the loyalists achieved in Jaquijaguana [Anta] in the year 1548. President Pedro de la Gasca, wishing to leave this land completely calm and pacified, consulted with the most experienced persons in the kingdom; he asked them what plan and method could be used to bring the Inca to peace and take him out of his mountainous hiding place in Vilcabamba, where he was withdrawn in the company of the rest of his brothers and kinsmen; finally he decided that there was no other way to put an end to this matter except to turn it over to Cristoual Paullu Inca, and in accordance with this decision, when he left Cuzco for the city of Los Reyes, the president left Paullu with ample authority, and he urged him to do everything possible to resolve the matter. Cristoual took this matter so seriously that he tried every means at his disposition to settle it. First of all, he decided to send an embassy and presents to Vilcabamba for his Inca nephews; the presents included things valued at more than one hundred thousand pesos—in gems and jewels of gold and silver and silk and other valuable cloth—all of which was carried by some noble Indian relatives of his. The Indians of Vilcabamba received this embassy with great pleasure and surprise, for they were very impressed that their uncle Paullu and their other Inca kinsmen of Cuzco would remember them. They kept the messengers for more than sixty days, giving them great banquets and fiestas, so that they would tell in Cuzco how pleased they were in Vilcabamba that out here so much importance was given to them. The Indians of Vilcabamba sent the messengers back with another present that was for Cristoual Paullu; it was no less valuable than the first one, because it included fine pieces of gold and silver, excellent *cumbi* cloth, of the kind that was made formerly during the time of the Incas, their ancestors, and various kinds of unusual birds and animals that were found in those provinces; and as their reply to tell their uncle Paullu Tupa that they had been pleased and singularly delighted to know the decision of his excellency President Pedro de la Gasca and to receive the demonstrations of love and friendship with which their uncles, brothers, and parents had asked them to come to their homeland, Cuzco, where they would be loved and served by their people and treated with much honor by the Spaniards; they were happy to do this, and without fail they would come the following summer, but since it was almost the middle of winter, they could not do it; and as proof that they were telling the truth and would keep their promise, they gave the messengers a certain sign that the Inca lords customarily used among themselves.

Cristoual Paullu was very pleased at the good reply that the ambassadors brought, and he took great care to arrange everything he needed to go in person the next summer to bring and accompany his nephews; and when the time came, he left Cuzco with a large accompaniment of important Indians, and entering through Lima-tambo, he reached the town of Guanipaco; there, after having sent his messengers to Vilcabamba, he became so gravely ill that he was forced to return to Cuzco, where he died in a few days.

Because of this death and more importantly because of the re-bellion of Francisco Hernandez Giron, which occurred at that time, the subjugation of the Indians of Vilcabamba was forgotten for a long time, until the arrival as viceroy of the Marques de Cañete, Andres Hurtado de Mendoza; owing to his prudence and efficient ad-ministration, the affairs of this kingdom were settled; therefore, this situation gave rise to a renewed interest in the matter of subju-gating the Indians. The viceroy sent a gentleman to Vilcabamba named Diego Hernandez, the husband of the Coya Beatriz Quispi-quipi, who was the aunt of the Inca Sayri Tupa; he also sent Juan Sierra and Juan de Betanzos, all residents of Cuzco and encomen-deros of Indians, and a Dominican friar, Fray Melchor de los Reyes. They were to persuade the Inca Sayri Tupa to fulfill the promise he had made to his uncle Paulla Inca; the viceroy, who was in the city of Los Reyes and was the second person of the King of Spain, also sent them to beg him to do this so that out here among the Christians the Inca could have the opportunity to learn about our holy faith and become a Christian. When the Inca found out the Christians had entered into his land and the reason for their trip, he was very pleased, as were the rest of the Inca *orejones*; and when Diego Hernandez came before him with his companions, the Inca received them with a great show of kindness and pleasure, and he held banquets and fiestas for them, and he gave them a large amount of gold in nuggets so big that some of them were worth two hundred pesos, and he also gave them a large number of silver bars.

The Inca Sayri Tupa decided to leave that land in the company
of those gentlemen, in spite of the fact that some important men
tried to dissuade him; he planned to present himself before the viceroy, offering his services as vassal of His Majesty. He left his two
brothers there in order to console the Indians of those two provinces; he also left orders for his brothers to leave right away if he
sent word from Cuzco for them to do so. He left by way of the Valley
of Andaguaylas; from there Juan Sierra went on ahead, because the
Inca so desired, so that Sierra could reach Lima and explain to the
viceroy that the Inca was already out of Vilcabamba; when the Inca
entered this city, the viceroy ordered the town council to go out and
receive him; and when the Inca entered into his palace, the viceroy got up from his chair and gave him a friendly hug and made
the Inca sit next to him, with the *oidores* and all the important
people of the city present. The Inca brought with him his wife and
sister, Cusi Huarcay; the viceroy also honored her very much and
seated her in the drawing room, where she was awaited by the ladies
of Lima, all dressed up with their best formal clothes and jewels.
He ordered that they be given good lodging and that they be waited
on by Spanish servants.

Many days were spent in Lima for the fiestas and rejoicing that
were held in their honor. All the Indians were pleased to see the
Inca, and the caciques from everywhere came to venerate him and
bring him many presents; this brought to mind the time of the Incas. In the name of His Majesty, the viceroy gave them for their
encomineda the Indians that had belonged to Francisco Hernandez
Giron; with this, they left for Cuzco, for they greatly desired to
see their brothers and relatives. In that city a solemn reception was
given to them; the Indians came out according to their *ayllos* and
kinship groups with their festive creations, as they used to receive
the Incas in the past; and the Inca and the Coya entered in their
litter richly dressed with brocade and precious stones. Sayri Tupa
represented very faithfully the person of Guayna Capac, his grandfather, whom he resembled very much according to the Indians.
Shortly after they arrived at Cuzco, they received the holy baptism,
and by order of the viceroy, the Inca was named Diego de Mendoza,
and the Coya was named Maria Manrique. The Archbishop of Lima
sent dispensation so that brother and sister could marry. The Inca
died one year after he was baptized, and it was suspected that he
had been poisoned by the cacique of Yucay, called Francisco Chil-
che, who, owing to this suspicion, was in prison for one year, although nothing was proven against him. Sayri Inca left one legiti-

mate daughter called Beatriz Clara Coya; she married Martin Garcia de Loyola, who was the governor of Chile when he died. They left only one daughter, who married Juan Henriquez, first Marques of the Valle de Yucay, also called Oropesa, because that is the [Spanish] name of the main town [Yucay] within the valley that falls within the Marquesado [see note 12].

Due to Sayri's absence, his brother Cusi Titu Yupanqui, who was second in line, governed in Vilcabamba; as long as Sayri was living out here, Cusi Titu refrained from raiding and robbing in our lands; but right after Sayri died, he took it upon himself to do as much damage to the Christians as he could; he assaulted the Valley of Yucay and many other places, bringing as many Indians as he could catch back to Vilcabamba and killing people traveling on foot; therefore, there was no safe place in the vicinities of Cuzco and Guamanga, nor was it possible to walk without escort from one place to another; and these attacks would have continued if the early death of the Inca had not put an end to them. The Inca left a son and three daughters. The son, named Felipe on being baptized, was brought to Lima by Viceroy Francisco de Toledo.

Cusi Titu Yupanqui was succeeded in the state of Vilcabamba by his younger brother Tupa Amaro Inca; the Spaniards tried very hard to bring this latter Inca to peace because they were very anxious to pacify the land infested by his people with continuous attacks and robbing. While Viceroy Francisco de Toledo was in Cuzco, he sent an Augustinian friar accompanied by three or four Spaniards to Vilcabamba; the friar was given ample powers to arrange a peace settlement with the Inca, pardoning him for all of the damage and insults that he and his men had committed. But the Inca refused, because actually his men would not let him make any agreement; instead they killed the friar and his companions.

Owing to these cruel acts, no one could be found who wanted to go with a message from the viceroy to the Inca. Finally, a resident of Cuzco named Tilano de Anaya offered to take a message; when Anaya reached the bridge of Chuquichaca, which was the edge of the lands that the Inca possessed, he was killed by the Indians of the garrison guarding that pass; they killed him because they found out that he was going to try to get their lord the Inca to come to Cuzco in peace; this was not to their liking, even though the Inca wanted very much to do it (according to what is said). The killers went to Vilcabamba, and they told the Inca how they had found certain Christians hiding at the bridge of Chuquichaca who were spying on the pass so they could come in and kill him; they went on to say that they had taken the lives of the Christians. The Inca was surprised at what had happened, and he was sorry that they had not sent word to him first.

When the news of these deaths reached Cuzco, it caused much grief and upset people; and the viceroy, who had sent them, felt very sorry about it; in order to find out more about the incident, he sent other messengers, but he took more precautions for their defense. When they reached Chuquichaca, they found Anaya dead, along with two of his servants, the bridge in ruins, and many Indian warriors on the other side of the river; our people asked the Indians why they had killed those Christians, and they answered that they acted on the orders of the Inca, who did not want to leave in peace or be a friend of the Spaniards; all of this was false; it was fabricated by the Inca's warriors. The messengers brought this reply to the viceroy, who, considering that nothing had been accomplished through peaceful means, decided to settle this matter by force of arms and not to leave Cuzco until he had eliminated that den of thieves from which the Christians received so much harm. To this end, he sounded the alarm and raised men; he named as commander Martin Hurtado de Arbieto, a resident of Cuzco, who made war on the Indians with all the good fortune that was desired; with the death of only three Spaniards, he achieved victory, and the Indians along with their king were defeated and put to flight; in the period of only six months that this war lasted, the provinces of Vilcabamba that obeyed the Inca were pacified; but they could not get their hands on the Inca, because when he saw that his men were getting the worst of the battle, he fled to rugged, inaccessible places.

Captain Martin Garcia de Loyola offered to go after him with only twenty select soldiers, even though it might be necessary to enter into hostile lands; and he fulfilled the mission as he promised; without losing the trail of the Inca, he kept on following him, and after a few days, he caught up with him. He captured him and brought him to Cuzco along with other Indian captains who were taken. By order of the viceroy, the Inca and the other culprits were put on trial, and they were sentenced to death. This decision was carried out in spite of the fact that all of the priests interceded on behalf of the Inca before the viceroy; not even the Bishop of Popayan, who begged him on his knees, could change the decision, nor could the lamentations that were made by the unfortunate Inca, who asked to be sent to Spain as a servant of the king. This execution was performed in the plaza of Cuzco, where a high platform had been constructed and a multitude of Indians had gathered; they were crying and lamenting the death of their king. When the Inca was already on the platform, so close to that critical moment, he showed himself to be so fearful and disheartened that he was hardly able to talk. At the urging of the priests who were there to console him, the Inca asked for the water of the holy baptism, and he took the name of Felipe Tupa Amaro. The sacrament of the holy baptism gave him so much courage and vigor that he got to his feet, and he made a certain movement of the hands which is a sign of courtesy among them; then he turned to where the majority of the Indian nobles were, and speaking in their language, he said in a loud voice, "Listen to me." Immediately the weeping and outcries of the Indians ceased, and the plaza became as quiet as if there were no people in it; this was a clear indication of how very respectful and obedient the Indians were to their Inca. What he told them on the advice of the priests is as follows: "Incas and caciques who have gathered here from the four *suyus* of the kingdom, be aware that I am now a Christian, and I have been baptized, and I want to die under the laws of God, and without fail I have to die now. I want you to know that everything that up to this point the Incas my ancestors and I have told you, that you should adore the Sun, the *guacas*, stones, hills, and rivers, all this is false and untrue; and when we told you that we used to go in to talk to the Sun and that he talked to us and told us that you were to do what we commanded you to do, that is also untrue and fraudulent, because the Sun did not talk; rather we did; since the statue is a piece of gold, it cannot talk; if I made you believe that, it is because my brother Cusi Titu told me that when I wished to order something, I should go in alone to the idol Punchau, and that no one should enter with me, and that the idol would not talk to me because it was a lifeless statue with no intelligence; and I was to come out afterward and tell you that the Sun had spoken to me and told me the same thing as I ordered you, so that you would obey me better; and I was to venerate what was inside of the idol Punchau, and that was the hearts of my ancestors the Incas." Having said this, he told them once again that everything that he had taught them was false and untrue, and he advised them to believe in one true God, Creator of all things, as was taught by the law of the Christians; he would die for his guilt, and he wanted to die a Christian, for them to forgive him for deceiving them up to that time and for them to plead with God for his sake. This was all said by the Inca with authority and royal dignity; it seemed that with the baptism God had given him new strength to be able to say that, since he was trembling and faint before.

After he finished his address, his head was cut off; this caused

the Indians incredible pain and made them shout to see the man
they held as their king end his life in such an unfortunate way;
and all of the Spaniards present felt no less compassion for him;
in general everyone felt sorry about the harshness of his execution.
Felipe Tupa Amaro left two young daughters who were brought
with him from Vilcabamba; they became Christians and took the
names Juana Pilcohuaco and Madalena; they have left successors,
and I know the son of one of them; he is named Felipe like his
grandfather.

Chapter 22: Of the name and locality occupied by the Kingdom of the Incas, and how these kings came to rule so many people and provinces

Since the lineage of the Inca kings has been concluded, from the first king who initiated this monarchy up to the last, where it ended, one thing is left to be dealt with now; it is the kingdom itself and the method of governing it that the Incas had. And starting from the beginning, I will say that they called their kingdom and dominions Tahuantinsuyu, which is the same as saying the four quarters or provinces; since the Incas resided in the city of Cuzco, which they always considered the capital and court of their empire, from there they designated the boundaries and divided it up into the aforementioned provinces or regions, according to their location in the direction of each of the four quarters of the world, and within each of the quarters there were many other smaller provinces of Indian nations differing in language, dress, and customs. These four quarters of the kingdom also had their own names, taken from the most important provinces included in each one of them. After one of the provinces to the east of Cuzco, called Anti, they gave the name of Antisuyu to the eastern quarter; they named the western quarter Contisuyu after another province with this name [Hispanicized as Condesuyo] located in that district; the northern quarter was named Chinchaysuyu, after the province of Chincha, located there; and the southern quarter, Collasuyu, was named after the great province of Collao [Hispanicized form of Colla], which is included in that quarter; and by these names they meant all the land conquered by the Incas that fell in each of those quarters.

In the middle of them was the royal city of Cuzco like the heart in the middle of the body, and from Cuzco four main roads went out toward each of these four areas. The length of this great kingdom extended from north to south along the seacoast for a distance of nine hundred to one thousand Castilian leagues; starting in the province of Popayan, it ran all the way to the Maule River in the Kingdom of Chile, forty leagues south of the city of Santiago;

although it is true that the Incas had not finished subjugating the entire province of Popayan when our Spaniards came, at that time they were in the process of conquering it, and the Incas had already reduced the whole province of Pasto, which today is under the jurisdiction of Popayan, and they had extended their dominion a few leagues beyond Pasto. Even though, for some time, the borders and boundary stones of this kingdom were located at the Maule River in the south and in the north along the Angasmayo River, which runs between Pasto and Quito, the valiant Guayna Capac enlarged his dominions more than fifty leagues in this northern quarter. For such a large area as this kingdom had, in width it was very narrow; in fact, at its widest point, it was not more than one hundred leagues wide from the sea over to the provinces of the Andes, where the dense forests and rugged terrain, more than the number and courage of its inhabitants, had curbed the ambition and greed of the Incas so much that they did not enlarge that part of their kingdom as they desired, although they attempted it several times. Even though the inhabitants of those sierras and woodlands are few in number, and these are quite barbaric, of different nations, divided in small *behetrias* without the skill and discipline of the Inca's vassals, nevertheless, with the help of the density and ruggedness of the *arcabucos* and woodlands and by the many rivers and swamps present there, the inhabitants were able to resist the powerful armies of the Incas, which, for the aforementioned reasons, won very little land in that place.

The Inca kings became such great lords and conquered so many provinces and nations first of all because they were never opposed by a united front; on the contrary, each province tried to defend its borders alone, without some allying themselves with others in order to increase their strength; and since they lived in *behetrias* or *cacicazgos* and small dominions, the major difficulty that the Incas had was in subjugating the territory around Cuzco; but those who had already been subjugated went with them to war; and therefore, the forces of the Incas were always greater than those of their opponents; and the Incas managed better because they surpassed the other Indians in intelligence, discipline, organization, and skill in fighting, and this ability gradually grew with their continued involvement in war. For this reason, although they did not always accomplish their purpose, they were very seldom or never completely routed, even though a few times many of their men were killed and they had to restrain themselves or even stop fighting for some time. In the second place, an important reason for their growth was the fact that no nation had tried to disturb the Incas in their own land; rather the other nations contented themselves with being left alone in their lands; there is no indication either in the records of the Incas or of the other nations that the Incas had been bothered. Moreover, after the Incas had pacified the surrounding territory, it was helpful to them to have their land very craggy and well defended. Of the four roads that extend from Cuzco throughout the kingdom, there is not one that, within twelve leagues of the city, does not cross a large river that is difficult to ford practically all year, and the land is very uneven, rough, and craggy by nature.

Another reason, more important than those just stated, is that from the time that these kings of Cuzco decided to conquer new lands and make others obey them, they sought a pretext on which to justify their designs, which is natural, and I think that all the nations of the world have done likewise no matter how barbaric they were. The first thing that these Incas proposed (although this was not the pretext which they ended up with and not the one that made them lords) was an imaginary idea that they held and feigned at first; namely, that from the Universal Flood only the first Inca and his brothers and sisters escaped in the cave called Pacarictampu and that from them the world was populated; on the basis of this they had a thousand fables and foolish stories; finally, whatever the case may be, they stated that all people originated from them and their descendants and that for this reason everyone must obey and serve them and this was everyone's obligation.

From another fable similar to this last one, they also took advantage of the opportunity to further their intentions, saying that they were children of the Sun sent by him to the world in order to teach mankind how to serve and honor the Sun. In effect, religion was one of the most important pretexts they gave for making war on other people, and in accordance with this, all of the people that they had under their power were treated in the following way. Not only did they try to hold them in submission as subjects, but they also compelled them to accept the Inca idols, hold Inca opinions entirely, learn Inca rites and ceremonies, and maintain the places of worship in exactly the same way that was customary in Cuzco. Besides this, the Incas took the major *guacas* of the vanquished from their provinces and brought them to Cuzco; the Incas believed that by this means the *guacas* would help them keep control over those lands from whence they came; nor did they lack the careful diligence needed to carry out all that has been mentioned, nor punishment for those who did not follow the Inca ways. And it is a proven fact that when some provinces rebelled, not only did they refuse to obey the Incas, but they also opposed the Inca religion; and this was the main pretext that the Incas had to conquer them again and the reason for punishing them so rigorously, as the Indians themselves tell.

Chapter 23: How the Incas administered newly conquered lands by putting in these lands outsiders whom they called mitimaes, and the types there were

of them Although it was very extensive and composed of many and very different nations, the entire empire of the Incas was a single republic, governed by the same laws, privileges, and customs, and it was observant of the same religion, rites, and ceremonies; however, before being brought under Inca rule, the several nations had their own common law and a different way of living and governing themselves. This union and uniformity was maintained everywhere; and it must be understood that what we say here that the Incas introduced into the nations that they subjugated was the same type of government that they maintained at the Inca court and where they ruled before.

The first thing that these kings did when they won a province was to take out of it six or seven thousand families (more or less, according to what seemed fitting to them, judging by the number and disposition of the people they found) and send them to other parts of the quiet and peaceful provinces, distributing them throughout a number of towns; and in exchange for them they put the same number of other people, who were made to leave the places where the first were settled, or from wherever the Incas wished, and among them were many *orejones* of noble blood. These individuals who settled in new lands were called *mitimaes*, which is the same as to say "newcomers" or "outsiders" in contrast to the natives; this name referred to the new vassals as well as to the old ones who were exchanged for them; in fact, both went from their own lands to strange lands; and even today we use the word in this way, calling all of the newcomers who are settled in all the provinces of this kingdom *mitimaes*. Care was taken in this transmigration that those who were transferred, the recently conquered as well as the others, did not move to just any land, in a haphazard way, but to the places that were of the same climate and qualities or very similar to those they were leaving and in which they were raised. Therefore, those who were native to cold lands were taken to cold lands and those from hot lands to hot lands, so that in this way they would not regret moving from their natural home so much and they would be healthier in the new lands, without falling ill from the change, which would be the case if they were taken to lands of the opposite climate of their homeland. The people who were moved by the Inca in this way were relieved from obedience to their former caciques, and they were ordered to submit to the rule of the caciques of the lands where they were placed; and there it was ordered that both types of *mitimaes* be given places to build homes and lands in which to prepare their *chacaras* and plant their crops, and they were to remain there as perpetual residents of the towns where they were placed; and they were to follow the practices and way of life of the local people, except that they retained the dress, emblems, and symbols of the people from their nation or province; moreover, this custom has been preserved up to the present time, for even now on the basis of the aforementioned things, we can distinguish between the natives of each town and the *mitimaes*.

The Inca introduced this change of residence in order to keep his dominion quiet and safe. The city of Cuzco, capital of the kingdom where the Inca had his court and residence, was far away from the most remote provinces in which there were many nations of barbaric and warlike people; therefore, the Inca felt that he could not maintain peace and obedience in any other way, and since this was the main reason why this measure was taken, the Inca ordered that the majority of the *mitimaes* who were made to go to recently subjugated towns settle in the provincial capitals so that they could serve as a garrison and presidio—not for a salary or for a limited time; rather, the *mitimaes* and their descendants would remain perpetually. And, as would be the case with warriors, they were given some privileges so they would appear to be more noble, and the Inca commanded that they always be very obedient and do whatever their captains and governors might order. With this skillful plan, as long as these *mitimaes* were loyal to the governors, if the natives rebelled, soon they would be reduced to obeying the Inca, and if the *mitimaes* made a disturbance and started an uprising, they would be repressed and punished by the natives; and thus, by means of this resolution to make the majority of their people re-establish themselves by shifting some to the places of others, the king kept his states secure from rebellion. Moreover, trade and commerce between provinces was more frequent and all the land better supplied with what was needed. Furthermore, with this transfer of their vassals from one place to another, the Incas aimed to achieve throughout their kingdom similarity and uniformity in matters pertaining to religion and political government, and they expected all of the nations of the kingdom to learn the language of Cuzco, which in this way came to be the general language of all Peru. With this shuffling of domiciles, the newly conquered, who were transferred within the kingdom, learned all this in a short time and without suffering or compulsion, and the old vassals who settled as *mitimaes* in the newly pacified areas taught the natives; great care was taken in this and the natives were compelled to learn, for the Incas obliged everyone to accept their language, laws, and religion, along with all of the opinions related to these matters that were established in Cuzco. The Incas eliminated, either completely or partially, the practices and rites that the conquered people had before Inca ways were imposed. In order to introduce and establish these things more effectively, besides the aforementioned conversion of the people, upon conquering a province, the Incas had the people's main idol taken away and placed in Cuzco with the same services and cult that it used to have in the province of its origin, and the natives were obliged to take care of all this, exactly as had been done when the aforementioned idol or *guaca* was in their province. For that reason Indians from all the provinces of the kingdom resided in Cuzco. These Indians were occupied in the care and ministry of their idols, and there they learned the practices and customs of the courtiers. Since they took turns by their *mitas* and assigned time for service, after returning to their own province they maintained the practices they had seen and learned in the court, and they taught all this to their people.

In the process of moving the *mitimaes*, no thought was given to the distance that there was from their lands to where they were ordered to go, even though it was very great. On the contrary, not infrequently, it happened that they were transplanted from one end of the kingdom to the other; other times they were moved three or four hundred leagues, more or less, as the prince deemed fitting; for this reason, today in the provinces of Collao there are *mitimaes* who are natives originally from the provinces of Chinchaysuyu, and in the latter provinces there are many Indians from the former. It is a proven fact that the Indians of different provinces were so mixed and thrown together that there is hardly a valley or town throughout Peru where some *ayllo* and tribal group of *mitimaes* would not be found. Mainly, the Inca took two things into consideration when moving his subjects. The first one was (as has been stated) that they not go to a climate that was contrary to their nature, and the other, that all the provinces of his empire be well populated and well supplied with food and everything necessary for human life. For this reason, he put people from elsewhere in the sparsely populated areas, and from the places that had more people than could be comfortably supported, the Inca took colonies to settle in the less populous ones; and these people who by order of the king left their own land and the jurisdiction of their caciques and settled in strange lands, giving obedience at the same time to the local caciques, are the ones who were actually called *mitimaes* during the time of the Incas. But after the Spaniards occupied this land, this name has been extended to others who were not actually *mitimaes* formerly; in fact, the word was extended to include the Indians who, by order of their caciques and with their permission or that of the Inca, lived away from their towns and provinces of origin in the districts of other caciques, although they were not under the jurisdiction of the latter, but under the caciques of the province from whence they came or where they were born. For an explanation of this, it is necessary to presuppose the existence of an ancient custom of these people, and it is that when some province did not produce certain foods, especially none of their bread, which was *maize*, but was suitable for other uses, special arrangements were made. For example, due to the extreme cold, the provinces of Collao do not produce maize or other seeds or fruits of temperate lands, but they are very abundant in pasture lands and most appropriate for raising livestock and producing *papas* [potatoes], from which *chuño*, their substitute for bread, is made, as well as some other roots. For the inhabitants of these provinces, the Inca had picked out lands which lie in the hot valleys of the seacoast on one side and on the other side of the mountains toward the Andes; in these temperate valleys they plant the crops that they lack in their own lands; and since these valleys were from twenty, thirty, and more leagues away from their land and they could not come to cultivate them as a community group the way they do in the rest of the kingdom, the caciques took care to send, at the appropriate times, people to farm there, and after the crops were harvested, these people returned to their own towns. Apart from this, by order of the Inca, on the outskirts of each town there were a certain number of Indians with their women and houses; they resided permanently with their children and descendants in the aforementioned valleys, in order to care for and cultivate the *chacaras* of their caciques and their communities. These people, although they lived in the land of others, were under the jurisdiction of their own caciques, and not those of the land where they resided; but after the Spaniards entered into this kingdom, at the time that the land was visited for the first time in order to parcel it out and entrust it to the settlers, these Indians who were found in the aforementioned valleys, put there by their caciques for the reason just stated, were counted and assigned in repartimiento along with the natives of the district where they were living. They were also relieved from obedience to their former caciques, and they were put under the control of the caciques in whose jurisdiction and land they were living. Consequently, they were entrusted to the same encomendero to whom the district in question was parceled out and not to the encomendero of the *cacicazgo* of which they were natives. To all of these people who, in the aforementioned manner, had remained in the lands where we find them, we also give now the name of *mitimaes*, without distinguishing them from the first ones, the only people that were *mitimaes* at the time of the Incas.

Chapter 24: How the Incas organized the people that they subjugated into towns, and the way they arranged the towns It has

already
been stated that before they were governed by the Incas, the Peruvian Indians did not have towns arranged with the design and form
of our towns; rather, they lived in small groups of dwellings, generally located on hills and slopes, as a defense against the attacks that
they made on each other. When the Inca subjugated a province,
he obliged the inhabitants to leave their former dwellings and come
down from the high and rugged places where they lived to other
more appropriate places that were designated for them, and there
they were to settle and live as a community under the authority
of superiors who were put in charge of them. It is true that, although we give the name of "towns" to these settlements or groups
of huts into which the vassals of the Incas were organized, the name
"town" is appropriate only by comparison with the groups of dwellings where they lived before; in fact, ordinarily these places were
so small and poorly designed (except for the provincial capitals,
which were usually larger and better constructed) that they did not
even resemble our most humble villages.

Later, in order to find out the number of people that there were
in each province, including both the natives and the *mitimaes*, nobles and plebeians, it was ordered that everyone be counted according to age, social position, and marital status; special lists were
made of the taxpayers and of those who were exempt, of children,
women, and old people. Within the ranks of the taxpayers were
included only the males from among the common people who were
between twenty-five and fifty years old, more or less, since among
them age was not counted in years, nor did any of them know how
many years old they were. For this grouping, they were accounted
for on the basis of the duty and aptitude of each person, and a
record was made of the exact number of boys, youths, and adult
males; and the women were grouped in the same way. Their language has special nouns for each one of these age grades, the same
as there are in the Latin language to name children, girls, youths,
and adult males, and the Indians still maintain this custom. Thus,

in Quechua, the general language, a girl who has not reached the age for marriage is called *tasque,* and from the time she is old enough to marry until she marries, she is called *sipas;* and they always use this name for girls of different ages, as long as they have not married, from the time they are fifteen years old until they are past thirty, but upon getting married, even though they are only between fifteen and twenty years old, they are called *huarmi,* which means "woman," and this is the way that the people were counted during the time of the Incas.

In the numeration that was made of the Indians for the purpose of assigning them superiors, since the latter were classified according to the number of subjects they had (as will be explained in the next chapter), the only people to be counted were the taxpayers, the ones who were registered in the census as residents. These census lists were brought up to date during the census inspections; those who had died were removed; those who had been born were added; and those who had changed their status were changed to other lists.

The Incas made the same division throughout all of their kingdom that they had made in dividing Cuzco into Hanan Cuzco and Hurin Cuzco. Thus they divided each town and *cacicazgo* into two parts, known as the upper district and the lower district, or the superior part or faction and the inferior; and even though these names denote inequality between these two groups, nevertheless, there was none, except for this pre-eminence and advantage, which was that the group of Hanansaya got preference in seating and place over those of Hurinsaya; this is the same thing done at court, where some cities precede others in place and in speaking first. In everything else they were equal, and the Hurinsaya people were considered to be as good as the Hanansaya people. The object the Inca had in dividing the towns and provinces this way into factions and tribal groups was so that with this division of *ayllos* and tribal groups, in some measure the will of his vassals would be divided, so that they would not join together in order to promote uprisings, and if some rebellion or insurrection occurred, the people of one group would not agree and unite with the other, since they were men of opposing factions and opinions. Besides this, it was so that by means of this division a better account could be kept of the people that there were in each tribal group for the cases that might come up in which they would be needed, whether it be for war or peace, such as for public works, apportioning some tribute, and other things of this kind; and also it was so that in the convocations and general assemblies there would be fewer problems, since the people of each faction had their places and seats designated. Another reason that moved them to make this division was to give their subjects occasion for competition and rivalry in the jobs and work that they were ordered to perform; since those of each faction considered themselves to be as good as their opponents, they made every effort to surpass them and they were embarrassed if they lagged behind; and since they were eager to gain honors in things of less importance, when these people were needed for some important undertaking from which they would come out with either glory or disgrace, owing to the fact that the people of each group were identified, they would do great and distinguishing things. Moreover, the Incas knew by this means who were the most diligent in serving them on the occasions that came up in peace and war because the members of each tribal group were always present together and the people of one group did not mix with the people of the other one; and in the fiestas and public festivities, each group took great pains to distinguish themselves and perform better than their rivals in the inventions and festive dress that they came up with.

The vassals were not permitted to move from one province to another on their own free will. In fact, all vassals had to reside in their towns; they could not leave or wander around or take trips through strange lands without permission from their caciques. The men and women of each nation and province had their insignias and emblems by which they could be identified, and they could not go around without this identification or exchange their insignias for those of another nation, or they would be severely punished. They had this insignia on their clothes with different stripes and colors, and the men wore their most distinguishing insignia on their heads; each nation was identified by the headdress. Although they all had long hair, some had it cut off under their ears and others had it very long there; some wore braids, others let their hair hang loose, and the majority had it banded and encircled with diverse kinds of ligatures. The Cañares, who were the natives of Tumibamba, put on their heads a round wooden crown similar to the ring for a sieve or the rim of the small box used for preserves. The Indians of Cajamarca had their hair tied with a sling, and their neighbors used thin cords made of red wool that they wrapped around their heads many times. The Indians of Guaylas wore cords over their heads that they called *pillos*, and they also wore white slings around their heads; the Indians of Bonbon wore red and yellow kerchiefs around their heads. The Indians of Jauja wore red bands about the width of a hand. The Indians of Andaguaylas wrapped around their heads wool cords that came down under the chin. The Indians of Cuzco and all those of Inca lineage used a certain ligature called a *llauto*; it was a wool band the width of a finger with a few twists. The Colla Indians wore some tight-fitting wool caps, which were cone-shaped because they molded their heads that way; and their women wore pointed hoods, similar in shape to the hoods of friars. Except for these Colla Indians, the headdresses of all the Indian nations were in the form of a garland, and the majority of them were made of cords and braids with many twists formed like a coil of thread the size of the head, and the headdresses were distinguished by the fact that some were made of wool, others of *cabuya* (which is their hemp), some thinner than others, and some of one color and others of another; with these and other differences the Indians of each province were distinguished, but these insignias are used by only a few now, because the Indians are adopting the use of our hats.

They were so well known by these insignia that on seeing any Indian or when any Indian came before him, the Inca would notice what nation and province the Indian was from; and there is no doubt that this was a clever invention for distinguishing one group from another. Since the different nations that gathered for any general convocation called by the king were almost innumerable, since all the Indians were beardless and of the same color, aspect, and features, and since they used the same language and dressed the same way, it would be impossible to distinguish each nation in any other way. Moreover, when they went to war, it was something to see the large army composed of such a variety of people as there were marching, distributed in various regiments and squadrons; and with these insignias the variety was evident at a distance, and each group was easily identified by its general and the rest of the field officers, and in battle it was impossible for the nation that showed the most valor to be overlooked.

Chapter 25: Of the governors, caciques, and other superiors to whom the Incas delegated the governance of their states

With respect to the governors, magistrates, and all different kinds of ministers of justice, we find very little diversity in the government of the Incas, because all those who had some jurisdiction served as judges in their districts for all kinds of trials and offenses which did not fall outside of their authority. Therefore, the governors and judges were not differentiated on the basis of the type of cases that they were authorized to judge or the nature of their jurisdiction, but they were differentiated by the amount and size of their jurisdiction, just as this was given to each one by the king. For some it was restricted and limited, and for others it was very ample and full; therefore, in order to give a general rule, it will suffice to say that since all the vassals were counted and superiors were assigned to certain numbers of them, more ample power was given to those who governed a larger number of Indians. Starting with the ones that were most restricted and that had the least authority, for every ten Indians who were taxpayers and residents, the Inca assigned one superior to look after the other nine; and for every five of these decuries, there was one superior who had charge of fifty; another person governed a century, which consisted of two decuries of fifty each; for every five centuries or every five hundred, there was another superior; and two of these superiors of five hundred were under a millenary, who was in charge of a thousand people; ten of the latter were subject to another person, who was more important, for he had ten thousand people under his obedience, which made up a jurisdiction called Hunu. These superiors took their names from the number of taxpayers in their decuries: the one who was in charge of ten was called *chunca camayu*; the superior of fifty, *hilacata*;[15] the superior of one hundred, *pachac camayu*; the superior of five hundred, *pichcapachac camayu*; the superior of one thousand, *huaranca*; and the superior of ten thousand, *hunu*; and all of those who governed one hundred or more were commonly called *curacas*. Over all of these officials the Inca put a governor or viceroy in each province;

he was a person of authority and ordinarily the Inca's near relative or close associate; this official was called *tocricuc*, which means "inspector." Under his authority were the *hunus* of his district; usually there were three or four or more of them, according to how far the borders of his district extended, and he was directly under the king and the king's council.

The Inca's council was composed of four judges or councillors, called *apucunas*, who always resided in Cuzco; each one of them took care of the matters pertaining to the part of the kingdom that belonged to him. Since it was divided into four regions or quarters, one had charge of the Chinchaysuyu quarter, another the Collasuyu quarter, the third the Contisuyu, and the fourth the Antisuyu. Among these governors and caciques there was strict subordination, because the five decurions responsible for ten subjects each were under the authority of the superior of fifty, and two of these were under the superior of one hundred; and in this order the minor officials were under the higher officials up to the most important one, who was directly under the king. The posts of the four councillors and the viceroys were not hereditary. The Inca filled them with captains and noble lords related to him who deserved these posts because of their prudence, their valor, and the services that they had performed for the crown. It is true, however, that if the sons of the latter had wealth and ability, they were preferred over others.

Within each province there was a principal town that was ennobled by the king with a greater number of residents and better buildings; this town was the capital and metropolis of the province and the Hunu districts that were within its boundaries. In it there were exquisitely constructed royal palaces, a magnificent temple dedicated to the Sun, which was like the metropolitan church of the district, a monastery of *mamaconas*, the largest storehouses of the area, well supplied with food to sustain the ministers and servants of the Inca and the warriors who might pass by there, a royal *tambo*, and a large number of Indians to perform various jobs. The latter were sent from the towns of the territory to take their turns at the *mita* labor service, not to mention the many *mitimaes* who lived there. Such were the towns of Quito, La Tacunga, Tumibamba, Cajamarca, Jauja, Pachacama, Chincha, and Vilcas, as well as the rest that were in the four *suyus* or quarters of the kingdom.

In these provincial capitals there was in residence a *tocricuc* or representative of the Inca; this official had the power to adminis-

ter justice and punish offenses in accordance with their seriousness
and even give the death penalty, unless the culprit was a noble
or gentleman, in which case no decision was made without inform-
ing the king, and the same procedure was followed in all difficult
or important matters. He also had the authority to raise men and
form an army if there was a war or an uprising against the king.
He went out to visit his district at certain times; he had the tributes
and royal revenues collected and placed them in the warehouses,
replenished the supplies at the *tambos*, took a census of the children that were born each year and those who reached the age to
pay tribute, and listed those who no longer had this obligation.
All of this information was given to him in great detail by the caciques, and he took it to the king when he went to court, which
was once a year for the fiesta of Raymi;[16] at this time he also took
the tribute that the Inca ordered him to bring from his district,
and then he informed the Inca about the state of affairs there. In
short, this viceroy kept vigil over the lesser lords and caciques, and
he restrained them when they would go beyond their limits, particularly for treating their subjects badly and for any other excesses,
and he endeavored to find out about everything that went on in
his province in order to provide a remedy when it was necessary.

Except for these two kinds of magistrates and governors, the
rest, from the *hunus* on down, were the lords and caciques that
the Incas found in the provinces when they were conquered. In order
to keep from being hated by the natives, the Incas left the local
caciques in charge of their *cacicazgos*, as if they had been worthy
of them. Certainly it is true that they changed their dominions, taking away part of what some had and giving more to others. And if
any of them was guilty of something for which he deserved to lose
the dominion that he possessed, he was removed from it and it was
entrusted to another person from the same province, a kinsman
of his if there was one. With regard to the succession of the *cacicazgos* and dominions, the Inca kept the following order. If the
eldest son was competent and able to take over his father's *cacicazgo*, he was appointed to the post, and he was given the *duho*,[17]
which was a low stool or bench on which the caciques sat on taking
possession of their *cacicazgo*, and after; only they used this seat;
and if the eldest son was not competent and the second-born was,
the post was given to the latter; but if the second-born died, he was
not succeeded by his son, but by his nephew, who had not inherited
the post because he was under age; and in case none of the sons

of the cacique in question qualified for the post, nor did the deceased leave any brothers, the second person in importance of the district was appointed cacique if he had the talents and requirements for it. This procedure was followed in the appointment and succession of all the *curacas* and caciques, who were appointed by the Inca or by the *tocricuc* as a special commission for the Inca; an exception to this were the *pachac camayus*, in charge of one hundred Indians, and officials in charge of less than this, because they were named by the *guarancas*, or caciques in charge of one thousand subjects, to whom they were subordinated. But these appointments were subject to the consent and approval of the higher-ranking caciques, and they could not be removed from office during their lifetime, unless it was for a serious offense, and then they would be succeeded by their sons in the same way as the others. The officials in charge of fifty and ten subjects were selected by their caciques, who also removed them from office when they performed their duties badly, and these minor posts were not hereditary.

We call these lords caciques because they were first given this name on the island of Hispaniola; in the two general languages of this kingdom they are called *curacas* in Quechua and *maycos* in Aymara. All of these superiors and foremen had limited jurisdiction, the lower ranking more so than the higher ranking; and those who had the broadest jurisdiction, who were the *hunus*, could not give the death penalty; they only passed judgment in cases of minor offenses and negligence. They took the responsibility to parcel out the farmlands to their subjects, designating for each Indian the amount of land that he needed and also the water that he was to take to irrigate his *chacaras* and sown fields, if it was irrigated land. Moreover, those who had mines in their districts had gold and silver extracted. Once a year they gathered the young men and the marriageable women in the plaza, and they permitted the young men as well as the young women to pick out the persons to whom they wanted to get married, and the Indians received as their wives the women that the *hunu* gave them. The minor decurions were responsible for keeping track of those who were under them, and they were to make a complaint against them if they committed some offense. Furthermore, they took care to inform the appropriate person of the needs of their subjects, to count those who were born or died, the young men and women who reached the age to marry, and the old and deformed individuals that were in their decuries, so that orders could be given which would remedy all of their needs.

These decurions made reports of all these things to their immediate superiors, and the latter would pass the information on to their elders along the chain of command up to the Inca, who in this way kept informed every year about the Indians of all ages that there were in every province for taxes and *mitas*, and how many could respond for war, public works, and the other jobs in which the Inca usually occupied them.

Chapter 26: Of the laws and punishments with which the Incas governed their kingdom

Since the Indians lacked writing, they had no written laws, but the ones that their kings had established were preserved by tradition, use, and observance. I will record here the most important laws that were most prominent in their memories.

Where the Inca was present, he alone was the judge, and before him all offenses committed were tried; and where he was not present, his governors and caciques administered justice. They were selected to serve as judges according to the nature of the case.

When someone committed an offense that was deserving of punishment, he was apprehended and put in jail, and in order to bring his case to trial, he was taken out of jail and brought before the Inca or the presiding judge and *curaca*. During the trial, witnesses were brought out and confronted the accused. Each one told what he knew about the case against the accused, and in this way they convinced the judge. After the case was heard, without other proceedings, time limit, or delay, the Inca or judge pronounced the sentence and ordered that the delinquent be punished in accordance with his guilt.

He that killed another in order to rob him received the death penalty, and before it was executed, the guilty person was tortured in jail to increase the punishment, and after being tortured, he was killed.

He that killed by treachery was put to death publicly and insultingly, even though he was a nobleman and the dead man was of much lesser station.

He that killed by casting spells received the death penalty. This punishment was executed with much publicity, bringing together the people of the surrounding towns so that they would be present at the execution, and likewise all of his household and family were killed because it was presumed that they all knew that craft.

If someone was killed in a quarrel, first it was determined who caused it; if the dead man did, the killer was given a light punishment at the discretion of the Inca; if the one who caused the fight was the slayer, he received the death penalty, or at the very best, he was exiled to the provinces of the Andes, a sick and unhealthy land for the Indians of the sierra; there he would serve for his whole life, as on the galleys, in the Inca's *chacaras* of coca.

The cacique that killed one of his subjects without permission from the Inca was punished in public by being given certain blows on the back with a stone (this was called stone punishment, and it was a great insult). It was done even though the Indian may have been guilty of some act of disobedience against the cacique in question. If after the cacique was reprehended and punished, he repeated the same offense, he died for it; and if this punishment was not executed, due to pleas and intercessions, the Inca took the offender's *cacicazgo* away from him and gave it to another.

The husband that killed his wife for adultery was set free without punishment, but if he killed her due to anger and passion, he received the death penalty if he was an ordinary man, but if he was an important gentleman who commanded respect, he did not die, but he was given another punishment.

The woman that killed her husband received the death penalty, and it was executed in this way: she was hung up by the feet in some public place, and she was left like this until she died, without anyone daring to take her down.

The pregnant woman that took potions in order to kill her baby received the death penalty, and the same punishment was given to the person that gave her the potions or maliciously made her abort by striking her or some other mistreatment.

He that forced a single woman was given the stone punishment for the first time, and the second time, the death penalty.

He that forcibly corrupted some maiden received the death penalty if she was a noble woman, and if she was not, the first time, he was given a certain torture that was used, and the second time, he died.

He that committed adultery with another man's wife who was not of the nobility was tortured, but if she was of the nobility, he received the death penalty and she died also.

He that took the daughter from her father against his will got no punishment at all, if the daughter consented and was not forced and both were from the same town; however, the father could punish her if he wished for having taken a husband without his consent, but the Inca would order that they be apprehended and separated because nobody could take a wife without his permission.

When someone was found in the house of another with his daughter, if the father made a complaint, the delinquent was punished at the discretion of the Inca and his governor.

He that scaled the walls of the house or retreat of the *mama-conas* was killed; he was hung by the feet and left that way within the very house where he committed the offense, and if any of the *mamaconas* let him inside and sinned with him, she was given the same punishment.

In certain cases marriage was prohibited, and fornication in the cases in which marriage was prohibited was punishable with the death penalty, and this punishment was executed without remission, if the guilty party was not a noble, because a noble got only a public reprimand.

He that robbed without reason, besides paying for the stolen item if he had the resources, was exiled to the Andes, nor would he dare to return without the Inca's permission.

He that stole things to eat from necessity was reprimanded and given no other punishment than being warned to work and that if he did it again he would be punished by being struck on the back with a stone in public.

He that stole some fruit from the fields or orchards by necessity while traveling was killed for it if the property belonged to the Inca; if the property belonged to someone else, the man was pardoned.

When one of the Indians that served in the *tambos* did not turn over the load that he was carrying to the proprietor, the town that the Indian in question was from had to pay for it because the town was responsible for the service of that *tambo*, and the Indian was punished.

He that stole the water with which the *chacaras* were irrigated and brought it to his *chacara* before it was his turn was punished with an arbitrary penalty.

He that insulted another was given an arbitrary punishment, but he that had provoked the words was given a greater penalty.

He that injured another or caused some similar harm was punished with an arbitrary penalty, and if it was done treacherously, he was tortured.

He that maimed another in a quarrel to such an extent that the injured party could not do ordinary work was obliged to support the injured party from his own property, apart from the punishment that was given to him for the offense, and if he had no property, the Inca fed the injured party from his property, and the delinquent was given a greater punishment.

He that maliciously burned a bridge received the death penalty, and it was executed without fail.

The Indian that was disobedient to his cacique for the first time was given the punishment that the Inca deemed appropriate: the second time he did it, he was given the stone punishment, and the third time, death.

The *mitima*[18] Indian that left the place where he had been put by the Inca to serve as *mitima* was tortured the first time, and the second, he was killed.

He that changed the dress and insignia of the province where he was born committed a great offense against the Inca, against his nation, and against the province whose dress he adopted, and thus he was accused by all of them and punished with rigor.

He that removed the stone boundary markers or entered into the land or property of another was given the stone punishment for the first time, and the second time, he received the death penalty.

He that hunted without permission on any land where trespassing was prohibited was castigated by being struck on the back with a stone and tortured.

If someone's livestock damaged someone else's property, the owner of the property could take as much of the livestock as the damage was worth, and they had established how many feet of maize equaled a certain unit of measurement, by which they assigned a specific penalty that was paid in proportion to the amount of damage done.

When travelers had something stolen from them in a *tambo*, first of all the cacique in charge of the *tambo* was punished, and afterward the latter punished the rest of his subjects for negligence and not having been watchful.

The Indian that did not show the proper respect for the Inca and lords was put in jail, where he was left for a long time, and if, in addition to this, they found him to be guilty of something else, he was killed.

He that was a liar and perjurer was tortured as a punishment, and if he was very addicted to this vice and did not mend his ways with this punishment, he was killed in public.

If a governor failed to administer justice or covered up anything for reasons of bribery or because he was so inclined, the Inca himself punished him, taking his *cacicazgo* and post away from him and denying him the right to have others, and if the injustice involved something serious, the Inca ordered that the offender be killed.

The Incas had two prisons in Cuzco. One of them was half a league away from the city, in front of the parish of San Sebastian, which used to be called Arauaya and was located in a place named

Umpillay; here thieves and other criminals were punished with the death penalty, which was executed by hanging the wrongdoers upside down and leaving them hanging there until they died. The other prison was underground within the city; in it they had enclosed lions [pumas], bears, tigers [jaguars], and serpents; and the people who committed the most atrocious offenses, such as treason against the king and the like, were thrown to these wild beasts and eaten by them. These Indians had many other laws which were very beneficial for governing their republic well. True it is that some of them were too rigorous, such as those that required the death penalty and other exorbitant punishments for light offenses. Also it should be known that justice was not uniform and equal among them; although they prided themselves on being just and punishing all offenses, they always gave different penalties to the nobles and the wealthy than they gave to the humble and poor. This was due to an illusion that they had which was to say that a public reprimand was a far greater punishment for an Inca of noble blood than the death penalty for a plebeian. They justified their follies as well as their lofty positions on the assumption that they were children of the Sun and the first ones to found the religion and sacrifices of the Sun. Therefore, in the enforcement of their laws, they paid careful attention to these privileges, and thus the punishments were different according to the social status of the person that broke the laws. It turned out that for the same offenses that a common person would get the death penalty, nobles of Inca lineage would get no other punishment than a public reprimand; but this reprimand was so feared that the Indians affirm that it has happened only a few times, and very rarely has a noble been executed.

Chapter 27: Of the distinction between nobles and taxpayers that there was in this kingdom, and of the way that the latter had of paying tribute, and the way the king paid salaries to his ministers and rewarded his vassals for the services that they rendered to him

In the republic of the Incas the way that tributes were paid was very different from the one used in our republics of Europe. In the first place, all of his vassals, no matter what their rank and social status, if they were capable and were not crippled and disabled, were employed to serve their king personally with unusual obedience and servility, each one in his own way; nevertheless, they were not called tribute-payers and taxpayers unless they really and truly were and showed that they were by the manner in which they paid their tributes. In this respect the Incas did not lack the system that all good republics maintain of making a distinction between nobles and plebeians. In the first place, all of the Incas of royal blood enjoyed the privilege of being nobles; they are called *orejones* by our Spaniards because they had unusually large holes pierced in their ears. These Incas by blood, along with other gentlemen of other lineages who by privilege of the king also pierced their ears, made up the order of knighthood, which we can say corresponded to our knights of the military orders, and these Inca knights were professional military men like them.

After these, the governors, captains, caciques, and judges of the Inca, along with their children, enjoyed the immunities and exemptions of nobles; not only were all of them exempt from the taxes paid by the common people, but they received salaries from their king and they were supported with the tribute of personal service that the *mitayos* and taxpayers rendered to them. In spite of this they were not excused from demonstrating their vassalage and proper recognition of their king with valuable gifts and presents that they gave to him at certain times, but since these were voluntary and without a given rate or enforced payment, even though they were commonly observed and customary, they were not accounted for as tributes. Similarly, we do not say that in Spain the nobles and grandees pay tribute because they aid the king with personal services and donations for wars and administrative needs. Besides this, the work that the ministers did in the service of the Inca and public administration, which was very arduous, equaled, but with added profit, the service and tributes of the common people.

Everyone else in the kingdom was registered as a taxpayer up to the *hilacatas* and foremen of less than one hundred men; therefore, those who were responsible for one hundred Indians or more were exempt from paying taxes, and those who had fifty men or less under them were counted along with the taxpayers, and as such they did manual labor in works and jobs along with the others. Only the *auca camayos* were included within the ranks of the taxpayers. *Auca camayos* means "people who are fit for war" or "able-bodied adults"; normally they were from twenty-five to fifty years of age, more or less, or married men even though they were not yet twenty-five years old; and one resident with his household and minor children was counted as one tribute-payer. The nobles and important people who were exempt from taxes, as has been stated, never did manual labor or artisan work. They served in honorable offices and posts, for which they received appropriate salaries, and they were much honored; and even though they were not employed in public offices, they were honored in accordance with their social status. Along with the nobles, women enjoyed exemption from paying tribute; this applied to all women of whatever age, marital status, or social standing, even though they were widows. Moreover, also exempt were all the blind, crippled, maimed, and sick people who were unable to work. In short, no one was registered as a tribute-payer except the males of the common people who were able to work at the time on the jobs which the people performed as a community.

All tribute was paid in personal services; they did manual labor in the works and jobs that I will describe in the following chapters. In place of paying tribute, the craftsmen worked in the service of the Inca, the Religion, or their caciques; each one performed the craft that he knew, such as making garments, working gold or silver, extracting these metals from the mines and processing them, making clay and wooden cups, and the other crafts; in these jobs they spent all of their time. As long as they were employed in fulfilling their quotas and tributes with these crafts and jobs, both the crafts-men and the artisans, as well as the communities of the towns and *mitayos*, were supported at the expense of the owner of the estate where they worked or the person they served, even though it might be the estate of the Inca or Religion; and from this same estate they were also given the tools along with the rest of their instruments and necessary equipment; they did not invest anything of their own except manual labor.

The pay and salaries that the Inca gave to his ministers, gov-ernors, and caciques for the work in the offices where they served was not a fixed and definite amount of something in kind, such as gold or silver, but was given in personal service of the subjects that they had in their districts and under their command. They were assigned a certain number of *mitayos*, the number that would suf-fice for their personal needs and for the jobs within their houses, to each one according to his social status and in order to maintain the authority of his office, and the ordinary rate was one *mitayo* for every hundred subjects that the official governed. Therefore, the *curaca* responsible for one hundred taxpayers was given one servant or *mitayo*; the one responsible for five hundred got five; the one responsible for a thousand got ten; and in this proportion the rest were assigned servants. Apart from these servants that were given to the officials for their retinue and service within their houses, the communities of their towns came to cultivate their *chacaras*, con-struct their houses, look after their livestock, if they had any, along with the other jobs on which, by order of the Inca, the subjects were obliged to serve them; and this service from their subjects was in place of a salary.

With regard to rewarding merits, they did not fail to proceed with care either. The ones that the Incas customarily rewarded were the captains who had distinguished themselves in war and the people who performed some special service for the Inca. The king remunerated these people by giving them valuable jewels or fine garments, and the most common gift and the one the vassals es-teemed the most was some of the maidens that used to be gathered as tribute, as well as livestock and farmlands that were retained as their property and that of their heirs.

Chapter 28: Of the division that the Inca made of the farmlands, and of the estate and rents that the Inca and Religion received

from them
When the Inca settled a town, or reduced one to obedience, he set up markers on its boundaries and divided the fields and arable land within its territory into three parts, in the following way: One part he assigned to Religion and the cult of his false gods, another he took for himself, and a third he left for the common use of the people. It has not been possible to determine whether these parts were equal in any towns and provinces; however, it is known that in many places the division was not equal, but depended on the availability of land and the density of the population. In some provinces, the part assigned to Religion was greater; in others, that belonging to the Inca was greater; and in some the portion belonging to the community exceeded either of the other two because it was always considered important that the people be well provided with food. Accordingly, in some regions, there were entire towns which, with their territory and all that it produced, belonged to the Sun and the other gods, such as Arapa [northwest side of Lake Titicaca] and others; and in other provinces (and this was more usual), the king's share was the largest. In these lands assigned to Religion and to the crown, the Inca kept overseers and administrators who took great care in supervising their cultivation, harvesting the products and putting them in storehouses. The labor of sowing and cultivating these lands and harvesting their products formed a large part of the tribute which the taxpayer paid the king. The boundaries of the lands and fields belonging to each one of these divisions were kept so exact, and the care and protection of these markers of the fields of the Inca and of Religion, the responsibility of cultivating them first and at the proper season, and their protection against damage or loss, were so impressed upon the Indians that it was one of the most important religious duties that they had; so much so that no one dared pass by these fields without showing their respect with words of veneration that they had reserved for the purpose.

The lands dedicated to the gods were divided among the Sun,

Lightning, and the rest of the idols, shrines, and *guacas* of general worship and *guacas* belonging to each province and town; the amount belonging to each god and *guaca* was specified, and these fields were cultivated before the others of the Inca and the community. The people came to cultivate them in the following way: If the Inca himself, or his governor, or any other important lord happened to be present, he started the work with a golden *taclla* or plow, which was brought to the Inca, and, following his example, all the other lords and nobles who accompanied him did the same. However, the Inca soon stopped working, and after him the other lords and nobles stopped also, and they sat down with the king to have their banquets and fiestas, which were especially notable on such days. The common people remained at work, and with them the *curaca pachacas*, who worked a while longer than the nobles; thereafter they supervised the work, giving any orders that were necessary. But the *hilacatas* and decurions in charge of ten subjects worked all day, as did the ordinary Indians who had no official position. These Indians divided the work they had to do by lines, and each task or section of work was called a *suyu*, and, after the division, each man put into his section his children and wives and all the people of his house to help him. In this way, the man who had the most workers finished his part, or *suyu*, first, and among them he was considered a rich man; and the poor man was he who had no one to help him finish his work, so he spent a longer time working. This same system was followed by each of the lords and *curacas* in his district, the most important man starting the work and soon leaving it, and the nobles following him according to their rank and social standing.

When the *chacaras* of Religion were finished, the fields of the Inca were immediately sown, and in their cultivation and harvest, the same order was followed. All of the people who were present came in a group, and with them the lords up to the most important caciques and governors, dressed in their best and singing appropriate songs. When they cultivated the fields of Religion, their songs were in praise of their gods, and when they cultivated the king's fields, in his praise.

The third part of the land, assigned to the people according to the division above, was in the manner of commons, it being understood that the land was the property of the Inca and the community only had the usufruct of it. It cannot be determined whether this share was equal to the others or greater, although it is true that each province and town was given sufficient lands to support its

population. Every year the caciques distributed these lands among
their subjects, not in equal parts, but proportionate to the number
of children and relatives that each man had; as the family grew
or decreased, its share was enlarged or restricted. No one was granted more than just enough to support himself, be he noble or plebeian, even though a great deal of land was left over to lie fallow and
uncultivated; and this method of dividing the fields is practiced to
this day in the provinces of Collao and elsewhere; I have been present when it was done in the province of Chucuito [western side
of Lake Titicaca].

When it was time to sow or cultivate the fields, all other tasks
stopped, so that all taxpayers together, without anyone absent, took
part, and if it was necessary to perform some job in an emergency,
like a war or some other urgent matter, the other Indians of the
community themselves worked the fields of the absent men without requesting or receiving any compensation beyond their food,
and, this done, each one worked on his own fields. This assistance
which the community rendered to its absent members caused each
man to return home willingly when he had finished his job; for
it happened that when the Indian returned to his house after a long
absence, he might find that a harvest he had neither sown nor reaped
would be gathered into his house. I even met a very old cacique
in the town Moho [northeastern side of Lake Titicaca] who had
lived at the time of the Incas, and he still practiced this custom.
For this reason that town was maintained better than any other in
Collao, and I was amazed to see how well populated it was, but
the people explained to me that this was due to the good administration of their cacique in having someone cultivate the *chacaras*
of the residents who were absent.

By judging from this division of lands, it is evident how absolute
the power of the Inca was over everything his vassals possessed.
In fact, no one was permitted to have a *chacara* or field, or even
power over one single span of land set aside, except as a special
favor of the Inca. And outside of this kind of a gift, there was no
other way to acquire real estate property. And the Inca usually did
this favor for some captains and individuals renowned for their
merits, in remuneration for their services, such as for having done
some heroic deed in the war, or having had the ingenuity to do
something of great usefulness for the republic, such as making some
bridge, irrigation ditch, or road, or for being sons of caciques that
had served him well, or for other reasons of this sort. And such
land granted to an individual was passed on to his descendants on

the condition that neither the first possessor nor his successors
could transfer it, exchange it, divide it, or dispose of it in any way
or manner. However, one who represented the legal person of the
ayllo and lineage, as the eldest member, had authority over it, and
he divided it each year among the kinsmen according to their customs. Therefore, they all benefited from it, and it was parceled out
according to the number of members. If a son of the first lord had
six children, and another had two children, each one, both the sons
and the grandchildren, got equal parts of the land, and it was divided
into as many parts as there were persons in the lineage; and in this
they used the following system. At the proper time, they all came
to sow the land; and the same ones who were present to do the sowing were required to harvest and divide up the products, and whoever was not present when the sowing was done did not get any
share, nor could he have anyone take his place as a substitute. However, even though he were absent for ten or twenty years, he did
not lose his rights upon returning; and although there were so many
kinsmen that there was no more for each one than an ear of maize,
this custom was followed. Therefore, according to what has been
stated, it is understood how the land used by the Indians belonged
to the community of an entire town; and the lands that were held
by individuals as a favor from the king also belonged in common
to the members of the lineage of the first owner, and these lands
were not divided, and the work of cultivating them was done on a
communal basis, and the individual who did not work in sowing got
no share of the harvest.

Chapter 29: Of the order in which the domesticated livestock was distributed, and the income that the Inca and Religion received in livestock and in clothing from its wool; and how the hunting grounds and woods were royal patrimony

The Inca had the same division made of all the domesticated livestock, assigning one part to Religion, another to himself, and another to the community; and not only did he divide and separate each one of these parts, but he did the same with the grazing land and pastures in which the livestock was pastured, so that the herds were in different pastures and could not be mixed. The Inca divided these pastures and had them marked in each province. The pastures of Religion and the Inca were called *moyas* of Religion and *moyas* of the Inca, and it was unlawful to put the livestock of Religion in the *moyas* of the Inca, nor could the opposite be done, for each herd or flock had its own specified district. The borders between provinces were also divided; the pasture lands of different provinces were not common, not even for the livestock of the same owner. For example, there were pastures in the province of Chucuito where the Inca's livestock was raised in that province; and the animals that the Inca himself had in the bordering province of Pacages could not cross over there to graze. In keeping these animals, great care was taken to assign herdsmen and foremen to count the increase in the flocks and the animals that died; and in contributing the people necessary for this purpose, the towns paid a considerable amount of their tribute. The part of the livestock that belonged to the common people was much smaller than either of the other two parts, as can be noticed by the names that were given to each one. The herds belonging to Religion and to the Inca were named *capac llama*, and the herds owned by either the community or privately were named *huacchac llama*, which means "rich herds" and "poor herds."

Moreover, the king took animals from the part belonging to the community; these were given to caciques and persons who served him as a favor to them; the king also ordered that the residents be allotted the number of animals they needed. None of the animals that the king gave as a favor to develop and start herds could be divided or transferred, any more than the lands; thus, the heirs of the first owner possessed his herds in common.

This domesticated livestock of llamas was one of the greatest riches that the Indians had. In order to conserve it so that it would always be on the increase, the Inca had ordered two very important things. First, any animal that got *caracha* (a certain illness like mange or scab which these animals often catch, and many die of it) was to be immediately buried alive and very deep, and no one was to try to cure the sick animal or kill it for food, and this was done in order to prevent the disease from spreading, for it is extremely contagious; second, the females were not to be killed for sacrifices or for any other reason. Owing to these measures, the vast number of these animals in their kingdom was incredible.

All of the animals were sheared at the proper time; the herds of Religion, those of the Inca, and those of the community were each sheared separately; the wool was placed in storehouses, which were also kept separate. Of this wool, that is to say the wool of Religion and of the Inca, the governors ordered all different kinds of clothing to be made each year, especially from *cumbi* for the Inca and Religion, and every town had craftsmen who made this fine clothing, and they were called *cumbi camayos*. With respect to the amount, there was no limit, but they were ordered each year to make whatever the Inca or his governors deemed appropriate, without giving the craftsmen any pay other than their sustenance; and this was another kind of tribute which was brought to the king.

The wool from the livestock of the community was distributed among the common people. Each one was given a sufficient but moderate amount for himself, his wife, and his children; and the cacique visited the people to see if they had made clothing, and he that was negligent in this was not left without being punished, and with this order and care, they all had clothing. On distributing this wool of the community, if the person to whom it was given already had wool from his livestock, this was not taken into consideration; wool was allocated to everyone, and it was not withheld from someone who had his own, and he was given the same share as everyone else, even though some families might have a great quantity of their own livestock.

Also marked were the hunting grounds and preserves of wild animals such as guanacos, vicuñas, and deer, but as for other such animals that are usually harmful, there were no restrictions. These hunting grounds were not divided into parts as was done with the farmlands and domesticated animals. The preserves of each province were set apart so that the inhabitants of one province could not go hunting within the borders of another province. Moreover, the Inca made all the hunting grounds part of the royal patrimony and his own property so that no one could hunt on them without his permission or that of his governors. This permission was granted at certain times for a limited number of animals according to the need, and killing females was also prohibited. With the hunting method they used, called *chacos* [public hunts], they could accomplish both these things very well.

The same thing was established with reference to the woods, *arcabucos*, and jungles in the places where they were of some importance; but where the land is rugged or the woods are thick, no attention was paid to them; only the level lands without dense forests were the property of the Inca and they were called *moyas* of the Inca, but the usufruct of these lands was also for the common use of the town in whose limits and district the woods and forests fell. However, the wood was cut with permission and on orders, according to the needs of each town.

Chapter 30: Of the storehouses belonging to the Inca and to Religion, the goods that were collected in them, and how these goods were used

By order of the Inca, large storehouses and granaries were made which the Indians called *colcas*. They were located in all the provinces of Peru; the tribute and goods belonging to the king and Religion were enclosed and stored in them. These royal and sacred storehouses were located particularly in three places. First, in the lands of the king and of Religion in each province where the products and tributes were stored immediately as they were collected; second, others were in the capital cities of the jurisdiction where the viceroys resided; and third, storehouses were located in the city of Cuzco. Moreover, for all of the storehouses, the same products and foods were allotted. The storehouses of the crown and of Religion were different, although they were always together, like the owners of what was stored in them and the uses to which it was put. The storehouses of the Inca were much bigger and longer than those of Religion; this implies that the Inca's share of lands and animals was greater than that which was given to the gods.

Ordinarily these storehouses or warehouses were built outside of town on a high, cool, and windy place near the royal road; today we can see the ruins of these storehouses on the sides of hills and slopes. There were many small square houses like ordinary lodgings, similar to small towers separated one from another by about two or three steps and placed in a very orderly and symmetrical way. In some places there were more, in others less, according to what was needed; and where there were more of these small towers and *buhios* together, we call them the bigger and longer storehouses and where there were less, smaller storehouses. Sometimes the rows had twenty, thirty, fifty, and more houses, and since they were located on high places in an orderly way, they looked very good, and in fact the same can even be said today of the walls that are still standing in some places, and these walls are so well preserved that the only thing they lack is the roof. The Indians put these storehouses in high places so that what was stored in them would be kept from getting wet and humid and from spoiling in any way; and by dividing the *buhios* in the aforementioned way, the Indians tried to prevent damage from fires so that if one of them caught on fire (which would easily happen because these houses had thatched roofs), since the fire could not be put out, no more would be lost than the contents of the house that was burning, and the fire would not spread to the rest.

All of the grain, seeds, and products that were gathered from the lands of Religion and those of the Inca, with everything else that the towns contributed in kind, was put by the Indians of the community in the first storehouses so that the Inca and his governors could distribute it as they wished. The collectors of the royal revenue and the revenue of Religion would gather from these storehouses at certain times the amount of goods that were ordered, and they had part of it taken to the storehouses of the provincial capital cities and part of it taken to the city of Cuzco at a specified time, which was before the fiesta of Raymi. The amount that was taken to Cuzco, both from the goods of the king and from those of Religion, was not always the same, but it varied according to how the harvests had been and the abundance or scarcity that there was in the storehouses of the provinces. Care was always taken to keep both these provincial storehouses as well as those of the capital cities of the provinces well supplied for ordinary consumption and special needs. In preparing these products after they were gathered, the same system was followed as in planting and cultivating them; that is to say that the people who were employed in this task ate at the expense of the owner of the aforementioned products; and from his property, the people were given all that was necessary for transportation from one place to another; therefore, the products belonging to Religion were transported on animals that belonged to Religion and the Inca's products were transported on his animals; and the goods, both those of Religion and those of the Inca, which were taken to Cuzco for the fiesta of Raymi, went on animals belonging to the owner of what was carried, and these goods normally were carried on the same animals that were taken to Cuzco at this time for the sacrifices to their false gods and for the royal fiestas. Therefore, the Indians who paid tribute by doing these tasks and jobs incurred no other expenditure, nor did they put forth anything other than their work.

The goods of Religion were used for no other purpose than the vain cult of their idols, namely for what was spent on the temples and *guacas* that were rebuilt and on repairing the old ones, for the sustenance and clothing of the priests, *mamaconas*, attendants, and caretakers of the temples, and for the sacrifices that were made during the course of the year to the *guacas* of the provinces and towns, according to what was ordained. The majority of these goods of Religion were taken to the city of Cuzco for the same purpose. The use and consumption of these goods brought from throughout the kingdom was on a very large scale. The concentration of their sacrifices was in that court because the temples of the principal gods of the kingdom were there, where a great many priests and persons dedicated to the cult of their gods resided, and their only function was to care for the idols and make ordinary sacrifices.

The Inca distributed his goods and royal income in the following order. What was brought for him to his court came there before the fiesta of Raymi, and commonly they brought him a large quantity of animals, clothing, and the other necessary things so that there would be an abundance of everything and enough left over to allot whomever the Inca wished. The finest and most valuable things, such as gold, silver, precious stones, feathers, exquisite clothing, and other things of this kind, were normally brought to the Inca by the cacique of each province himself or by one of the cacique's sons or kinsmen. When the Inca received these tributes, which, as has already been stated, belonged to him because these goods had been worked and prepared in his name and for him, he had some cups of gold, silver, or precious wood given to the bearer; according to who it was, the Inca would also give the bearer some of the exquisite clothing that was brought or some other clothing similar to it, in order to do him a greater favor and good turn. Then the Inca would have the storehouses that were in Cuzco furnished with all the necessary supplies that would be consumed during the year, particularly for sacrifices and offerings to the gods. In the sacrifices made by order of the Inca in the ordinary and special fiestas, a large part of the income and tributes was burned and consumed.

Finally, all of the royal goods that were gathered and kept in the storehouses were distributed and used by the king in the following way. The Inca ordered that of the exquisite clothing and other precious objects from each province, a certain amount was to be given to lords, *curacas*, and important people of the area, according to the social status and rank of each one. Although it is true that the women and Indian servants of the aforesaid lords made clothing for them, it was ordinary and coarse, used only to dress their servants; but the magnificent clothing made of fine *cumbi* worn by the caciques and lords could be made only for the Inca, and he hand-

ed it out to these lords. Apart from this, at many of the fiestas
that were held during the year, as a favor to the lords, caciques,
and nobles, the Inca gave out magnificent shirts and blankets, gold
and silver cups, necklaces, bracelets, and other jewels of emeralds,
turquoise, and other precious stones set in gold. Moreover, all of the
service done for the royal household and for the bodies of the dead
Incas was supported from the Inca's property; and the king provided
food for his relatives and the lords he had with him, and all of his
garrisons, presidios, and soldiers, who got no other salary except
their food and clothing, and the pay was two garments for each
soldier. Furthermore, the Inca would give his caciques permission
to allow part of the clothing and food that was in the storehouses
of their districts to be given out, even though there was no need for
it, in order to keep his vassals happy.

Therefore, it seems that all of the work done by the Indians
would turn out to be beneficial to them, especially if they were
in need of it; and since the clothing that some made and the products that they harvested were not needed by the workers themselves, the Inca gave it to others, but not a thing left his kingdom for
foreign kingdoms. In fact, from these same storehouses he ordered
alms to be given to the poor and needy, and after the province was
supplied with the necessary provisions, he had them supply the
needs of other surrounding provinces; and thus foods were carried
from one province to another, and not infrequently, foods were transported from the storehouses of the coastal plains to the sierra and
vice versa. All this was done with so much care, order, and speed
that nowhere was anything lacking nor was anyone in dire straits,
even though there were lean years; for the provisions went from
person to person where they were needed, and what was left over or
not necessary was kept in the storehouses for times of need. These
storehouses were always very well supplied because ordinarily there
was food gathered from ten or twelve years back. There were in
these storehouses and warehouses inspectors, overseers, and accountants for the administration of the royal goods; these officials
kept careful records of all goods received or consumed of everything
that was sent away.

These storehouses were always kept full, and all of the things
that the towns gave as tribute were the supplies and provisions
kept in them. There was a large amount of maize, *quinua*, *chuño*
[dried potatoes], beans, and other vegetables; ample amounts of
charque or dried meat from llamas, deer, and vicuñas; different
kinds of clothing made from wool, cotton, and feathers; shoes that

they call *ojotas*; arms, according to which ones were used in the provinces, to supply the soldiers when they moved from one place to another; and a large amount of all the other things that were sent from throughout the kingdom as tribute to the king; this even included red sea shells, which were taken to Cuzco from Tumbez, more than three hundred leagues, to make *chaquira*, which were very thin beads that looked like coral. Our Spaniards found these storehouses full of all of these things; even during the time of the wars that, on entering this land, our men waged with the natives until our men subjugated them, the towns charged with supplying their respective storehouses continued to gather in them, as they used to do, the products from the lands of the Inca and from the lands of Religion as well as the rest of the royal income, and part of this was consumed and used in sacrifices, for the products were given to those who were in charge of doing it before, and the rest was kept in the storehouses, for they believed that the time would come when they had to give an account about it to the Inca; and thus when President Pedro de la Gasca passed through the Valley of Jauja with His Majesty's army on the trail of Gonzalo Pizarro, although la Gasca stayed there for seven months, there was no scarcity of food for the soldiers during this entire time. The products of many years were found in the storehouses; there were more than five hundred thousand fanegas[19] of food; and it was understood that, had it been necessary, there was much more available in the many storehouses of that valley.

Chapter 31: Of the roads that the Incas made throughout their kingdom and the labor service that was provided by the provinces to

repair them The Incas had two royal roads constructed that ran the length of their kingdom from the province of Quito to the Kingdom of Chile, which is nine hundred leagues, one along the plains and seacoast and the other inland through the provinces of the sierra. In some places it was thirty leagues from the coast, in others fifty or sixty, more or less, according to the lay of the land. Apart from these roads, which ran together from one end of the kingdom to the other like parallel lines, there were in different places four to six other transverse roads going from one side to the other; these cut across the two main roads already mentioned. The length of the transverse roads was equal to the width of the Peruvian Empire. The most important of these ran through the city of Cuzco, crossing the long road of the sierra in the city plaza, and on one side it ran toward the province of Contisuyu and the Arequipa region, and on the other side it ran through the province of Antisuyu, which we call the land of the Andes now. Another road passed from the port of Tumbez to the sierra; another from the Valley of Trujillo to the provinces of Cajamarca and Chachapoyas. Two others ran through the district of this Archbishopric of Lima, one through the Valley of Paramonga and another from the valley of this city of Los Reyes [Lima] up to the Valley of Jauja; through the province of Chuquiabo there was another from the seacoast to the provinces of Chunchos. Apart from these, which were the most important, others went up from the valleys of the seacoast, cutting across the snow-covered cordillera, reaching the towns farthest to the east and most remote in the kingdom. But none of these transverse roads was as celebrated or as well known and famous as the first two, which, truly, considering the lack of equipment and tools, were magnificent constructions, which could be compared favorably with the most superb roads of the Romans.

First I will treat the coast road, and then the sierra road. The length of the coast road has already been stated. Its width is not the

same everywhere; this is due to the different kinds of land where
it passes; but if the differences are reduced to generalities, there
are three kinds, namely, level, fertile valleys and [two kinds of]
wasteland. In some places the latter is level and in others it is broken by rugged and uneven sierras. On the plains as well as on the
slopes, most of the wasteland is dry, sandy ground, although firm
ground is not lacking in some places and in others there are craggy
sierras with boulders and slabs of stone. Through all of the level
land, both fertile valleys and fields as well as desert wastelands,
the road runs in a perfectly straight line, but with this difference,
in the valleys it is so narrow as to be no more than twelve to fifteen
feet wide, and only two or three men on horseback can go abreast
on it at one time; and on either side it was enclosed by thick mud
walls which were two or three *estados*[20] high. Some parts of these
walls are still standing, although with the passage of time the majority have fallen down by now, and since the road through these valleys is so narrow, we call the stretches of walls that have remained
callejones del Inca [lanes of the Inca]. An example is the part of
it that we see running across this Valley of Lima from the Cara-
guayllo River to the slopes near Surco; it passes by the last houses
of this city of Los Reyes, and commonly we call it the Callejon
de Surco because it goes on the road to the town of this name. On
the basis of this stretch of road that cuts across this valley and other
such roads of the seacoast that I have seen and walked on, one un-
derstands what the coast road was like formerly. The road that
crosses this Valley of Lima, which is four or five leagues in length,
goes in a perfectly straight line; and during the time of the Incas,
it was enclosed by mud walls, and the surface was flat and clean,
without rocks or gullies where one could stumble.

The part of this road located on level desert wasteland did not
have a specific width, nor was it enclosed on the sides, nor are there
any signs of it having been made by human skill or work. The
majority of the earth is such loose sand that the tracks of those
who passed yesterday cannot be seen today, and with the least wind
that blows the road is blurred so much that no sign remains of
where it goes. Thus it would hardly be possible to make anything
durable on it, especially since almost all of the land of this kind
is full of sand heaps or dunes that the wind blows from one place
to another and commonly many of them are shifted into the middle
of the road in such a way that the travelers are obliged to go curving
around these dunes. Nevertheless, so that those who traveled across
this sandy ground would not get lost, since the trail was usually

covered, during the time of the Incas there were heavy posts driven into the ground at intervals within sight of each other that served as signposts and guides for the travelers. According to the Indians, the reason why the road was enclosed with mud walls in the valleys of *chacaras* and sown fields was so that when the armies marched through there, the soldiers would be kept within those walls and would not stray out into the *chacaras* and fields and damage them. As proof that orders were given to build walls along this road for this reason, a strong argument is the fact that not only this main road was lined with walls, but also all the little roads and paths that crossed these valleys from one place to another. We see this today in the Valley of Lima, where there are still innumerable large walls and small lanes lined with tall, thick walls, so narrow that two men cannot ride abreast on horseback along them, but must go single file.

The part of this road of the plains that reaches the sierra and broken land was made by hand with much work and skill. If it passed through hillsides with cliffs and slabs of rock, a narrow path, only wide enough for one person leading a llama or sheep, was dug in the boulder itself; and this type of construction did not run very far, but as soon as the boulder or slab of rock was passed, the road widened again. On some rugged slopes where the road could not be made across the middle of the hillside, strong steps were made of flat stones that still endure. Across all the other sierras and slopes, the road was as we see it today, leveled off and ten or twelve feet wide. Where the slope was very steep, there was a wall of dry stone about one to three *estados* high, and inside it was filled up with earth so that it was made even and perfectly level on both sides; in other places, on the upper side, they had a wall made of stone without mortar, one-half *estado* high, like a terrace, that would hold back the earth and rocks that rolled down from above, so that the road would not be blocked. Along the parts of these hills and slopes where there was some ravine or narrow gorge that cut off the road, even though it was three or four *estados* deep, rock walls were also made from below and built up to the level of the road. Therefore, the most work and skill necessary to construct and repair this road was in the sierras and places subject to landslides, where, if the road was broken up, it would be impossible to walk until it was mended; and so much for the road of the plains and seacoast.

The sierra road ran uninterrupted and open because, since it did not pass through sandy ground like the coast road, it was not blocked anywhere like that one. With respect to its construction,

design, and width, it was similar to the coast road, except that,
since the sierra is rainy, having lakes, springs, and marshes, it was
necessary to make frequent repairs where the water washed away
and ruined the road, and in the very flat places subject to flooding,
with marshes and bogs, they had carefully constructed causeways
that were one, two, and three leagues long in some places and fifteen
to twenty feet wide, perfectly straight and raised above the level
of the ground as much as was needed, in some places from two
to four cubits. The material from which they were normally made
was the sod from the ground next to the causeways, and since with
time the ground had been compacted and grass had grown along the
edges, the causeways were very solid and strong, as we see them
today in many places, particularly in the Valley of Jaquijaguana,
next to Cuzco, and in the Dioceses of Chuquiabo, on the road between Chucuito and Zepita [western side of Lake Titicaca]. Since
the royal highway goes along the banks of Lake Titicaca, when
the lake fills up during the rainy season, the area around the road
is inundated, and only the causeway remains in view; and people
walk along the road, while water covers the ground on both sides,
sometimes one-half *estado* deep and other times more. Beneath
these causeways there are culverts and drains with small bridges
made of large stone slabs under which the water runs from one side
to the other without stopping or overflowing. In some places these
causeways are made of rocks and large, flat stone slabs, and generally, where there are quagmires and bogs, the road is well paved with
these stone slabs and large rocks for many leagues. Such is the one
that passes through the province of Conchucos and other parts of
the sierra. At the present time these causeways are not as complete
as they were when we found them; this is due to our carelessness
and neglect. In many places the rains have washed them out and
ruined them, and since no effort is made to repair them, they are
deteriorating more and more, and over these marshy places it becomes impossible to walk except during the dry season. Across the
level and firm ground that was not sown with maize, there was
nothing constructed except the road, which was well made and
marked, and the rocks and grass were cleared away. Between the
chacaras and fields of maize and other vegetables that grow in mild
climates, the road was lined on both sides, although not with such
large walls as we see on the coast; at least such large ruins and
clear signs of them do not remain. I have walked three hundred
leagues on this sierra road, and I have not seen it lined with walls
anywhere, and in any valley that the road crosses along the coast

there are extensive stretches of the ancient walls. I think that the reason for this is that since it rains so much in the sierra, the rains have been wearing away and breaking down these fences because they were made of earth, and on the plains of the coast, since it never rains, these unfavorable conditions have not been present to destroy them.

The task of repairing these roads and the bridges that were on them for crossing the rivers was the responsibility of the inhabitants of the provinces and towns that the roads ran through. The people came to these tasks in community groups, according to the number of workers required from each province in the work distribution that the caciques and governors made for this purpose, and the service and work that they rendered for this type of tribute was very hard. In fact we see now that the power and authority of the viceroys and corregidores is not enough (although some of them normally attend to it more carefully than others) to keep these roads mended and repaired. However, it was not as much work to repair them in Inca times as it is at the present time. This is true on the one hand because there were so many more people then than now that there is no comparison, and there were fewer roads; on the other hand, at that time the only traffic was pedestrians, generally barefooted, and the animals of the land. Therefore, the roads did not wear out before as much as they do now, because now they are used by horseback riders, mule trains, and, in some cases, wagons.

Chapter 32: Of the tambos and chasques and the tribute that the Indians gave in providing the labor service for them

The two royal highways of the sierra and the coastal plains, as we have said, passed through the principal towns of the kingdom, which were the capital cities of the provinces, such as Cajamarca, Jauja, Vilcas, and other places of the sierra, and on the coast, Tumbez, Chimo, Pachacama, Chincha, and other large towns. The ones on the sierra road were located at intervals of twenty to thirty leagues, more in some places and less in others, and on the coast road, there was one in every important valley. In these towns there were royal lodgings and storehouses called *tambos*, supplied with a great abundance of all the things that could be obtained in these places. Thus the Inca could be accommodated when he passed by there and be served with no less luxury, majesty, and splendor than he would in his court, and everything necessary could be given to the garrison soldiers and the armies when they passed through these towns. Apart from these large towns and many other small ones located on these royal highways or not very far from them, there were well-supplied *tambos* and storehouses at intervals of a day's journey, which was every four to six leagues, even though it was an uninhabited place and a desert. These *tambos* were the same as our inns and hostelries, except that they were used in a very different way because they were not privately owned. The community of the town and province constructed them and had the obligation to keep them clean, in good repair, and provided with servants. In them the armies, governors, and the rest of the royal ministers were given accommodations, and they were given their meals and everything else that they needed from the Inca's storehouses that were in the *tambos*; and the governors who resided in the capital cities of the provinces took great pains to see that the people cared for the *tambos* very well.

With respect to their design and form, they were large houses or *galpones* with only one room, one hundred to three hundred feet long and at least thirty to a maximum of fifty feet wide, all cleared and unadorned without being divided into chambers or apartments, and with two or three doors, all on one side at equal intervals. Many of the ancient *tambos* endure intact and are still in use; and of those that have caved in, which is the majority of them, vestiges and ruins of them can be seen; of those that are still standing, the best, most spacious, and best maintained that I have seen are the one at Vilcas and the one at the town of Moho, the first in the Bishopric of Guamanga and the second in the Bishopric of Chuquiabo.

Apart from the *tambos* and storehouses, along these two royal highways every quarter of a league there were also some huts or small houses built in pairs facing one another near the road, and these huts were only large enough for two men to fit in them. The material and form in which they were made was different in different regions. In the provinces of Collao the huts were made of coarse stones without mortar, and they were about the size and shape of an oven for baking bread. Some of them are still standing, because they are made of dry stone and the rains have not washed them away, nor have they been burned by travelers who wanted to warm themselves. In each one of these huts two Indians always resided, and therefore, in every pair located together at the intervals stated above, four men were stationed. They performed the job of runners or messengers, who with incomparable speed carried the orders and commandments of the Inca to the governors and caciques of the whole kingdom, and the runners brought the news that was sent to the Inca at his court or wherever he was located. Therefore, in a very brief time the Inca knew what was happening in all of his states and word was spread there of all that he ordered. These messengers and runners were called *chasques* in the Peruvian language; this word means "he that receives" because the runners take and receive the message one from another.

The manner in which this job was performed is as follows: of the two Indians who were stationed in each little hut, called a *chuclla* by them, one was on the watch while the other rested. They took turns standing four-hour watches; and when the king sent some message to any province or when his governors answered and sent news, the Indians at the first post were told what was being ordered with the least number of words that would convey the message, because they did not have letters, and the runner whose turn it was committed the message to memory very well and left at once in great haste and, without stopping, ran the mile up to the second post, and when he came near, he raised his voice and repeated the message he was carrying. At his call, the other runner came out all ready and received the message while both continued to run without stopping, and after the first runner finished passing on the message, he returned to his place, and the second runner carried the message with the same speed to the third *chasque*; and in this way the message went from person to person to where it was being sent. These *chasques* ran with such speed that in ten or twelve days the Inca had an answer in Cuzco from the orders that he sent to Quito, even though these two cities are four hundred leagues apart, and in one day, twenty-four hours, it was normal for a message to travel fifty leagues.

The Incas also used the runners and messengers when they felt like having something especially delicious that needed to be brought from far away; if, while he was in Cuzco, the Inca felt a desire for some fresh fish from the sea, his order was acted upon with such speed that, although that city is over seventy leagues from the sea, the fish was brought to him very fresh in less than two days. These *chasques* carried a certain insignia in order to be recognized and so that credence would be given to the message they carried. Let it suffice as proof of the speed at which they ran their relays that when the Spaniards ordered them to make runs as they used to do, in situations that came up where it was needed, such as during the time of the civil wars, since it was an ancient custom of theirs, immediately the caciques, each within his own jurisdiction, had Indian *chasques* put in place, and although they could not be so well coordinated that runners were not lacking in some places, because there was not the diligence and order of the Inca times, nevertheless, letters were carried from this city of Lima to the city of Cuzco in three days over one hundred and forty miles of very bad road over very broken sierras. Now it takes the Spanish mail by horse twelve to thirteen days to do the same. The post service of the *chasques* was held to be one of the great accomplishments of the Inca kings. Nevertheless, it was no light task for his vassals, who considered that the contribution of Indians for this job and serving and supplying the *tambos* was a very oppressive kind of tribute, particularly, supplying the *mita* labor service of these *chasques* and messengers, because it was excessively hard work, even though they changed shifts every month; and as such they have regretted it very much the times that the Spaniards have ordered them to do it.

Chapter 33: Of the rest of the tribute that the Indians paid their king in personal services

Apart from the work that the people did in place of tax or tribute by cultivating the fields and raising the livestock of the Inca and Religion and by doing the other jobs and tasks that we have told about, they had to make a very great contribution of men and laborers for all of the jobs and work done throughout the kingdom for the service and utility of the king as well as for the republic. The taxpayers came to these jobs by turns or *mita* (as they say), when each person was called; and they all took part in the occupations and chores that the Inca and his governors assigned to them, and the most common and ordinary ones were the following. In the first place, they provided what was needed for war, and the number of men that commonly served was very great, both in the armies that were formed and reassembled, and in the garrisons and presidios that were in the capital cities of the provinces and on enemy borders. Many soldiers also served in the ordinary conquests, *guazauaras* [skirmishes] that the Incas had with many nations adjacent to their empire, such as the Pacamoro Indians, the Popayan Indians, and other nations bordering on the province of Quito, and to the south next to the provinces of Charcas with the Chiriguana Indians and the Araucan Indians of Chile, barbaric and very warlike peoples.

Another part of the *mitayos* was employed in the service of the Inca and his kinsmen and all of the governors and caciques of the provinces, as well as in the care and upkeep of all the *guacas* and temples, both those that were in Cuzco and those in the rest of the kingdom. Moreover, some of these *mitas* provided the labor for the mines of gold, silver, and other metals; the mines that the *mitayos* worked for the Inca were numerous and very rich, such as those of Porco [south of Potosi], from which they extracted such rich metals that they contained 50 percent silver, but the most famous were the ones at Tarapacá, in the Diocese of Arequipa. These mines were located in some dry sandbanks where no water is found within twelve leagues of the area and were so rich that the majority of the metal that was extracted from them was white, refined silver without a mixture of scoria. Lodes were not found in these mines, but rather pockets or isolated nuggets of pure silver

that the Indians call *papas*; some of them weighed from one-half
to one and two arrobas,[21] and a nugget has been found that weighed
four arrobas.

There is information about a lode that the Indians have covered
up, and they say that it belonged to the Sun, that it was two feet
wide and all of pure silver. This came to be known because of the
following incident. One of the first conquistadores of this kingdom
and one of the first settlers of Arequipa, named Lucas Martinez,
being the encomendero of Tarapacá, worked these mines. It happened that at the same time, an Indian of Pedro Pizarro's repartimiento, which happened to be nearby, told Pizarro that he would
show him another mine richer than Lucas Martinez's mine. While
they were out looking for it, Pizarro came upon some pits that
the Indians had worked formerly, and while digging in them, he
found some rocks similar to adobes, and these rocks were of white
silver that was richer than usual. After each rock was extracted,
no more processing was done than to hit the rock a few times on
top with a big hammer, and a thin outer crust flew off, and the
remainder was a sheet of silver.

When Lucas Martinez found out about this, believing that Pizarro's mine was the rich lode, he threatened to kill the caciques
of his encomienda because they had not told him about the lode
that Pedro Pizarro had found. The caciques answered that he should
not be vexed, that they would give him the mine of the Sun, which
they had not dared to reveal because the sorcerers said that if they
disclosed its location to the Spaniards, all of the Indians involved
would die. Lucas Martinez encouraged them by saying that the sorcerers were not telling the truth. But the day before the Indians
were going to show it to him, there was an eclipse of the sun, and
since the Indians believed that the Sun had become angry because
they were going to uncover his mine, they told their encomendero
that they would not dare to do it because they feared that they
would surely die if they showed him the mine, because the Sun
had gotten angry and for this reason the Sun had stopped in that
way. Lucas Martinez encouraged them to talk again by explaining
the cause of the eclipse, and while he was well on the way to showing them the cause, a strong earthquake occurred. Owing to this,
the Indians said that even if he were to kill them all, they would
not reveal the mine to him. This happened while Vaca de Castro
was governing in this kingdom, during the year of 1543. Many other
mines of silver and gold were worked by the Incas. Very well known

among them is the gold mine that was in the area of the city of Chuquiabo.

The number of Indians that worked on the construction of fortresses and royal palaces was incredible; actually the Indians say that in building the fortress of Cuzco ordinarily thirty thousand men were employed. And many of these magnificent constructions were built throughout the kingdom.

None of the tribute-payers was exempt from these personal jobs; and service was required everywhere, and it was executed in the following way. After the Inca and his councillors had agreed in Cuzco on the number of *mita* laborers to be raised that year for the tasks mentioned above, people came immediately from the whole kingdom. Each province sent its share; in order to get the proper amount from their towns and provinces, each *hunu* gathered the taxpayers of his district, who numbered ten thousand, and from among them he levied the number of men that were requested from him. Commonly it was however many the Inca and his councillors happened to want; and the lower caciques made the proportionate distribution. For example, if they had to raise one thousand men, each cacique contributed the appropriate number. Therefore, once it was known how many men were to serve in the *mita* labor, the towns could not be treated unfairly in the distribution, nor could some towns be more burdened than others. Similarly, even though all the livestock that they gave in tribute was for the Inca and Religion, the same kind of distribution was made. If one hundred thousand men were ordered to be brought to Cuzco, they were levied according to the number of men under each superior, and they were so careful and orderly in setting and executing the levy that there was no disputes or delay in bringing forth each one his share of men. In order to get the thousand men mentioned above, the cacique of the *huno* divided up the levy among the ten caciques in charge of one thousand subjects who were under his command, and each one of the ten superiors distributed the one hundred men to be raised among the ten caciques in charge of one hundred subjects, who were under his obedience; and these superiors, in the same order and method of subordination, continued down to the decurions over ten Indians. Each one of them came forward immediately with his *mitayo* laborer for his immediate superior, and the latter passed his five laborers on to the superior of one hundred, and in this way they went up the ranks until the thousand men of the levy were turned over to the *hunu*. And in this way the tribute of *mitas* and personal service was equal in all of the provinces, just as in cultivating the land and the other contributions that were made to the king, except that in some places, where there was an abundance of notably important things or where the people were more suited for some kind of jobs, then the residents of that place were not subject to the common and general levies, but worked on what the Inca ordered them to do; and as a compensation for the work they did on the job they were designated to perform, they were exempted from other *mita* labor service. For example, because the people in the province of Lucana were suited for bearing the litters of the Inca, since (as they say) the Lucanas walked at an even pace, all of the litter bearers of the Inca were from that province; and because the Chumbivilcas were excellent dancers, the Inca designated many of them for this occupation; and since there was in the province of the Chicha Indians a red firewood that was excellent for carving, even though it is two hundred leagues from Cuzco, the Chichas brought the wood themselves, all carved and prepared to be burned in the sacrifices and in the fires that were made in the plaza in the presence of the Inca and the bodies of the embalmed lords.

The same was observed in the provinces in which there were mines that were worked. Since they provided the men to work the mines, they were relieved from other contributions. Therefore, from everywhere, the things that were special there were brought to the Inca, and besides this, the ordinary products from the fields were brought; although these were brought in proportion, I mean so much less of the ordinary products according to how much more work was done to fulfill the special obligations that were required of their province. One thing should be pointed out with respect to the amount of tribute that they brought to the king, and it is that there was no other rate or limit, either of the people that the provinces gave for the *mita* labor service or in the other requirements, except the will of the Inca. The people were never asked to make a fixed contribution of anything, but all of the people needed were called for the aforementioned jobs, sometimes in larger numbers, other times in lesser numbers, according to the Inca's desire, and the result of those labors was the royal tribute and income; and in this way the people extracted all the gold and silver that the Incas and the *guacas* had.

Chapter 34: *Of the tribute of boys and girls that the Inca collected from his vassals and for what purposes they were used*

It seems that the vassals of the Inca were overworked with the many abuses and tributes that he assigned to these poor people. Actually whatever they produced by the sweat of their brow, except their personal sustenance, was all for the king, and they were not permitted to possess anything or enjoy any liberty. They were kept in very severe servitude by the ambition and tyranny of their princes, and nevertheless, if that were the extent of the oppression and misery in which they lived, it could be tolerated. But besides the tributes already mentioned, another was added; willingly or by force, the people were compelled to contribute their own children, who were killed in their abominable sacrifices. This cruel act was progressively more inhumane in proportion to the innocence of those youngsters, who least deserved such treatment. Women and children were exempted by the Inca from the obligations and impositions that we have described up to this point (nevertheless, they still had to do a considerable amount of the work of the tribute-payers, because on all of the jobs they helped their fathers and husbands when the men were occupied in their *mita* labor, except for the military service). This brutal contribution was levied only on these poor children, and in truth, this alone was much more terrible, incomparably more so than any of the other kinds of tribute, even worse than all of the others together, not only for the distressed, innocent children, who like tender little lambs were taken to be slaughtered, but also for their bereaved parents, who, no matter how hard and barbaric they may have been, in the last analysis were parents, and nature did not fail to make them feel parental love, for this is not even denied to wild animals. The apportionment of this tribute in children that the king ordered his subjects to pay every year was no more limited than the other contributions; it depended on what the Inca desired. All these children had to be from nine to ten years old or younger, and all the males gathered in this way were sacrificed; and they were killed by strangulation with a cord, or by a blow with a club, and then they were buried, and sometimes they got them drunk before having them killed.

The number of girls that were gathered was much larger than the number of boys, as can be seen by the assignments the girls were given. The method of gathering them was as follows. A judge or commissioner named by the Inca was dispatched to each province, and his only responsibility was this matter of collecting girls, watching over them, and sending them to Cuzco when they were the right age, and this official was called *apupanaca*. He wandered about the towns within his jurisdiction, and he had the authority to pick out any girls that seemed to him to have beauty, a good figure, and a good disposition, if they were between eight and nine years of age or younger; these girls were called *acllas*, which means "chosen women"; they were brought to the house of the *mamaconas*, and for this reason it was called *acllaguaci*, which means "house of the chosen women"; and there was one of these houses in the capital of every province. The young girls were raised in these houses until they were fourteen years old; they remained in the company of the *mamaconas*, who were the cloistered women, dedicated to the service of their gods in the manner of nuns or like the vestal virgins of Rome. The *mamaconas* taught these girls all of the women's work and activities such as spinning, weaving wool and cotton, preparing food, making their wines or *chichas*, as well as other jobs that are appropriate for women. There was income designated for their support which came from the fields belonging to Religion, and there were also overseers who were in charge of supplying them with what they needed and watching over them very carefully with the object of protecting their virginity.

Every year at the time of the fiesta of Raymi, the commissioner who chose this tribute took from these houses of seclusion the girls who were thirteen or fourteen years old or older, and with no less watchfulness than had been used up to that point, he took them to Cuzco, according to the number that each province had to send that year. Once the girls that were sent from all the provinces, which was an excessively large number, were gathered together in that city, they were placed in the presence of the Inca, who distributed them immediately, according to the present need, in the following order. Some were assigned to the monasteries of *mamaconas* to replace the number of those that died, and these took the vows of that order, living always in confinement and chastity, occupied in the service of the temples of the Sun, Thunder, and the other gods that were served by women.

The Inca took another considerable number aside and ordered that they be kept to be killed in the sacrifices that were made during the course of the year; these sacrifices happened often and for many different reasons, such as for the health of the Inca, when he got sick and when he went to war in person; and in case he died, those that were to be sent to the other life in his company would be killed; and for many other occasions they felt a need for this sacrifice, because they were under the influence of the devil. And it was a necessary prerequisite that the girls for these sacrifices be virgins. The Inca assigned the most noble and beautiful girls to be his servants and concubines, and gave a large number of them out to his captains and kinsmen, remunerating with this kind of prize the services that they had rendered to him; and for the same reason, he gave some of these virgins to other people when he wanted to do them a special favor, and receiving one of these virgins from the Inca personally was considered to be an extraordinary favor. This is because these Indians do not value anything as highly as having many wives, and other than their legitimate wife, they could not have another except as a special favor from the king, and he would normally give these women out for different reasons, that is to say, for someone being eminent in some art or for having exhibited special skill in something pertaining to the public welfare or for having done some brave deed in a war.

The Inca would normally concede to his governors the authority to distribute some women among the caciques and important men of each province from where the women were taken. Finally, the number of women ordered to be gathered for these purposes was very large; and no consideration was given to the matter of whose daughters they were, except that the choice and decision was made by the *apupanaca*, and the parents of the girls could not protest for any reason or show any signs of sadness at the loss of their daughters. In this kind of contribution there was no fixed rate or specified number, the same as there was none in the others either, and therefore the number of girls that were gathered each year was not the same.

Although this was such a hard and oppressive tribute, it was made somewhat more endurable by the fact that the Indians believed that the virgins killed in the sacrifices made in honor of the gods, for the health of the king or other needs of the republic, would be favored by having their souls rest in great peace, and for this reason, of their own free will, some parents would offer their daughters, especially in Cuzco and the surrounding regions, when the Inca or some great lord became ill. Nevertheless, it is true that what usually happened was due to the normal fruits of parental love, that is to say that the parents felt sorrow and pain, and in point of fact they felt it very intensely on seeing themselves deprived of such loved ones, so close to their own innermost being. Paternal authority being lost, their children were snatched away from them much to their regret, and before their very eyes these children who had hardly started to enjoy a flicker of life were delivered into the hands of death. This was the main reason why they were not very watchful with the daughters; on the contrary, it is said that they were happy to see them seduced at a very early age; this way the girls were safe from the *apupanaca*, since virginity was a prerequisite for selection. The only reason for this was to make use of the girls as soon as they reached marriageable age, and neither the parents nor the girls had any freedom of choice in this matter.

Chapter 35: Of the control and great power that the Incas had gained over their vassals, and the fear and reverence with which the vassals obeyed and served the

Incas When the government of the Incas is seen in the light of the nature and condition of the Indians (for they are all subservient people who obey and comply with the obligations that they have more out of fear and rigor than love and kindness), it may seem proper and good. Nevertheless, if it is contemplated by itself and for free people who are reasonable and law abiding, it was the most unjust and tyrannical government imaginable. Although the Incas were men of sound judgment, nevertheless, by their form of government they did show that they were barbarian in the way they treated their subjects. The fact is that the closer man comes to a reasonable government, the more humane and benign he becomes; thus, on the contrary, where the barbarians show their barbarism the most is in the way they treat their vassals with extraordinary rigor, harshness, and cruelty, not looking upon them as their equals in status and nature but as if the vassals were inferior in both these respects. Barbarian rulers expect to be venerated as more than men, and at the same time they treat their vassals like beasts. The yoke that these miserable Indians carried on their necks was so heavy that if all the men in the world were brought together for the purpose of inventing a kind of subjugation and tyranny as severe as the conditions under which the Indians lived, I doubt that they could invent anything that would surpass what these Incas had achieved to subjugate their people.

And whoever considers carefully the order that the Incas maintained in administering and keeping their empire will find that everything was directed toward subjugating the people, with no other objectives at all. I could easily go into details in order to prove it, by telling about all of the things that they required to be done for this oppression of their subjects, but let it suffice to say that the poor subjects did not even have the liberty to possess anything of their own without permission from the Inca or his governors, even though it was nothing more than killing a domesticated animal or having two sets of clothing; they did not have the right to eat whatever they wanted, but what the Inca felt they should eat, nor could they marry whomever they wanted, much less arrange the marriage of their daughters. And (what is more) they were not even lords over their own women and children, but some men's wives were taken away from them and given to other men, and their children were taken away to be killed in the sacrifices.

The caciques went through their districts during the year, checking to see that the Indians had no more than what they had been assigned, that they did not possess gold or silver, that they were not wearing valuable clothing, and that they did not have more than ten head of livestock without special permission; this privilege was normally given by the Inca to the caciques, but for a specified number of animals. Not even the caciques themselves could wear valuable clothing unless the Inca had given it to them for some unusual service. Daughters were commonly under the authority of their parents only up to the age of ten years, and from then on they were at the disposition of the Inca. All people, no matter how noble they were, who came from outside of the court to enter into the presence of the Inca, took off their shoes and put some sort of load on their shoulders as a sign of vassalage and respect. They spoke to him with unusual humility and reverence, keeping their eyes down so as not to look at his face, and the Inca acted with notable gravity and answered with so few words and in such a low tone that he was barely understood. In his presence no one sat down except the great lords as a special privilege.

And inasmuch as the Incas had no other goal in their form of government than to place their vassals in greater subjection and servitude every day, in order to placate the Incas, their governors and important as well as lesser caciques, each one in his own office, attempted to further this objective. The Incas endeavored to break down all of their subjects' power so that they could not raise their heads; and since the Incas were very astute, they did not lack the cunning and skill necessary to complete such a difficult task as taming these barbarous and unruly people. The principal means that they used to this end was to make certain that their subjects were poor and that they kept continuously busy with an excessive amount of work so that, being so oppressed and humiliated, they would lack the vigor and spirit to aspire to rebel. With this objective in mind, they built great fortresses, made roads, constructed terraces on the hillsides, and made their subjects bring tribute to

Cuzco from more than three and four hundred leagues away. For this same reason the Incas introduced so many idolatries to their subjects and loaded them down with so many rites and sacrifices that when the Indians were completely free from other labors and jobs, the work of making sacrifices alone was sufficient to keep them from taking a deep breath and relaxing.

They made their subjects accept in their towns the same arrangement of shrines, dedicated to diverse deities, that there was in Cuzco, showing them the order in which they were to make sacrifices to each one and for what reasons. Besides this, they invented new kinds of cults and ceremonies every day; and all of their vassals were obligated to participate, so much so that this subjection to idolatries alone was so great that whatever they harvested and raised, including their own children, they were forced to use up in the sacrifices. Moreover, so that they would not even have freedom of thought, when necessary works were lacking for them to do, the Incas made their vassals work everywhere in things that were not needed for any useful purpose, and we find many such works that were done. Therefore, owing to the established order, no one could get involved in anything except what he was ordered to do. It is the truth that, although the main intention the Incas had with these continuous occupations and jobs was to have their people subjugated and under control, nevertheless great care was taken to maintain their health and to insure that they never suffered from need. Therefore work was done in moderation, except that it was continuous, keeping them occupied in both matters pertaining to religion and in the needs of the Indians themselves, because no less care was taken in one endeavor than in the other.

Furthermore, their reputation and the high esteem in which the Incas were held by the Indians was of very great importance. On the basis of it, these primitive people came to have the opinion that the Incas were not only different from other men in valor and strength, but closely related to the Sun and to the other *guacas*, and on such friendly terms with these gods that they conversed with them. The Indians accepted as proof of this error the testimony of the Incas themselves, who boasted about all of this, as well as the authority of the religion that the Incas always held up before the people in all of their conquests. The Incas had introduced the veneration of all this with such care, consuming in the name of religion such a large amount of goods and so many children that this had come to be the main occupation of the whole land. And the Incas justified this great burden and obligation by the idea that they were gods to the Indians, who should not fail to further the Inca's designs. This opinion was strengthened every day as the people saw the many victories that the Incas achieved over all kinds of people; and it was further strengthened by the fact that although the Incas were so few at first, they had subjugated this whole kingdom, and their authority among the people was increased in no small way by the admirable order and harmony that the people saw imposed by the Incas on everything, both for the utility of the republic and for the growth of the cult of their gods. The Incas made the people listen to this nonsense every day, so the people thought that the Incas were very much like gods and full of more than human wisdom.

The people were particularly impressed on seeing the adornment and majesty with which the Incas had brilliantly decorated their court, which the Indians held in great veneration. Moreover, the city of Cuzco was the capital of the empire, where the laws that were to be obeyed were given, with regard to religion as well as government; from there the governors came to rule all of the provinces, and those who concluded their term of office returned there to give an account of what had happened. Aside from all this, the devil had forged in the capital the customs, idolatries, fiestas, and sacrifices that seemed appropriate to him for his ends, which were none other than to attract these blind people to himself. Therefore they believed that the capital was the home and dwelling of the gods and the abode of heavenly things. This is what the Incas made them think, because by this means they furthered their designs and strengthened the power that they wanted to have throughout all of their kingdom. The esteem in which Cuzco was held continued to grow as strangers saw how it was venerated by its residents and because of the mysteries that these residents made people believe were in every hill, spring, road, and canyon, as will be seen in the next book[22] when we treat the temples, *guacas*, and holy places that were around Cuzco.

In spite of all this, I am not persuaded that the methods mentioned above would have been sufficient to establish the domination and subjugation of these people, if the Incas had not also taken advantage of rigorous measures such as death and exemplary punishments which were executed on those who got out of line. In fact, the people did not fail to rebel many times in order to gain their liberty, as men whose natural inclination moved them to seek it, just like the rest of the men in the world. Many of these dreadful punishments that the Incas imposed are still very fresh in the memories of those living today. As something notable, they have continued to pass the tales of these incidents on as a tradition from father to son; and I will relate here two or three examples. In a place near Payta, one of the Incas killed five thousand men at one time, and in order to create even more terror and fear in his subjects, he had the hearts taken out of the dead, and a circle was made around their fort with these hearts. Guayna Capac had all the males (except the boys) killed in the towns of Otavalo and Carangue, and owing to this event the inhabitants of these towns were called *guambracuna*, which means "boys." And in the valley of Jaquijaguana, four leagues from Cuzco, another Inca killed all of the males that lived there, including even those that were still in their mother's womb. This was done by cutting open the women to look for males. For this reason, those towns were called, in memory of this deed, towns of females. Apart from these great punishments, for the most atrocious offenses not only were the guilty killed, but also all their relatives.

It must be added to this that the Incas took a long time to put the Indians in the state that I have described and in which we found them; and during this period of conquest the Indians rebelled many times, fighting for their liberty, for which they were given cruel and horrendous punishments. And the Incas had so much good fortune after they started to rule that it would frighten the most brave and arrogant people in the world. Therefore, after so much time passed, with the continuity and custom of being subjugated, where children go through the same thing that their parents had seen, it is natural that the people's spirits would be dimmed and their wrath be forgotten, which are the natural arms that man possesses to defend himself. Therefore, I conclude that by way of rigor and cruelty more than by other means, the Incas came to break the spirit of their subjects and put them in this rigid servitude in which they had them and to establish the subjugation and submissiveness with which they were obeyed and respected; and this was such a harsh form of slavery that it is difficult to imagine a more severe one, even though we review all the governments of the people in recorded history.

Chapter 36: Of the order they followed in installing the Inca, the royal insignias, and the Inca's great majesty and splendor

When the king died, he was succeeded on the throne by the eldest of his legitimate sons, and the son held as such was the one borne by the queen and principal wife of the Inca, called Coya, which means the same as queen. The rest of the sons borne by the many other women or concubines of his were excluded from the succession and considered to be ineligible for the crown. The prince was not crowned until the funeral rites of his father were concluded, and after this, all of the great lords and gentlemen who resided in the court and whoever could comfortably come from all over the kingdom gathered in the plaza of Cuzco for the installation and coronation. This very important act was celebrated with special ceremonies, solemn fiestas, and a multitude of sacrifices, as we will tell in the following book, which is about their religion.[23] The Inca took possession of the kingdom when he put the fringe on his forehead, which was like the royal crown, and after it, he put on the rest of the insignias that the Peruvian kings used; besides the fringe there was the *sunturpaucar*, the *champi*,[24] the rainbow and two serpents, and the other emblems that each one picked out.

The way his vassals installed him and swore allegiance to him is as follows. Once all the lords were together in the plaza and the king was seated in the middle on his *duho*,[25] one by one the lords stood up, first the *orejones* and after them the caciques and lords in charge of the most towns. In their hands they had some little feathers called *tocto* from certain birds that are found in the paramo. They stood barefooted before the Inca and turned the palms of their hands toward him, showing their reverence. Then they passed the feathers in front of their faces, shaking the feathers, and they gave the feathers to a nobleman who was standing next to the Inca. The nobleman took the feathers, gathering them all; then he burned them. They also swore allegiance by the Sun, raising their faces toward it, and by the earth, to be loyal to the Inca and serve him in whatever he ordered them to do.

The king was dressed and adorned in the same clothing as the

Inca nobles and *orejones*. The king was distinguished only by having larger holes pierced in his ears and larger and more lavish earplugs, by having his hair cut short to the breadth of one or two fingers, and by his *llauto* [headband] which was many-colored. The braided headbands worn by other members of the Inca lineage were of a single color. The Inca wore a cloak and a shirt, with *ojotas* on his feet; in this respect he followed the custom of the common people, but his clothing was different from the usual in that it was made of the finest wool and the best cloth that was woven in his whole kingdom, with more brilliant colors and finer-quality weaving. The *mamaconas* made this clothing for him, and most of it was made from vicuña wool, which is almost as fine as silk. Some of his clothes were ordinary and simple, of one single thickness or cloth without a border or material added to the surface; other clothing was very colorful and showy with very small feathers woven into it, and other clothing was covered with ornaments of gold, emeralds, and other precious stones; this was the finest formal attire and corresponds to our embroidery, cloth of gold or silver, and brocades.

He changed his clothes after a brief time without putting the ones that he cast aside on again, especially if he got a spot on them, no matter how small. While Atauhualpa was held prisoner by the Spaniards in Cajamarca, one day it happened that while he was eating in the presence of the Spaniards who were guarding him, as he was taking a bite of food, a drop fell on the clothes that he was wearing, and, waving his hand to the maid who was holding his plate, he left the table and went to his chambers to change clothes, and he came out again wearing a dark gray shirt and cloak. Coming up to him, a Spaniard touched his cloak, and, noticing that it was softer than silk, he asked him what his clothes were made of; the Inca responded that they were made from some birds that fly about at night in Puerto Viejo and Tumbez and bite people. In pursuing the matter, he said that it was from bat wool, and when the Spaniard asked him where so many bats could be gathered, he answered with these words: "What else would these dogs from Tumbez and Puerto Viejo have to do but catch these birds to make clothing for my father Guayna Capac?"

The fringe (royal insignia that they always wore in place of a crown or diadem) was called *maxcapaycha*; it was made of very fine red wool, four fingers' breadths wide and one finger's breadth thick. They had it sewn to the *llauto* and hanging in the middle of their forehead, and it reached down to their eyebrows. From the middle up, this fringe was very carefully put through some little gold tubes, and the wool inside them was spun and twisted, and from the little tubes on down, which was what dropped down on the forehead, the wool was untwisted and not spun. The *sunturpaucar* and the *champi* were two of the king's other insignias, besides the royal standard. The *sunturpaucar* was a staff, a little shorter than a pike, all covered and adorned from top to bottom with short feathers of various colors which were placed with such skill that they made an elegant effect, and to finish it off, the tips of three large feathers rose up from the top. The *champi* was a certain kind of weapon with which they fought in wars. In front of the Inca, at the sides of the royal standard, two *champis* on two long staves were held, and the Inca himself, instead of a scepter, carried a short *champi*, like a baton with a golden head. The royal banner or standard was a small, square pennant, about ten or twelve palms[26] around the edge, made of cotton or wool cloth; it was fixed on the end of a long pole so as to stand out stiffly and not wave in the wind. Each king had his arms and emblems painted on it, because each of them chose different ones, although the most usual for the Inca lineage were the rainbow and two serpents stretched out the length of it, parallel with the fringe that served as a crown. To this, each king would normally add as his emblem and symbol whatever figures he liked, such as a lion [puma], an eagle, and other things. For a fringe this standard had certain long red feathers placed at intervals.

The Incas made a majestic display both in their personal style of life and adornment and in the pomp and splendor that accompanied them and with which they were served inside and outside of their homes. The multitude of servants that they had in their palace was incredible. Many of these servants were the children of caciques and noblemen. These youngsters were raised in the royal house so that they would learn civil customs. The Incas felt that it was a sign of grandeur to support many servants and have many wives and concubines. They were served all the exquisite, precious, and rare things that the land produced, and they had these things brought for their pleasure from the most distant corners of their empire. The king ate while seated on a small stool, hardly more than one palm high, which was the seat of the lords, called *duho*; it was made of very exquisite red wood, and it was always covered with a fine cloth, even when the Inca was seated on it. The table was the ground, as it was for the rest of the Indians, but it was set with great ostentation and richness, including gold and silver service, sumptuous food, and luxurious *chichas* or wines, as well as the pomp and bustle of servants. Serving women brought him all of his food on gold, silver, and pottery plates and set them before him on some very thin, small green rushes. When he pointed out the dish that he wanted, it was brought to him, and one of these serving women would take it to him and hold it in her hand while he ate. At some big fiestas he came out to eat in the plaza with a noisy accompaniment. All leftovers from the meal and whatever the Inca touched with his hands were kept by the Indians in *petacas* [chests]; thus, in one chest they kept the little rushes that they placed before him when he ate; in another, the bones of the poultry and meat left over from his meals; in another the clothes that he discarded. Finally, everything that the Inca had touched was kept in a *buhio* [hut] that an important Indian had charge of, and on a certain day each year it was all burned. They said that since the Incas were children of the Sun, whatever they touched had to be burned, made into ashes, and tossed into the air, and no one was to touch it. The king's bed was not very luxurious, because he slept on the ground, on top of a large cotton quilt, and he was covered with woolen blankets.

Wherever he went, and many times within a town, the Inca was carried on the shoulders of bearers supporting a splendid litter covered on the inside with gold; carrying this litter was a special favor and honor. When the Inca traveled, he had a large following of *orejones*; these were the nobles and military men, who added security as well as authority to the Inca's group. Two or three hundred bearers of the Lucana nation preceded the litter or portable platform. These Indians were the official litter bearers, and they wore a special livery. Those out in front cleared the road where they were going to pass and relieved the bearers as they got tired. The Inca also showed his majesty by traveling slowly; thus, when his services were not urgently needed, he traveled no more than four leagues a day, and wherever he stopped, accommodations were prepared for him as elaborately as if he were in his court.

The riches of these barbarian kings were so immense that it is not easy to describe. They never found that their wealth was insufficient, nor were they ever worried about finding a way to remedy their needs, because they never had any; rather they had peace of mind and abundance of everything, for they were more concerned about how to divest themselves of what was left over from their large income than in seeking new ways to obtain and keep treasures. This was due to the fact that whatever their vassals produced or acquired was at their service and disposal, and everything precious and valuable that was found in their states, like gold, silver, precious stones, fine wood, clothing, livestock, along with everything else, finally came to them, and it was produced and harvested in their name. In short, all of their riches consisted in the multitude of vassals that they had, and these vassals were always occupied and attentive in their service just like slaves, with no other pay or salary except their sustenance. At the same time the vassals were occupied in following orders in the interest and utility of the Incas.

With a good team of officials and workers these Incas constructed many very sumptuous palaces in which to live in Cuzco and the countryside and valleys of the region, where they had houses for relaxation. In fact, there was not a province in their entire kingdom where they did not have houses and royal palaces to stay in when they visited their states. These houses or alcazars were made in their style—large, strongly fortified, and expensive—as we see from the large, thick walls and vestiges that still remain in Cuzco and other places as well. They had them all furnished with the same adornment and service as if they always lived in them, with their storerooms and wine rooms well supplied, rich gold and silver service, living rooms and chambers adorned with unusual richness. Diverse representations of animals, birds, and other things of this kind, sculptured in pure gold, were seen on the walls. All of the service and the cups for the dining room as well as the kitchen were of silver and gold, and not counting this service, there was a great amount of these metals still not worked, which was kept in large earthen jars, and a great amount of fine clothing of incalculable value. They kept very careful care and accounts of all these things; and the overseers or magistrates made sure that there were artisans and silversmiths in each one of these houses to make the aforementioned things.

The riches that were collected and gathered together just in the city of Cuzco, as the capital and court of the empire, were incredible; in it there were many important houses of the dead kings with all the treasure that each one had accumulated in his life. Since the one who ascended to the throne did not touch his predecessor's property and riches, which were given over to the *guaca* and service of the deceased, the new king had his own house built and acquired silver and gold and all the rest; thus the treasure in that city was immense, especially since each king tried to surpass all of his ancestors in having a richer, more illustrious and splendid house than they did.

Moreover, in that city there were the most sumptuous temples of the whole kingdom as well as the most numerous *guacas* and important gods of the provinces and the illustrious and highly venerated sanctuary of the Sun, called Coricancha, which means "house of gold," and it was one of the richest temples in gold and silver that there has been in the world. People came there from everywhere with their most precious things to make their vows and sacrifices. So Cuzco was the richest city that has been found in this New World, and the reason why it had such a great amount of wealth in silver and gold and precious stones was because the caciques and governors made presents of all of these things to the Inca when they visited him in his court and when he passed through their lands as he was visiting his kingdom. And this wealth grew steadily every day, because there were numerous provinces and because other provinces were continuously reduced to his obedience and also because there were very few who used these metals, with the exception of the great lords and noblemen, who adorned themselves for war with some jewels made of gold and silver. Thus, almost all of these metals that were taken from the many mines that there were and that there are today throughout the whole kingdom came into the possession of the Inca. Some of these mines were worked at the expense and under the auspices of the Inca himself, and others, constituting the majority, were worked at the expense of the caciques of the districts where the mines were located. This was so that they would have things to give as presents to the Inca. Added to this was the prohibition against anyone taking silver or gold out of Cuzco. Therefore, there came to be incomparable treasures amassed there from long ago for the magnificence and authority of the kings, and not only was removing precious metals from the aforementioned city prohibited, but things of this kind could not be removed from other parts of the kingdom to foreign places. Moreover, the people spent nothing on things that are consumed with use, as we do, except on idols, molded figures, decorated sheet metal, cups, and gems for the service and decoration of the temples and for the king and great lords, nor did the kings pay the salaries of their servants and officials in these precious metals. The salaries were paid in the clothing and food that the towns contributed. From all this it is clearly understood that over so many centuries[27] the Incas had gathered and accumulated incomparable riches, and it was only a very small part of this treasure that came into the possession of the Spaniards, even though there was such a large amount of it.

On seeing how anxious the Spaniards were to find these metals and how much they esteemed them, the Indians hid and buried the majority of the treasure.

Finally, the Inca's sisters took turns one at a time in serving him. Each sister was aided by a large number of ladies who were the daughters of noblemen. These ladies, who were relieved every eight days, always stayed with the Inca to serve him, because his servants and distinguished assistants did not enter into the room where he resided; rather they remained outside in the patios, and if one of them was called, he entered barefooted into the presence of the Inca.

Chapter 37: Of their computation of time, of the quipos or recording devices, and the method of counting that the Peruvian Indians had

The movements of the heavenly bodies are an admirable thing, well known and manifest to all peoples. There are no people, no matter how barbaric and primitive, that do not raise up their eyes, take note, and observe with some care and admiration the continuous and uniform course of the heavenly bodies. Since the revolutions of the sun and the moon are the most visible and common of all, more than the other planets and celestial orbs, all nations have used them rather than any others to classify time. This was done by these Peruvian Indians, who, owing to the knowledge that they achieved concerning the course of these two heavenly bodies, learned to keep track of their year and measure time. They took account of the diurnal revolution which the sun makes around the earth in one natural day in order to recognize and distinguish between day and night, and they used the movement of the sun from one tropic to another in order to keep track of the years. They also used the movement of the moon to identify the months. These constitute the three specific and fixed parts [day, month, year] into which they divided time. They identified our solar year by observing the solstices and starting the year by the summer solstice of this Antarctic Hemisphere, which falls on the twenty-third day of December and ends at the same point where it started. Therefore, their year turned out to have the same number of days as our year, with the exception of the bissextiles or leap years, which they did not understand. For this reason, it is impossible to ascertain how accurate their year was; but I really do not think that their observations were so accurate that they avoided making many errors, in spite of the fact that they utilized the best means that they knew in order to fix their year and keep an accurate record of the passage of time.

So that their record would be correct and accurate, they used the following method. On the crest of the hills that surround Cuzco, two markers or pillars were placed on the eastern side and two more such pillars were placed on the western side of that city, on the spot where the sun rises and sets when the tropics of Cancer and Capricorn come; and at the time when the sun rose and set exactly along the pillars of the south side, as observations were taken from the city of Cuzco, it was considered to be the beginning of the year. Since that city is located at twelve to fifteen degrees to the south, that was the time when the sun reached the farthest point on that southern side. From there, returning to the quinoctial line, it passed its zenith, and when it moved to the farthest point away on the northern side, as the sun rose and set it was aligned over those other pillars that marked the farthermost point on that side; and on returning from there to the point where it left, the Tropic of Cancer, which the first pillars marked, the year was concluded. The word for year was *huata* in Quechua and *mara* in Aymara.

Their year was composed of twelve months, and these months were counted by moons, and thus they use the same word for "month" and "moon," which is in Quechua, the language of Cuzco, *quilla*, and in Aymara, *pacsi*. The days that were left over each year were incorporated into the moons themselves. Thus, on the eastern as well as the western sides, where they had their markers placed at the point where the sun rose and set when it reached the tropics, between these two posts or markers, they had others placed, each one at the point where the sun reached that month; all of these pillars together were called Sucanca, and they were important objects of worship, and sacrifices were offered to them at the same time as the rest of the sacred objects. The two pillars that marked the beginning of winter were called Pucuy Sucanca, and the other two that marked the beginning of summer were called Chirao Sucanca. All the months had an equal number of days, and each one had its own name. The first month, which corresponded in part to December, was called Raymi; the second, which started about 20 January, was called Camay; the third, Hatun Pucuy; the fourth, Pacha Pucuy; the fifth, Ariguaquiz; the sixth, Hatun Cuzqui Aymoray; the seventh, Aucay Cuzqui Inti Raymi; the eighth, Chahua Huarquis; the ninth, Yapaquis; the tenth, Coya Raymi; the eleventh, Homa Raymi Puchayquiz; and the twelfth, Ayamarca.

By these twelve months they regulated the times to sow and till the soil and for the other work done during the year, and also for their fiestas and sacrifices, and not for anything else. They did not count their age in years; neither did they measure the duration of their acts in years; nor did they have any fixed points in time from which to measure historical events, as we count from the birth of our Lord Jesus Christ. Thus, there was never an Indian who knew his age, and there are hardly any today who know how many years old they are, much less the number of years that have elapsed since some memorable event. When they are asked about things of the past, if something happened more than four to six years back, what they usually answer is that the incident occurred *ñaupapacha*, which means "a long time ago"; and they give the same answer for events of twenty years back as for events of a hundred or a thousand years back, except that when the thing is very ancient, they express this by a certain accent and ponderation of their words.

They did not divide their year up into any parts other than months and days. The word for day in the language of Cuzco was *punchau*, and in the language of Collao, which is Aymara, it was *uru*; and in Quechua night was called *tuta* and in Aymara, *aroma*. They did not use weeks, nor did they give proper names to the days of each month as we give proper names to the days of the week, calling them Sunday, Monday, etc.; they only used the common noun *day*. Neither did they succeed in dividing the day up into hours, nor did they have any kind of clock to know how much time they used in what they did. However, they did have a certain way, although it was not very exact, of dividing up the day into parts for the purpose of knowing how much time they took in the occupations which they undertook. This method of counting time was done in two ways. First, it was done by pointing with their finger to the part of the sky where the sun was located when they started their work. For example, if a traveler was asked when he had left the inn, he answered by raising his finger to the sky and pointing to the place where the sun had been at that time; from this they were able to calculate more or less how long the traveler had been walking, and they did the same in the rest of their jobs and activities. The other method was very homespun. Throughout almost all of this Kingdom of Peru certain roots called *papas* [potatoes] are raised. They take the place of bread, and it takes more or less an hour to cook them. This time that it took to cook *papas* is used by them to measure the duration of the things that can be done in a short time. Thus, they will say that in doing such and such a thing it took them the amount of time necessary to cook one pot of *papas*. And this is what these people achieved with regard to time, and these are the methods of counting and fixing it that they had.

In place of writing they used some strands of cord or thin wool strings, like the ones we use to string rosaries; and these strings were called *quipos*. By these recording devices and registers they conserved the memory of their acts, and the Inca's overseers and accountants used them to remember what had been received and consumed. A bunch of these *quipos* served them as a ledger or notebook. The *quipos* consisted of diverse strings of different colors, and on each string there were several knots. These were figures and numbers that meant various things. Today many bunches of very ancient *quipos* of diverse colors with an infinite number of knots are found. On explaining their meaning, the Indians that know them relate many things about ancient times that are contained in them. There were people designated for this job of accounting. These officials were called *quipo camayos*, and they were like our historians, scribes, and accountants, and the Incas had great confidence in them. These officials learned with great care this way of making records and preserving historical facts. However, not all of the Indians were capable of understanding the *quipos*; only those dedicated to this job could do it; and those who did not study *quipos* failed to understand them. Even among the *quipo camayos* themselves, one was unable to understand the registers and recording devices of others. Each one understood the *quipos* that he made and what the others told him. There were different *quipos* for different kinds of things, such as for paying tribute, lands, ceremonies, and all kinds of matters pertaining to peace and war. And the *quipo camayos* customarily passed their knowledge on to those who entered their ranks from one generation to the next. The *quipo camayos* explained to the newcomers the events of the past that were contained in the ancient *quipos* as well as the things that were added to the new *quipos*; and in this way they explain everything that transpired in this land during all the time that the Incas governed. These *quipos* are still used in the *tambos* to keep a record of what they sell to travelers, for the *mitas*, for herders to keep track of their livestock, and for other matters. And even though many Indians know how to read and write and have traded their *quipos* for writing, which is without comparison a more accurate and easier method, still, in order to show the great subtlety of this method of preserving history and keeping accounts for people who had no writing and how much they achieved with it, I wish to give the following example of what happened in our times.

Two Spaniards left together from the town of Ica to go to the city of Castro Virreina, and arriving at the *tambo* of Cordoba, which is a day's travel from Ica, one of them stayed there and the other continued his trip; at this *tambo* this latter traveler was given an

Indian guide to accompany him to Castro Virreina. This Indian
killed the Spaniard on the road and returned to the *tambo*. After
some time passed, since the Spaniard was very well known, he was
missed. The governor of Castro Virreina, who at that time was Pedro
de Cordoba Mejia, a native of Jaen, made a special investigation
to find out what had happened. And in case the man had been killed,
he sent a large number of Indians to look for the body in the puna
and desert. But no sign of him could be found, nor could anyone
find out what had become of him until more than six years after
he had been killed. By chance the body of another Spaniard was
found in a cave of the same desert. The governor ordered that this
body be brought to the plaza so that it could be seen, and once
it was brought, it looked like the one the Indian had killed, and,
believing that it was he, the governor continued with the investigation to discover the killer. Not finding any trace or evidence against
anybody, he was advised to make an effort to find out the identity
of the Indian who was given to the deceased as a guide at the *tambo*
of Cordoba. The Indians would know this in spite of the fact that
more than six years had passed because by means of the record
of the *quipos* they would have kept memory of it. With this the
governor sent for the caciques and *quipo camayos*. After they were
brought to him and he continued with the investigation, the *quipo
camayos* found out by their *quipos* the identity of the Indian who
had been given as a guide to the aforementioned Spaniard. The Indian guide was brought prisoner immediately from his town, called
Guaytara, and, having given his declaration in which he denied the
crime, he was questioned under torture, and at once he confessed
to having killed the man, but explained that the wrong body had
been brought. However, he would show them the place where he
had killed the man and where the body was located. Police officers
went with him to the puna, and they found the body where the Indian guide had hidden it, and it was in a cave located some distance
from the road. With the great cold and dryness of the paramo, the
body had not decomposed, but it had dried out, and thus it was
whole. The first body that was brought was never identified, nor was
the killer. The extent of the achievement of the record and memory
of these *quipos* can be appreciated by this case.

    In their way of counting, the Indians have the same kinds of
numbers that we do. Counting up to ten units, and from there on
up reduplicating on the denary numbers, one, two, three units, etc.,
up to twenty. This number is expressed by two denaries, the number thirty is expressed by three, and in this way the denaries are

added in exactly the same way as in our system on up to one hundred, and the hundreds are multiplied up to ten, which is one thousand. This number is called *huaranca*. With regard to their kind of numbers and manner of counting, the system used by both the Peruvian and the Mexican Indians is very similar. And it is worth noting that though all of the Indians' things are different from ours, there is no difference between their system of counting and our own.

I do not know what to attribute this to, except that the people that came to populate this New World must have kept the method of counting that they learned in the Old World from where they came, and this system must be the same one that has been perpetuated by us and by them.

Notes

INTRODUCTION

1. Although the biographical data are sketchy, by far the most important source of information on Cobo is found in his own works. To date, the most reliable articles are the following: (a) Francisco Mateos, "Un misionero naturalista, el padre Bernabe Cobo," *Missionalia Hispánica*, 13 (Madrid, 1956): 225–315. This article also appeared as the introduction to Cobo's *Obras*, Biblioteca de Autores Españoles, 91–92 (Madrid, 1956): vii–xlvii. This is the edition of Cobo used here; it is cited simply as *Obras*, or BAE 91 or 92. (b) Raúl Porras Barrenechea, *Los cronistas del Peru* (Lima: Sanmartí y Compañía, 1962), pp. 405–411. (c) Philip A. Means, *Biblioteca Andina*, Transactions of the Connecticut Academy of Arts and Sciences (New Haven, 1928), pp. 349–357. In addition to the foregoing, a note of caution must be added. Much misinformation can be traced to M. González de la Rosa in his introduction to Cobo's *Fundación de Lima* (Lima, 1882), pp. vii–xxii. Even authors like Means have made the mistake of using González.

2. *Obras*, 91: 4, 165; 92: 279–280. There is no documentation of Cobo's ever having gone to Venezuela. The possibility was first suggested by González de la Rosa, *Fundación*, p. ix.

3. *Obras*, 91: 399; 92: 321.

4. Ibid., 91: 240–241, 311, 342. The dates for the trip to New Spain are explicitly stated by Cobo in three places. There is no basis for placing the return in 1650, a date found for the first time in González de la Rosa, *Fundación*, p. x.

5. *Obras*, 91: 101, 362; 92: 60–61, 438.

6. Although Cobo indicated that he had finished the *Historia* in 1639 (*Obras*, 92: 280–281), he continued work on it at least until dating the prologue fourteen years later (91: 7). More documentation on Cobo can be found in my dissertation: R. C. Hamilton, "Americanismos en las obras del padre Bernabé Cobo," Tesis doctoral, Madrid, 1974; under the same title a booklet containing a condensed version of the introduction and selections from the text was published in Madrid by La Muralla in 1976.

7. See Book II, Chapter 2, of this translation.

8. John H. Rowe, "Inca Culture at the Time of the Spanish Conquest," in *Handbook of South American Indians*, ed. Julian Steward, 2 (Washington, D.C.: Smithsonian Institution, Bureau of American Ethnology, 1946): 194. See also Porras Barrenechea, *Los cronistas*, pp. 408–409.

9. See Jesús Domínquez Bordona, *Manuscritos de América*, Catálogo de la Biblioteca de Palacio, 9 (Madrid, 1935): 182–183; and Real Academia de la Historia, *Catálogo de la Colección de don Juan Bautista Muñoz*

(Madrid, 1954), p. lvi. In addition to the Muñoz copies, there is another copy of the volume on natural history, made around 1800; it is in the New York Public Library, Span MSS. 19—Rich 8.

10. Bernabé Cobo, *Historia del Nuevo Mundo*, ed. Marcos Jiménez de la Espada. Vol. 3 (Seville, 1892) contains Books 11 and 12, plus Book 13, Chaps. 1–11; vol. 4 (1893) has the remaining chapters of Book 13 and Book 14. See note 21 for more details on this publication.

11. Means, *Biblioteca Andina*, p. 353. Means thought that all fourteen books of the first part of Cobo's *Historia* were included in this MS.

12. González de la Rosa, *Fundación*, p. xvi, states as follows: "Según hemos podido saber en nuestros viajes por Europa, el manuscrito de la *Historia de Indias* de Cobo se conserva hoy en tres volúmenes, que forman parte de la llamada Biblioteca particular del S. M. el Rey, situada en el real palacio de Madrid." ("As we have been able to determine in our travels through Europe, the manuscript of the *History of the Indies* [sic] by Cobo is kept today in three volumes that form part of the private library of His Majesty the King, located in the Royal Palace of Madrid.")

13. R. Vargas Ugarte, *Manuscritos del extranjero*, Biblioteca Peruano, 1 (Lima, 1935): 351. ("416.—MSS. 83-3-36. 1 vol. in 4to, bound in vellum, 363 numbered pages. On the back [of the first page]: History of the New World. 2 pages. 1 History of the New World, First Part. Book Eleven, Chapter 1 Concerning the Sparse Population of America and Its Causes. It continues up to Book Fourteen inclusive. The text is all done in the same handwriting. Original. As the reader has probably noticed, this is the work of Father Bernabé Cobo.")

14. Porras Barrenechea, *Los cronistas*, p. 410.

15. See the introduction to Cobo's *Obras*, p. xliv.

16. F. 320 and f. 324, *Biblioteca Nacional de Lima*.

17. This letter is found at the beginning of the *Fundación de Lima*, MS. 332–33.

18. This identification was verified by a professional handwriting expert, Mr. Charlie Cole, Campbell, California.

19. D. Antonio Josef Cavanilles, "Discurso sobre algunos Botánicos Españoles del siglo XVI . . ." *Anales de Ciencias Naturales*, 7, no. 20 (Madrid, 1804): 126–211.

20. MS. 84-4-18; Biblioteca Capitular Colombina de Sevilla. This MS. was identified by Don Bartolomé José Gallardo, *Ensayo de una Biblioteca Española*, 2 (Madrid, 1866): 486, no. 1851; here the handwriting is said to be "Letra como principios del siglo XVIII" ("writing like that of the early eighteenth century"). It certainly is not Cobo's hand as González de la Rosa stated (*Fundación*, p. xvi).

There was an earlier publication of parts of the *Fundación de Lima* added as an appendix by M. Jiménez de la Espada to his *Relaciones geográficas de Indias*, 1 (Madrid, 1881): iii–cxxxvi. The Muñoz copies were used.

21. This edition was published in four volumes; vols. 1 and 2 contain Books 1–10; vols. 3 and 4, Books 11–14, as stated in note 10. Later editions were reprinted from this text: (a) *Historia del Nuevo Mundo* (Madrid: Colección Cisneros, Ediciones "Atlas," 1943). This edition contains the first two chapters from Book 7 and Book 10. The prologue is based on an article written in 1882 by Enrique Torres Saldamando for his book, *Los antiguos Jesuitas del Perú* (Lima, 1882), pp. 98–106. This article has much of the same misinformation published by González de la Rosa. (b) *Historia del Nuevo Mundo* (Cuzco: Publicaciones Pardo-Galimberti, 1956); this book is a reprint of vol. 3 of the Jiménez de la Espada edition; the introductory material is based mainly on the pieces already mentioned by Torres Saldamando and González de la Rosa. (c) The most recent edition has already been mentioned in note 1, under the title, *Obras*, BAE 91–92. It contains all of Cobo's works known to have survived: a complete reprint of the Jiménez de la Espada volumes; a corrected edition of the *Fundación de Lima*, including the cover letter of 1639, based on the Muñoz copy; and Cobo's other letters, taken from an article by C. A. Romero, "Dos cartas inéditas del P. Bernabé Cobo," *Revista Histórica*, 8 (Lima, 1925): 26–50.

22. For further details, see Rowe, "Inca Culture at the Time of the Spanish Conquest," in *Handbook of South American Indians*, ed. Steward, 2: 185–186.

BOOK I

1. The first three parts are Europe, Africa, and Asia.
2. The Castilian league used here equals about three miles.
3. Father Cobo did an elaborate geographical study of the Andes, which includes a classification of six zones according to differences in flora, fauna, and climate. See Book 2, Chapters 7–17, of Cobo's *Historia del Nuevo Mundo*, not included in this translation.
4. A *behetria* is an independent Indian community having no hereditary ruler or government.
5. An encomienda was a grant by the Spanish crown of Indian vassals. The Indians were required to perform labor service and give tribute. The grantee, or encomendero, was supposed to Europeanize the Indians.
6. Repartimiento was the distribution of Indians for labor service. Often used interchangeably with *encomienda*, *repartimiento* refers only to the system of forced labor exacted from the Indians. Especially in colonial Peru, repartimiento was known as *mita*, a labor system used by the Incas (see glossary).
7. The space between the equator and each of the polar circles was divided into twenty-four climes.
8. Each vara is three Castilian feet, or about thirty-three inches; thus two varas would be five feet, six inches.

9. *Cuarteron* refers to a person who is three-fourths European and one-fourth Indian.

10. One arroba equals about twenty-five pounds.

11. *Baquiano* means an old hand, experienced in the ways of the Indies.

12. Father Cobo refers to a part of his *Historia del Nuevo Mundo* that has been lost.

13. This reference is found in 4 Esdras 13:40–47; this apocryphal book is often given as an appendix to editions of the Latin Vulgate Bible. Cobo supposes that his readers are familiar with this biblical reference, which tells of the Ten Lost Tribes of Israel. Other references by Cobo to the Bible will be found in the Latin Vulgate translated by Saint Jerome. The standard English translation is the Douay Rheims version. The King James version is significantly different.

14. This refers to the *Historia del Nuevo Mundo*.

15. The West Indies.

16. Cobo seems to give a rough estimate of these distances, as the Juan Fernández Islands are about 400 miles from the coast of Chile and the Galápagos Islands about 650 miles from the coast of Ecuador.

17. Pliny, *Natural History*, Book 8, Chapter 83. [This note appears in the left margin of the MS.]

18. De Reb. Salom. Reg., lib. 4, cap. 16. [This note appears in the left margin of the MS. It is an abbreviation of the following Latin title: "Ioannis de Pineda hispalensis e Societate Iesv. Ad suos in Salomonem commentarios. Salomon praevivs, id est, De rebus Salomonis regis, libri octo. Lvgdvni, apvd H. Cardon, 1609." First edition. See page 212, where Cobo got the preceding references to sixteenth-century theologians who wrote on the origin of the American Indians. The names and titles used in the Cobo MS. are abbreviated and/or Hispanicized. I have given the equivalents used in modern reference works. Some of these writings are found as commentaries in editions of the Bible. This is the case for Benito Arias Montano; he edited the Polyglot Bible of Antwerp, which was published between 1569 and 1572. Included in the commentaries on Genesis there is a section called "Phaleg" dealing with the Ophirian theory.]

19. This refers to the Seventy Interpreters of the Septuagint, a Greek translation from Hebrew of the Old Testament.

20. Cobo refers here to authors like Pliny; see *Natural History*, Book 2, Chapter 112, and Book 6, Chapter 37.

21. Meroe was a kingdom on the Nile in the vicinity of the modern city of Khartoum; Borysthenes, the river now named Dnieper; the Fortunate Islands, now called the Canaries; Cattigara, a city which was the farthermost place to the east, just below the equator, on Ptolemy's map.

22. This refers to the Line of Demarcation established by the Treaty of Tordesillas on June 6, 1492.

23. The MS. contains the following Latin abbreviation in the text: "In

Africae descript." This is a reference to Herodotus' section on Africa (which he called Libya).

24. Here Cobo refers to his *Historia del Nuevo Mundo*, Book 10.

25. Marañon refers to the Amazon River and its tributaries.

26. Hevilath is mentioned in Genesis 2:11.

27. Here Cobo refers to the turkey. In pre-Columbian times the Spanish word for "peacock" was *pavo*; after the conquest the turkey was called *pavo* or *gallina de la tierra*, "chicken of the land." The peacock became known as *pavo real*, "royal peacock."

28. Cobo's references are found on page 216 of *De Rebus Salomonis*. See note 18 above.

BOOK II

1. Cobo was writing in 1652; see Book I, Chapter 16, of this work. Compare Book I, Chapter 10, where Father Cobo states that the traditions of the Indians hardly date back five hundred years.

2. Father Cobo had good reasons for believing in the existence of giants. Genesis 6 states that "giants were upon the earth" before the Flood. Many classical authors also mention giants, and some of the most reliable chronicles state that giants were present in America.

3. See Book I, Chapter 10, of this work.

4. See Book 13 of the *Historia del Nuevo Mundo*.

5. The books on religion and customs, 13 and 14 of the *Historia del Nuevo Mundo*, are not included in this volume.

6. Father Cobo does not give the authors or titles of these manuscripts. However, he seems to refer to accounts like the *Memorias antiguas historiales y politicas del Peru*, written about 1642 by Fernando Montesinos. In this work Montesinos states that America was peopled by Noah's grandson [*sic*] Ophir and his followers. As has been seen, Cobo took great pains in Book I, Chapters 15–20, to disprove the theory that Hebrews came to America. Montesinos also gives a long list of pre-Inca and Inca kings. In this next passage, once again Cobo seems to be disagreeing with Montesinos.

7. In the prologue to the *Historia del Nuevo Mundo*, Cobo says that he also had a manuscript copy of Pedro Pizarro's chronicle.

8. See *Historia del Nuevo Mundo*, Book 13, Chapter 2, not included in this volume.

9. "Fringe" here refers to one of the major symbols of Inca royalty, a series of tassels worn in the center of the forehead. For more details, see Chapter 36.

10. Chucuito, an administrative center, is also referred to as a province, in the area of the Lupaca tribe. In addition, Lake Chucuito means Titicaca.

11. Hatuncolla is an administrative center of the Colla tribe.

12. This is a reference to the Marquisate of Oropesa, the only feudal estate in South America, granted to Ana Maria de Loyola Coya in 1614. It comprised the towns of Yucay, Huayllabamba, Urubamba, and Maras, just to the northwest of Cuzco.
13. *Guazauara* is a Taino word meaning "battle" or "skirmish"; it was unknown to the Peruvians before the Spaniards introduced it from the West Indies.
14. Unfortunately, this part of Cobo's *Historia* is lost.
15. *Hilacata* is an Aymara word meaning "cacique." The other designations are Quechua. The first word in each case is a number: *chunca* means "ten," *pachac* "one hundred," etc. The other word, *camayu*, means "official."
16. Raymi was a month approximately equivalent to December. In it the Incas celebrated some of their most important rites and festivals.
17. *Duho* is a Taino word unknown to the Peruvians before the arrival of the Spaniards.
18. *Mitima* is the singular of *mitimaes*.
19. The fanega is a Spanish measure, approximately 1.6 bushels.
20. Each *estado* equals the height of the average man, or about five feet, six inches.
21. An arroba equals about twenty-five pounds.
22. Reference is made to Book 13, Chapter 13, of the *Historia del Nuevo Mundo*, not included in this translation.
23. See note 5 above.
24. These insignias are described more fully later in this chapter.
25. A *duho* is a low stool; see note 17 above.
26. One palm is equivalent either to the breadth of the hand or four fingers, i.e., about three to four inches, or to the whole length of the hand from the tip of the thumb to the end of the little finger. Since Cobo seems to be using the first measure, the royal banner would be about fourteen inches square.
27. See Chapter 1 of this book, in which Father Cobo states that the Incas had ruled for about four centuries.

Glossary Loan words from American Indian languages: Q, Quechua; A, Aymara; T, Taino; and N, Nahuatl.

aclla. Q. Chosen woman. *Acllas* were selected at about eight or nine years of age.

acllaguaci. Q. House of the chosen women.

agi. T. Capsicum or chile pepper.

apucuna. Q. The Inca's highest judges or councillors. There were four of them, one in charge of each of the four quarters of the empire. The word *apu* means "lord," and the suffix *cuna* can mean either plural or a member of a class. (Cobo uses the Hispanicized plural *apucunas*.)

apupanaca. Q. Judge or commissioner assigned by the Inca to pick out the girls who were to fill the ranks of the *acllas*.

arcabuco. T. Dense woodland.

Ariguaquiz. Q. The fifth month, corresponding in part to April.

aroma. A. Night.

auca camayo. Q. An able-bodied man, fit for military service. *Auca* means "soldier" and *camayo*, "official."

Aucay Cuzqui Inti Raymi. Q. The seventh month, corresponding in part to June.

Ayamarca. Q. The twelfth month, corresponding in part to November.

ayllo. Q. An extended family or lineage believed to have a common ancestor.

ayllo. Q. A weapon made of a long cord with balls at the end, used in the game of the same name. The *ayllo* was used in hunting as well as in war. This word and the word above meaning "lineage" are homonyms. The Spanish word for the weapon is *bola* or *bolas*, also used in English.

baquiano. Uncertain origin, but possibly from Taino. Old hand, experienced in the ways of the Indies.

buhio. T. House. Used in Spanish to designate an Indian hut with a thatched roof.

cabuya. T. Fiber of the agave or maguey.

cacao. N. *Theobroma cacao*. The chocolate tree and its seeds or beans.

cachua. Q. A dance in which both men and women were free to select their partners. The dancers moved about in a circle with joined hands.

cacica. T. The Hispanicized feminine form of *cacique*.

cacicazgo. T. Derived from the Taino *cacique* and the Spanish suffix *azgo*. The dominions of a native chief.

cacique. T. A native chief.

Camay. Q. The second month, corresponding in part to January.

camayu. Q. Official. Also spelled *camayo*.

cannibal. T. A person who eats human flesh. The Spanish spelling in the MS. is *canibal*. A variant of the same word in the MS. is *caribe*.

capac llama. Q. Rich herd.

caracha. Q. An illness similar to mange that llamas often catch.

caribe. T. Cannibal.

cassava. T. Bread made from the manioc root or yuca. The Spanish form used in the MS. is *cazabi*.

chacara. Q. A piece of ground or field under cultivation.

chaco. Q. Public hunt in which several thousand men made a great circle and drove the wild animals toward the center; designated hunters would go in when the circle was small and kill as many animals as were desired.

Chahua Huarquis. Q. The eighth month, corresponding in part to July.

champi. Q. One of the Inca's royal insignias; a mace with which the Inca fought in wars.

chaquira. Uncertain origin, but probably from an Indian language of Panama. Thin beads made from red sea shells.

charque. Q. Dried llama meat.

chasque. Q. Runner or messenger who carried the Inca's orders to the governors and caciques of the empire. These runners were stationed at intervals of one-quarter of a Spanish league (a little less than a mile), and they used a relay system.

chicha. Uncertain origin, but probably from an Indian language of Panama. Any of various alcoholic beverages made by fermenting maize, other seeds, or fruits.

Chirao Sucanca. Q. Two pillars that marked the beginning of summer. The word *chirao* means "summer," and *sucanca* refers to "pillar" here. One pillar was on the eastern side of Cuzco and the other was on the western side. Observations were taken from Cuzco, and when the sun was seen to rise and set by these pillars, it was the beginning of summer.

chuclla. Q. One of the huts or small houses built in pairs along the royal highways every quarter of a league (slightly less than a mile). They were large enough for two messengers, or *chasques*, to fit into them and were used to shelter the *chasques* as they waited to receive messages.

Chunca. Q. Ten. Used with *camayu* to mean the superior of ten taxpayers, the lowest-ranking official.

chuño. Q. Dried potatoes.

coca. Q. *Erythroxylon coca*. A plant similar to a rosebush; or the leaves of this plant, which contain a stimulating narcotic. The Andean Indians chewed these leaves. The word *coca* is used in both Spanish and English.

colca. Q. Large storehouse; *colcas* were located in all of the provinces of the Inca Empire. Goods collected as tribute were stored in them.

condor. Q. *Vultur gryphus*, the huge Andean vulture.

Coricancha. Q. Golden House. Located in Cuzco, this was the most sacred Inca shrine.

Coya. Q. Queen or principal wife of the Inca.

Coya Raymi. Q. The tenth month, corresponding in part to September.

coyote. N. *Canis latrans*. Prairie wolf.

cumbe. Q. The finest quality of wool cloth made for the Inca. Also spelled *cumbi*.

cumbi camayo. Q. Craftsman who made fine cloth and clothing for the Inca. *Cumbi* means "fine cloth" and *camayo*, "official."

curaca. Q. Title given to the higher-ranking officials in the Inca government; they were in charge of one hundred or more taxpayers. The *curaca* with the highest rank was the superior of ten thousand taxpayers.

duho. T. A low stool or bench which was a symbol of high public office.

galpon. Uncertain origin, but probably from some Indian language of South America. A large storehouse or shed with only one room.

guaca. Q. Any object or place worshiped as a deity. The Incas had numerous such shrines, including temples, burial places, idols, stones, springs, etc.

guambracuna. Q. Boys. *Guambra* or *huarma* means "boy"; the suffix *cuna* indicates plural.

guanaco. Q. *Lama guanicoe*, the wild species of llama.

guaranca. See *huaranca*.

guazauara. T. Battle or skirmish.

hammock. T. A hanging bed. The Spanish equivalent used in the MS. is *hamaca*.

hanan. Q. Upper moiety or subdivision of most Inca towns and provinces. See also *hurin*.

Hatun Cuzqui Aymoray. Q. The sixth month, corresponding in part to May.

Hatun Pucuy. Q. The third month, corresponding in part to February.

hatunruna. Q. Rustic. The word *hatun* means "big," and *runa*, "man."

hilacata. A. Government official in charge of fifty taxpayers.

Homa Raymi Puchayquiz. Q. The eleventh month, corresponding in part to October.

huacchac llama. Q. Poor herd.

huaranca. Q. One thousand. Used here to mean the superior of one thousand taxpayers. Also spelled *guaranca*.

huarmi. Q. Married woman.

huata. Q. Year.

hunu. Q. Ten thousand. Used here to mean the superior of ten thousand taxpayers, the highest-ranking official of the *curaca* class.

hurin. Q. Lower moiety or subdivision of most Inca towns and provinces. See also *hanan*.

hurricane. T. Violent storm with heavy winds. The Spanish equivalent used in the MS. is *hurracan*.

Inca. Q. King or emperor. A member of the royal *ayllos* or nobility.

llama. Q. *Lama glama*, the well-known domestic animal of South America, used as a beast of burden and a source of meat and wool. It was also used often as a sacrifice to the gods.

llauto. Q. A wool headband worn by the Indians of Cuzco and all those of Inca lineage. It was not a symbol of royalty, but was used to support the royal fringe. Also spelled *llautu*. See also *maxcapaycha*.

maguey. T. Agave, especially the century plant.

maize. T. *Zea mays*, the native corn of America. The Spanish equivalent used in the MS. is *maiz*.

mamacona. Q. Cloistered women, dedicated to the service of the Inca gods. These women also trained the newly chosen girls, the *acllas*, in household occupations such as spinning, weaving, and cooking. The word *mama* means "mother," and the suffix *cona* can mean either plural or a member of a class. (Cobo uses the Hispanicized plural *mamaconas*.)

mara. A. Year.

maxcapaycha. Q. Royal fringe attached to the Inca's headband in the middle of his forehead; it reached down to the eyebrows.

mayco. A. Native chief.

mico. Uncertain origin, but probably from an Indian language of Venezuela. Monkey.

mita. Q. Labor service, performed by taxpayers who came by turns lasting up to several months. This labor service supplied soldiers, laborers for public works, servants for the nobles, and workmen for other official jobs.

mitayo. Q. Laborer or workman in the service of the *mita*.

mitimaes. Q. Settlers or newcomers who were brought into a recently conquered province to propagate Inca culture. In exchange, an equal number of newly conquered people were sent to take the place of the settlers. The term *mitimaes* was also applied to these new vassals who were moved from their native lands. The word *mitimaes* and its singular *mitima* are Hispanicized forms of the word *mitma*.

molle. Q. *Schinus*, Peruvian pepper tree. Its rose-colored berries were used to make a potent *chicha* beverage.

moya. Q. Pasture land.

ñaupapacha. Q. A long time ago, ancient times.

oca. Q. *Oxalis crenata*, a plant cultivated for its edible roots.

ojota. Q. Sandal or shoe.

pacsi. A. Moon.

pachac. Q. One hundred. Used here to mean the superior of one hundred taxpayers, the lowest-ranking member of the *curaca* class.

Pacha Pucuy. Q. The fourth month, corresponding in part to March.

Pachayachachic. Q. A name of the creator. *See* Viracocha.

papa. Q. Potato. This word is also applied to nuggets of pure silver.

petaca. N. Case or chest.

pichca. Q. Five. Also a kind of dice game.

pichcapachac. Q. Five hundred. Used here to mean the superior of five hundred taxpayers.

pillo. Q. A cord or band worn on the head.

Pucuy Sucanca. Q. Two pillars that mark the beginning of winter. The word *pucuy* means "winter," and *sucanca* means "pillar" here. *See also* Chirao Sucanca.

pulque. Probably from Nahuatl. A fermented drink made from the juice of an agave called "maguey."

puna. Q. The highest lands of the Andes. The word is used in both Spanish and English.

punchau. Q. Day.

purupuru. Q. Round plumage used as an insignia by the first Inca, Manco Capac.

pururauca. Q. Hidden thieves, according to Cobo. *Auca* means "soldier, enemy, or thief"; *puru* is used here in the sense of "hidden"; however, this meaning is not found in Quechua dictionaries or vocabularies.

quilla. Q. Month. This word also means "moon"; the months were counted by moons.

quinua. Q. *Chenopodium quinoa,* a plant cultivated for its seeds; it replaces maize in the higher lands of the Andes. Usually spelled *quinoa* in English.

quipo. Q. A device used to record numbers; it was made of strands of cord or thin wool strings. From the main cord, smaller strings hung like fingers. Knots tied in the smaller strings indicated the numbers in a decimal system. Usually spelled *quipu* in English.

Raymi. Q. The first month, corresponding in part to December.

runa. Q. Man. This word came to mean "Indian" after the Spaniards arrived. *See also* Viracocha.

Rutuchico. Q. An elaborate ceremony in which a child was named; it was celebrated after the child was weaned and involved, among other things, cutting the child's hair. The word also means "hair cutting."

savanna. T. Grassland, open plain. The Spanish equivalent used in the MS. is *zauana.*

sipas. Q. Marriageable woman.

sunturpaucar. Q. A staff covered from top to bottom with short feathers of different colors; three of the feathers rose from the top. This staff was one of the royal symbols of the Inca.

suyu. Q. A section or division of land assigned to one man and his family for their share of agricultural labor. This same word is also used in the toponym Tahuantinsuyu, "Land of the Four Quarters."

taclla. Q. Foot plow.

tambo. Q. One of the royal lodgings and storehouses located at convenient intervals along the royal highways.

tasque. Q. A girl who has not reached the age for marriage.

teçonte. N. Volcanic rock.

Ticciviracocha. Q. A name of the creator. *See* Viracocha.

tocricuc. Q. Governor of a province. The *hunus* of his district were under his authority.

tocto. Q. Little white feathers used in a ceremony for installation of the Inca.

tuta. Q. Night.

uru. A. Day.

vicuña. Q. *Lama vicugna*. Found wild in the Andes, it is related to the llama but smaller.

Viracocha. Q. Creator of the world. He was the Inca's major deity, and he was also known as Viracocha Yachachic, "Viracocha the Creator," or Pachayachachic, "Creator of the World." After the arrival of the Spaniards, the term *viracocha* was applied to the Europeans in contrast to the Indians, who were known as *runa*.

yanacona. Q. Retainers. As officials of the Inca government, they were exempt from the *mita* labor service. *Yana* means "retainer"; the suffix *cona* can indicate either plural or a member of a class.

Yapaquis. Q. The ninth month, corresponding in part to August.

yuca. T. *Manihot*. The many varieties of this manioc root were grouped in use as poisonous and nonpoisonous. Cassava bread was made from the poisonous kind after the poison juice was squeezed out.

yunca. Q. Hot, humid lowlands. The term is applied to the lands east of the Andes. It is used as an adjective: *temple yunca* and *provincias yuncas*. Unlike a number of other writers of the sixteenth and seventeenth centuries, Cobo never uses *yunca* to refer to the coastal desert of Peru.

Bibliography

HOLOGRAPH MANUSCRIPTS BY COBO

1. MS. 331-2. Biblioteca Universitaria de Sevilla. One bound volume containing a cover page and a text of 568 folios. The first page reads: "Historia del Nuevo Mundo, por el P. Bernabe Cobo, de la Compañia de Jesus. Primera parte. Prologo al Lector." At the end of the prologue the date is found: "7 de Julio de 1653." The following pages contain the first ten books of Part One of the *Historia*.
2. MS. 83-4-24. Biblioteca Capitular Colombina de Sevilla. Colombina-Cobo MS. One bound volume containing 363 folios which measure 217 × 155 mm. The text is written in a clear and careful style of handwriting, generally twenty-five lines to a page with paragraphs indented. The first page reads: "Historia del Nuevo Mundo, Primera parte, Libro undecimo. Capitulo primero, Que la America estaua poco poblada y por que causas." The following pages contain Books 11–14 of Part One of the *Historia*.
3. MS. 332-33. Biblioteca Universitaria de Sevilla. One bound volume containing a cover page, 5 blank folios and a text of 208 folios plus a 3-page index. The title page reads: "Fundacion de Lima por el Padre Bernabe Cobo de la Compañia de Jesus." The prologue is a letter written to D. D. Juan de Solorzano Pererira del Consejo de S. M. y del Real de las Indias. At the end of the letter the date is found: "Mexico, 24 de Enero de 1639."
4. F. 320. Biblioteca Nacional de Lima. Letter by P. Bernabe Cobo. "Mexico, 21 de Junio de 1633."
5. F. 324. Biblioteca Nacional de Lima. Another letter by P. Bernabe Cobo. "La Puebla, 7 Março de 1630."

MANUSCRIPT COPIES OF WORKS BY COBO

1. MSS. 202 and 203. Biblioteca del Palacio Real, Madrid. Muñoz Collection. Volumes 19 and 20 contain the *Historia del Nuevo Mundo*, Part One, Books 1–10. This is a copy of Holograph MS. 1 (MS. 331–2, Biblioteca Universitaria de Sevilla).
2. MS. 19—Rich 8. New York Public Library, MS. Division. Spanish American Collection. Purchased from O. Rich. This MS. contains the first ten books of Part One of the *Historia*. It may be a copy of the Muñoz MS. above.
3. There seems to be a lost copy of the Colombina-Cobo MS. It was used by Marcos Jiménez de la Espada in Madrid.
4. MS. 84-4-18. Biblioteca Capitular Colombina de Sevilla. One bound

volume with the following title: "JHS. Fundación de Lima escripta por El P. Bernabe Cobo de la Compañia de Jesus año 1639."
5. MS. 204. Biblioteca del Palacio Real, Madrid. Muñoz Collection, volume 18. One bound volume with the title "B. Cobo, Historia de Lima."

MAJOR EDITIONS OF COBO'S WORKS

1. *Historia del Nuevo Mundo.* Edited by Marcos Jiménez de la Espada. Sociedad de Bibliófilos Andaluces. 4 vols. Seville, 1890–1893.
2. *Fundación de Lima.* Edited by M. González de la Rosa. Colección de Historiadores del Perú. Lima, 1882.
3. *Obras.* Edited by Francisco Mateos. Biblioteca de Autores Españoles, vols. 91–92. Madrid, 1956.

Index